Political Language and Rhetoric

Political Language and Rhetoric

Paul E. Corcoran

University of Texas Press, Austin

International Standard Book Number 0-292-76458-8
Library of Congress Catalog Card Number 79-63529
Copyright © 1979 by University of Queensland Press
Printed in Hong Kong

To

Annie Barlow Corcoran

When a reality of human existence has completed its historic course, has been shipwrecked and lies dead, the waves throw it up on the shores of rhetoric, where the corpse remains for a long time. Rhetoric is the cemetery of human realities, or at any rate a Home for the Aged. The reality itself is survived by its name, which, though only a word, is after all at least a word and preserves something of its magic power.

José Ortega y Gasset

Contents

Introduction

The subject of this study is language. Language is an embracing form of human activity that has an effect on every aspect of life. In various ways we speak, listen, read and even think with language. It is the stuff of which we build, destroy and re-build individual and social identities, a fact which is especially interesting because it distinguishes man from other animals and appears to be his unique contribution to biological evolution. It is understandable therefore that language has become the object of intense investigation from any number of different points of view. Indeed, the study of language—like many another academic discipline—has become so specialized that it has invited the criticism that the ideas and findings produced by this effort are increasingly remote from language itself and the way it is used in ordinary life. It is probably not a matter of consolation to either linguist or critic that specialization in the study of language has existed for over two thousand years.

The special point of view in this study of language has to do with politics: language as a social force and as a kind of political behaviour. To establish this interest is not to suggest that other approaches to the study of language are in any way mistaken, or even that the present emphasis can be adequately accomplished without the assistance of ideas from many other kinds of linguistic analysis. There will be enough problems simply in the attempt to establish an examination of language as a form of political analysis. To illustrate this difficulty, as well as to give a clearer impression of the outlines of the present approach, we need only to take note of the initial assertion that language is an all-embracing activity, and therefore characteristic, of individual and social life. If this is true, it is clear that the delineation of a particular category of language must be arbitrary, and a prima facie violation of the axiom that it is a pervasive, continuous and all-embracing form of human activity. We shall, in brief, be plagued with the thought that a focus upon "political language" is arbitrary—or academic—in character simply because it is a special interest, and that any of our "findings" will be the fruits of partial labour.

Political language seems, despite these reservations, to be a category that bears some relationship to ordinary experience. In the absence of careful reflection, at least, "political language" appears to be a term referring with simple plausibility to things we say, hear or read as we go about our daily routine. We may read an editorial in the daily newspaper, hear a campaign speech on the television or even make a comment about the government of the day over luncheon, knowing in each case that certain words or phrases used in such situations are not normally convenient for other subjects: for example, policy, legislation, national interest, vote, etc. Nevertheless, we are more apt to think that "political language" is really language about politics, and that save for a small number of words, there is no evident shift to a special vocabulary or grammar to read or speak about politics. Of course we may associate certain stock phrases, clichés or a sanctimonious delivery with a politician's campaign speech or press conference, but eccentric language is familiar in other settings—the pulpit, board room or magazine advertisement—so that there is no necessary reason to acknowledge that politics, somehow, has its own proper dialect. On first reflection, therefore, we would identify political language by its content, rather than by its form. This casual definition, or "recognition", of political language will be of some assistance to the reader in the pages to follow. It will serve as a reminder that, even as the treatment becomes technical and abstract due to the introduction of linguistic terms or the discussion of special cases or classes of language settings, our subject is based upon ordinary and familiar experiences. An additional, and very important, point is that the aim of the present study is to shed some light on the subject of political language as it appears to us in the contemporary setting. If the following chapters pursue this aim by means of theoretical and historical analysis of language of an occasionally esoteric character, it is only with a view to a clearer perception of the role of language in contemporary society.

The initial acceptance of a loose definition for political language raises a question about the title of this study, *Political Language and Rhetoric*. Why is "rhetoric" apportioned a distinct title apart from the inclusive first term of the title? An exhaustive answer to this question cannot be given here without introducing matters that are actually treated at length in this book. By way of prefatory comment, however, it can be said that "rhetoric" has been given special recognition simply because it is a term that is understood to refer to a special form of political language, and it would be unfortunate not to use a term that has been, with remarkable consistency, taken to mean the appropriate family name of the subject of our present interest. Rhetoric is a word which we associate with the making of political speeches and has stood for a method of discourse—ranging in aim from swaying the masses to teaching schoolboys—for more than two thousand years. To use this word in our present title, then, is actually to under-score the fact that our subject is larger than rhetoric, and that there are political aspects of language that cannot be expressed or comprehended solely within an investigation of a formal method of political communication. The need for a broader and more encompassing approach, represented by the term "political language", becomes especially important as we consider the relationship between language and the numerous technologies that have been created which either directly or indirectly affect language performance. The association of "making a speech" with rhetoric is simply too narrow an approach to the many ways in which the spoken, written, printed and broadcast word has come to be a significant feature of social life and political power.

We have stated that political language is the subject of this study. It is equally important to acknowledge that the particular treatment of this subject will be based upon the assumption that language is a technology or, to be less dependent upon mechanical images, a technique of human performance. A further assumption will be that this technique—which has indeed given rise to forms of technology—is achieved on behalf of the aim of expression or communication, two terms which we shall take as substantially synonymous since each has reference to an activity which creates or conveys what we might broadly call information, that is, physical (visual, aural, etc.) representations of ideas, emotions, descriptions, quantitative or qualitative characterizations, and the like. The idea of language as a technique will be developed at considerable length in the following chapters, but it is important to introduce this perspective now so that the reader will find the major propositions and hypotheses of this study comprehensible.

Except as a way to introduce the point, it is actually misleading to say that language is *a* technique of expression of human performance. Much of the argument in this study, in fact, will be directed toward establishing the idea that language, as a form of human expression has given rise to a great variety of techniques. It will be our task here to identify these techniques, the conditions under which they emerged, the particular relationship of each technique to its predecessors and successors, and, most importantly, the political uses and social implications of each of these language techniques. A full demonstration of these relationships is clearly beyond the scope of a single book. The special aim of the present study is to examine the political and social implications of communications while relying on the diverse literature devoted to the emergence of language and its associated technologies.

A term that will be used often in this study is "public discourse". This is another phrase that is common enough, and seems to refer to a process that actually exists in society, but it is a phrase that also seems to defy careful definition, and may mean different things in different historical epochs. We shall use "public discourse" in this study as a very general term referring to the use of language, by whatever technique, to give expression to ideas or other utterances about the social order. This definition, general as it is, seems to rule out a number of uses of language that need not be considered as a part of our present investigation, while still providing a sphere of linguistic expression essentially equivalent to political language or "language about politics". A campaign speech, a letter to an editor about economic inflation or a slogan attacking the government sprayed on a public wall would be within the sphere of public discourse; a recipe to bake bread, a telephone directory or an automobile repair manual would not.

Thus far we have set forth the boundaries of interest for this study. The subject of immediate interest is political language, the various forms of which we shall trace according to their techniques of expression within the realm of public discourse. The effort will be aimed at a comprehension of the political effects of each of these techniques, particularly with a view to understanding the role of language communication in contemporary society. Having at least general familiarity with the essential terms of these statements of intention, we may now turn to four specific propositions about political language and rhetoric, the demonstration of which is the ultimate goal of this study.

1. The evolution of successive techniques of language communication has led to different forms of public discourse, with differentiations in social function and political importance at each "technological" stage of development.
2. Political rhetoric, as a technique of political expression, was a concomitant of literacy as a distinct language technology.

Subsequently, innovations in language technology, primarily mechanical printing and more recently other techniques of communication, transformed the social function and political importance of rhetoric.

3. Political rhetoric—understood as a public address, a speech—in the twentieth century is a technologically superseded form of communication; it is obsolete. Its residual cultural aspect bears no resemblance to its original social and political function, i.e., to inform and to persuade.

4. Contemporary political language—as opposed to formal rhetoric—has assumed a peculiar and in some senses an inverted social function as a technique of linguistic expression. This is borne out in the uses to which political language is often put: not to persuade, but to control; not to stimulate thought, but to prevent it; not to convey information, but to conceal or distort it; not to draw public attention, but to divert or suppress it. In short, contemporary political language may play precisely the reverse role from that classically conceived for political rhetoric. Instead of a rhetorical "method" to inform, persuade and enlighten, contemporary political language aims at an etiolated monologue which has no content, which placates, and which bears no relationship to the organization, coherency and clarification of information and ideas.

The reader will note that these propositions are ambitious and wide-ranging. They can, indeed, be expected to go close to, if not beyond, the border of political polemic, a fact which the author admits, wishes it were not so and promises to make every effort to resist in the interest of understanding the subject at hand.

Another difficulty encountered in addressing these propositions is the need to draw upon a vast expanse of human experience with language, dating from pre-history to the present day. This indebtedness is made possible by the existence of a large body of literature devoted to language and communications, but this debt requires the present study to form its demonstrations with great dependence upon, and only brief discussion of, that literature. This disadvantage, some may feel, is counterbalanced by several advantages. The treatment of language from its earliest appearance in a very condensed and selective (at times superficial) fashion enables the present study to focus upon contemporary political language from an encompassing perspective, even if the historical context is not, as it could not be in a single volume, exhaustive. It is also true that many of the elements encountered in a discussion of political language—such as rhetoric, linguistics, literary traditions, anthropology and technological development—have entire bodies of literature unto themselves. A constructive approach to these fields in any work hoping to benefit from them is to use them as a bridge of concepts and information, and as a bibliographical source. A final recommendation of the broad scope of this study is that the investigation of a subject as elusive and yet as pervasive as political language certainly is requires all it can get in the way of historical balance and methodological rigor. If this balance can be obtained from a consideration of language in successive historical epochs, perhaps breadth of scope will provide a sense of measured change, even though no single period can be dealt with exhaustively. Similarly, if the fields of anthropology, linguistics and classics can provide analytical concepts and reliable information, our interest in a subject as universal as language and as ideologically sensitive as political discourse will surely profit from the methods and evidence of these specialized disciplines.

The reader will discover that the four propositions outlined above conform to the larger structure of this book, and will be treated, not as individual hypotheses to be tested independently, but in their given order as a single, inter-related argument that moves from chapter to chapter. Chapter I develops the subject of language from its very psychological and social foundations, and endeavours to emphasise the social and cultural aspects of language. This emphasis is particularly important for any study intending to focus upon language as an object of political analysis. The treatment of language as a "political institution" is carried over into Chapter II, where more specific illustrations are given of the social and political character of language performance in societies which are predominantly oral cultures. Chapter III is an analysis of classical rhetoric, a technique of expression developed by a growing literate culture whose use demonstrates not only the social impact of a new language technique, but also appears to be a source of tension and eventual readjustment *vis-à-vis* the customs and interests identified with pre-literate techniques of expression.

Chapters IV to VI carry this evolutionary development forward into the "modern" era of printing and broader literacy, with a view to comprehending the changes in political rhetoric and the character of public discourse as a result of a new technnology of communication. Chapters VII and VIII trace this evolution in the techniques of human expression into the contemporary world of "mass" and "electronic" communication, endeavouring to explain the essentially changed character of both rhetoric (as a formal use of language) and political discourse generally. This transformation does not suggest the disappearance of political language, but only the conditions and techniques in which language assumes a new role as a form of political expression. Chapter IX pursues several of the implications of contemporary political language and communication techniques, especially with regard to the idea that the most recent and predominant techniques of communication may be giving rise to a kind of "post-literate" culture in which, perhaps not surprisingly, there are introduced elements of language expression bearing resemblance to features of oral culture. Any final evaluation of these trends must be, of course, highly speculative, but it may not be entirely impossible to imagine, on the one hand, the future of public discourse and the specific forms of political language in a post-literate world. On the other hand, the particular viewpoint of this study obliges some speculation as to the implications for political power and cultural growth in a society which finds the spoken and written word to be obsolete forms of expression and wholly inadequate to communicate the "information" deemed necessary for the preservation of the given social order.

Language, Communication and Culture

> *Language.* 1. The whole body of words and of methods of combination of words used by a nation, people, or race; a 'tongue'.
>
> *The Oxford English Dictionary*

It is our present interest to draw attention to the social or public character of all language. Language is a part of the social environment. There are many fields of study concerned with language as the product of internal and largely inexplicable mental processes, and it is true that the appearance of language, in speech and writing alike, is always a personal performance. This performance, nevertheless, whether in the creation of sounds or symbols, has a public character. Even when language is used for the articulation of intensely private utterances, such as prayers or confessions, the individual is taking advantage of a form of expression that was acquired as a right of common experience and social circumstance.

The whole of language has a public dimension. Speech is an effort that somehow assumes a public, even if it has to create one as with the cry of a hungry infant, or the alarm sounded at the discovery of danger. Whatever the profound internal complexities of mind and body which produce the lingual utterance, the sound of this subtle work is out there, offered to the community formed by and sharing that sound. In much the same way, language that is precipitated in symbolic form—written, printed and graphic language texts—is public in character. The word, in its many manifestations, is a sign, a signal: the book that is published, the headline or poster that catches the eye, the text that is handed down from generation to generation. Grammar itself, in both the unconsciously adopted rules learned by the yet unschooled child and the caveats of formal grammar, serves as a common guide in forging a public currency. The availability of language as sound and symbol extends to its presence as a cultural artifact. The ability to read, write and speak ties the present to the past, making possible not only public access to a cultural heritage but also an opportunity to experience the past in the many ways that literature makes possible. Literature becomes the past, as well as the means to it. In this sense, language is an important part of the public domain, embodying the tradition itself and providing the means by which it remains accessible and alive in public discourse. Language, then, is a birthright, but one whose value depends upon its being held in common.

Viewing language as a cultural phenomenon or an accessible public resource should not imply that language is an "artifact" or a system that is an exclusively objective social reality. There is, without doubt, an objective character to language, in the sense that the individual confronts bodies of literature, a vocabulary, and more or less definitive rules of grammar. But language is far more than that, as is recognized in the distinction which de Saussure makes with regard to *langue* and *parole*—a distinction which actually emphasizes the unity of the objective composition and the active performance of language.[1] The idea of language as an available public resource can be expanded to the broader conception of language as a "natural" resource, in recognition of the fact that successful language performance is an integral part of personality development within a social setting.

The analogy of language as a public "resource" can be extended further by recognizing its kinetic quality. Far from language simply serving as a method of concretizing and preserving the past, it is clear that language has a potency, what might be called an energy source, that operates within the public domain and can be placed at the service of designs to shape and change society. Thus, if language is a resource of cultural value and creative power, and is the sort of resource whose use is unavoidably public in impact, it is plain to see that the use of language is bound to have social and political consequences. Simple illustrations of this can be seen in the various public reactions to proposals for censorship, the teaching of phonetic spelling in grammar schools, an unhappily-edited Shakespeare play, or the unnecessarily obscure wording of a bureaucratic regulation.

It is one thing to say that language is a public resource available to all in common, but quite another to demonstrate that this has ever been substantially the case. Indeed, exceptions to the fully public character of language are numerous and perhaps the most interesting, especially for political analysis. Imagine, for the moment, that the opposite is true of language: that it is a faculty of expression that is private and privileged in character; that only certain members of a society are to speak, certain others to read, and others still to do both. Imagine that these privileges are guarded by special orders, access to which depends upon the possession of other privileges or stations. Imagine further that there are actually different languages used by varied classes of citizens, some of which are accorded the support of a formal grammar and orthography for the production of written texts, while others are not.

Developing this imaginary society of privileged language, of course, brings to mind any number of familiar cases in which access to and the performance of language is restricted and deeply reflective of the patterns of social rank and privilege. Only very recently in Western civilization has public authority taken upon itself the responsibility to engender literacy among both sexes and all classes. No one has yet made the claim that this endeavour has been very successful in reducing the opportunities for discriminations that can so easily be made on the basis of accent and widely disparate levels of attainment. It was not until the seventeenth century that a break was made in the separation that previously existed between the learned and the vernacular tongue, when Latin served as the official language in the Church, the schools, and the privy documents of State. This separation of language is recognized even today in nations around the world which retain imperial languages as the official discourse of school and government, primarily English and French—a distinction that is all the more significant in cases where the indigenous language has a completely different orthography. George Orwell's *1984* depicts a society in which language plays a crucial role. While the proles are left to their vulgar cockney, members of the inner and outer party are devising "Newspeak", an increasingly reduced language aimed at the elimination of the possibility to express ideas, feelings, and qualities. Until this aim is achieved, an enormous bureaucracy is busy revising and destroying all written records so that "history" will conform to the policy of the day.[2]

If the use of language is the birthright of social man, it is clear that its acquisition, and the sometimes frustrating conditions under which this right is exercised, must be the subject of political inquiry. Having alleged that language is a public resource from the standpoint of actual political community it must be conceded that it is a scarce one. And, if it is possible to pursue the analogy without excessive objectification, where there is scarcity there will be customary relationships of possession and exchange. To suggest that there is a "political economy" of language is probably not a grossly misleading metaphor, and may well be a provocative way of expressing the relationship between the distribution of language and power. A few illustrations of this economic viewpoint will provide a basis for the proposition that language is a significant feature of political life.

It has already been suggested that the quantitative and qualitative distinctions in the use of language follow, reflect and certainly reinforce other major social distinctions such as class, profession and degree of learning. This is not just to say that educated people obtain better jobs and material rewards, while the illiterate—a term that is itself relative—perform menial and unremunerative tasks, although this is generally true. An example that takes our attention away from the common assumptions of modern society, with its putative commitment to democratic education and universal literacy, will be more helpful. There is good reason to believe that in pre-literate tribal life oral and written expression were subject to official restriction and recognition of status.[3] These restrictions and privileges were maintained by the observance of chants, public ceremonies, prayers, oaths, traditional *rites de passage* having to do with fertility, coming of age, the hunt and harvest, and the proceedings associated with taboos. In such a society, where the word and the symbol were actually magical, complex social differentiations were used to insure the proper use of symbolic and oral language. Shamans, astrologers, and "medicine men" were the guardians of the most powerful words or symbols, and were thus the most powerful members of society or, at least, the most feared and respected for their access to the deities. Other ranks, such as the chieftain, the hunter, or the warrior were initiated to that status upon the revelation to them of oaths, totems, wall paintings, genealogies, stories and other expressions that were restricted from others. Even the language in common to the tribe was restricted through the use of taboos, formal ceremonies, and prescribed rituals for feast days and special occasions, such as funerals, weddings, and so on.[4] In brief, language played a specifically public function, and this function was identical to the maintenance of social distinctions and individual identities. Prestige and power were conferred upon those who were allowed, by tradition and the passing down of secret expressions, to appropriate the language of power: curses, prayers, invocations of the deities, oaths, and the interpretation (and performance) of magical signs and symbols. Others in the tribe who had need of these powers—to remove illness and evil spirits, to bless the hunt, to solemnize birth, wedding and death, to seek strength in battle—could do no other than be faithful supplicants.

In modern society, the political economy of language is practically the same as in earlier times. The medicine man has changed from priest to scientist and lawyer. The guardian of tribal totems, holy days and "dream time" allegories has been replaced by the academic, librarian and curator. And the chieftain? The tribal chieftain, who presided over public ceremonies and whose quarters represented the magnificence of tribal artisanship, culture and wealth, has changed from oligarch to king to politician. His language and the symbols of political authority will be found, in later chapters, to be no less reliant upon a kind of magic for their special powers.

In addition to these official roles language discriminates in many other ways. Language, more than clothes, is the mark of a man even today, when the importance of one's accent is apparently on the decline. This is particularly true because of the appearance of seemingly impenetrable nomenclatures that have grown up with technological specialization, a phenomenon which threatens to reintroduce distinctions between restrictive languages and the vernacular. Those whose work is to produce and speak technological languages constitute private orders of discourse to which the public may not be admitted. Finally, there remains in contemporary society a qualitative range of schooling which produces a very small proportion of the population with a certified claim to being conversant with "the literary tradition" (a group just large enough to support "the arts"), and a larger number who are introduced to the new technological languages. A still larger proportion, whose inferior schooling allows no such claim to even these modest skills, might at best be called "functional literates", and at worst, "functional illiterates". This discrimination roughly divides the population into those who work with their heads, using the skills of reading, writing and calculation, and those who work with their hands. The literate few are distinguished by their proper accents, reasonably literate journalism, adeptness at gaining a livelihood from literary or technological pursuits, and use of literate traditions for entertainment. The semi-literate population is confined to a linguistic world of largely oral traditions—slang expressions, dialects and sub-cultural idioms—and a diverting exposure to cinema, television and newspapers which flaunt a sub-literate style. But the population as a whole has in common a dependency upon the guardians of language, the educator, the publisher and journalist, the lawyer, politician and bureaucrat, and the broadcasting establishment. The power and status enjoyed by these groups flow directly from their identity with and control over the means of communication in both common and specialized language.

In addition to the sanctions and privileged limitations which survive in the use of language, there remains something similar to the taboo. Censorship is an obvious example. Some things cannot be said, by law or custom, in certain settings or certain forms, especially in print. Another restriction upon the public use of language is secrecy which, given the advancing state of military technology, is perhaps more pervasive and obsessive than ever before. As in the tribal setting, the real aim of secrecy is power over others, a use of language that, far from being public in character, has the direct aim of privacy. Secrets, of course, would have no significance if it were not the aim of those who have control over them eventually to initiate others into them, thus to extend the sphere of influence their existence makes possible. This process is particularly notable in the conduct of modern foreign policy, which would not be able to survive unless it had abundant supplies of secrets to reveal in formal secret ceremonies. Finally, a restrictive use of language that is somewhat analogous to taboos and their related mythical adumbrations is the official myth or lie. The official lie is another way of using language with a view to control and power, not the least because it presumes a possession of the information that is the object of suppression. One must have a certain status to produce a myth: one must be an authority, a source. A writer or speaker having this status is thus able to produce a myth or lie, the very success of which reinforces his status. The combination of these limitations—one might say privations—upon the public use of language amounts to the creation and maintenance of social power. The appropriation of certain elements potentially available to public discourse creates a "scarcity" of language as well as a group in possession of "intelligence" for whose political profit it may be returned to the market.

The study of language as a political phenomenon must take account of the fact that the use of language has always been a matter of technology. This idea is especially confirmed if we consult the definitions of the Greek word *technē*, which point to such concepts as art, creativity, craftsmanship and method. Regarding language as a technology may initially seem to contradict the argument that it is a public—even a psychologically natural—resource, a kind of elemental component of society. This paradox is easily resolved if we hold, as anthropologists and historians do, that a prime characteristic of man is that he is a tool-making creature. In at least a theoretical sense, the emergence of man and a rudimentary tool of communication (be it utterance or sign) are coincidental phenomena.[5] This process may indeed be seen to occur throughout the life of the species in the emergence of the lingual infant.

The history of language as a technology only begins with the appearance of the earliest simple tools. Some writers have developed the idea that human history is substantially the history of the technologies that man has created.[6] Others have narrowed even this approach by holding that human history might as well be interpreted in the light of successive developments in "communications technology".[7] These are, at least, provocative arguments, and will be given closer attention in later chapters. What is of present interest is the viewpoint itself that language, broadly considered, can be regarded as a class of technological innovation and production. This proposition immediately suggests the idea that "language technology" encompasses within a single category several forms of skilful human (bodily) performance, such as speech, reading and writing and an enormous variety of "communications" devices that have aided man to use language in different ways to extend the very form of producing, symbolizing and reproducing language. This technology comprises the entire range of "techniques" which are commonly understood to have expanded man's ability to express himself in ways that are meaningful to others: calligraphy, phonetic symbols, scrolls and books, printing presses, the typewriter, telegraph, telephone, radio and television, to mention only the most obvious ones.[8]

Of related interest to the technological view of language is the idea that the successive appearance of these techniques is subject to contemporaneous social and political forces. It may be conveniently assumed that the predominant techniques of communication in any given era do not necessarily present revolutionary forces, and are actually taken largely for granted. It is, nevertheless, equally apparent that the evolution of language technology is an organic function in the life of that culture, and is perhaps uniquely both a participation in the *status quo* and an articulation of changes in the political ethos. This point is adequately demonstrated in the introduction of mechanical printing, a technological innovation closely related to breaks in secular and religious traditions. Looking ahead, it is not clear what the extent will be of the changes accompanying the introduction of television, but it is already clear that its use has had an impact upon language, literacy and political life.[9]

The emergence of language as an increasingly complex technology is at the same time an evolution of a cultural texture containing, in different degrees of preservation and restoration, representations of "superseded" techniques. It is to be expected that, just as language plays a changing role throughout this evolution, the surviving forms will assume different functions and produce transformed social and political effects. The impact of the industrial revolution upon society at large, as well as upon political institutions, is a case in point. Clearly, the tools of manufacture provided by advanced technology have transformed the social, economic and political relationships at all levels of society, from family to State. It is to be anticipated that the tools of communication, which have made language into a social force far different from the simple spoken and written word, have played their part in this same transformation.

The next four chapters will attempt to trace the development of language—both *langue* and *parole*—as an emerging technology.[10] The implication of an organic continuity introduced by the term "emergence" is intended only in a metaphorical or thematic sense, although this disclaimer is probably made with an excess of caution. A technological continuity in successive forms of human expression is not a radical idea,[11] and it will be further argued that there are definite connections between the particular stage of language technology (some readers, as well as the author, might prefer to replace this term with the phrase "forms of discourse") and the use of language in society, especially from the standpoints of politics and power.

The idea of language as a technology carries with it two important implications. The first is that a technology is a method by which to shape or fashion things: for example, cultural artifacts (poetry, song, literature or religions) or one's fellow man. The second implication is that, as a technology, there arises the question of its becoming obsolete. Both of these corollaries will be examined in this study. The first is the central question of the active power, the actual creative effect, of language in political life. The second raises the question of finitude or temporality in the function or use of specific techniques of communication, a condition that must be presupposed by the proposition that language is actually a technological evolution of new and, at least in some ways, more useful techniques. Language, taken in this broad evolutionary sense, manifests a range of forms and uses at any given time. The range expands with the passing of time, although certain expressive techniques, rendered technologically obsolete, may survive in an altered form or in the service of different social functions. Thus in historical perspective, linguistic culture is an amalgam of all communication technologies, including the anachronistic and idiosyncratic as well as the innovative and the "modern".

This line of argument presupposes a "time lag" in which technically obsolete modes of expression are retrenched and redefined. New uses are found for them, or they are preserved indefinitely in a supporting institution, and their original social function changes in both character and importance. An example, perhaps not of the greatest political importance, will serve to illustrate this transformation. "Folk-singing" as a use of oral language, with the technical refinements, let us say, of rhyme, meter and phonic modulation, is a technique whereby a pre-literate society (or simply an illiterate sub-group within literate society) may preserve and "communicate" cultural identity, heroes, events and values from generation to generation. The intrusion of literacy and printing into this society will produce a number of unsettling effects. The very recording and printing of these folk-songs will, for the first time, produce them as a "type" or model. This in turn will have the effect of making it possible for new songs to be "written" by "songwriters", thus enabling the literate to compare the old songs with the new ones, and with entirely different song styles. The folk-songs are now seen, inevitably, as anachronisms—consciously so on the part of anyone attempting to write a "new" one. This process of obsolescence is compounded with the introduction of still newer techniques—new "instruments", phonographic recording, amplification and radio, for example—which radically change the scope and scale of the audience to the point that the very social character of the expression is transformed. It might be said that its identity is lost the moment it becomes apparent—apparent, that is, by contrasting its identity with alternative forms of expression.

Following this example further, we are able to see precisely how this transformation takes place. The original social function of the technique (folk-singing) was, as noted above, retentive and conservative in character: a means of reproducing ideas, values and information deriving from the society's past. The moment that this medium is revealed for what it is by a far more powerful rival—the techniques and resources of literacy—to those who sing and listen to it, the function of this use of language changes. Now the performance of such expression is, in a sense, reactionary or romantically revolutionary. In either case, it is a recidivist form. Cases to illustrate this point are easy to produce. An early example might well be the troubadours and their nomadic wanderings

throughout Europe prior to the Renaissance, performing their
sophisticated pastoral *chansons* in provincial dialects which were
gradually losing ground to linguistic standardization.[12] Much more
recent examples are to be found in the revolution, temporary though
it was, in popular music in the 1960s by "folk music". This
revolution was at once fostered by the growing protest against
American involvement in the Vietnam war and the rejection of the
mannered stylization and cumbersome hardware of rock music. The
"folk" reaction as a demand for peace and simplicity and artistic
primitivism was epitomised by the performer typically appearing
in "country" clothing and playing only a modest acoustic guitar.

A study of political language must give careful consideration to
"obsolete" forms of communication. Although important consequences arise from the introduction of the very latest forms of
expression and communication—in this age, television and electronic data processing—the phenomenon of linguistic performances
within the cultural time lag requires inseparable attention. In short,
we must examine the new, if in some ways obsolescent, functions
of language as they assume their new lease on life in the underlayer of language culture beneath the level of contemporary
technology. Geology provides an appropriate image for the growth,
decline and preservation of language techniques in the process of
stratified sedimentation. The forms of communication in any
historical period may be seen as a changing texture which appears
distinct at any specific point, although obviously related to the
textures which appeared earlier and later. Each form—a song, a
book or a grammophone recording—is unique, and yet part of a
larger cultural formation. Each supports, and is supported by, the
others and assumes a part of the culture in which language is
periodically reincarnated.

This view is an expression of the idea that an investigation of
political language and rhetoric will ultimately focus upon several
"anachronisms" within language. This point of view may be useful
in approaching a subject which practically as well as theoretically
appears to the contemporary eye and ear to be, in fact,
anachronistic. Such a study will justify itself if we are able to go
beyond description, with a view to raising theoretical questions
about the common opinion that modern political discourse has a
curious and unproductive relationship to effective communication.

Notes

1. Ferdinand de Saussure, *Cours de linguistique générale* (Paris, 1916). *Langue* can be translated as "tongue", although in linguistics it is meant to suggest a language system with a complete grammatical system used by a group or community. *Parole*, or "speech", refers to the actual performance of an utterance which more or less conforms to the boundaries of the *langue*. Technical terms in the field of linguistics are provided with helpful definitions and illustrations in Mario Pei and Frank Gaynor, *Dictionary of Linguistics* (New Jersey, 1969).

2. In the U.S. edition of *1984* (New York, 1961), Erich Fromm has an Appendix entitled "The Principles of Newspeak" that provides an interesting and detailed discussion of the role and effects of Newspeak in Oceania.

3. See Gilbert Durand, *Les Structures anthropologiques de l'imaginaire* (Paris, 1963), pp. 451–59. The formal uses of language in magic and religion is extensively documented in J.G. Frazer, "The Magic Art", Vol. I, of *The Golden Bough, A Study in Magic and Religion*, 3rd ed. (London, 1911), Chs. III and IV.

4. J.G. Frazer, *The Golden Bough*, Vol. II, "Taboo and the Perils of the Soul" (London, 1911), provides voluminous documentation on this subject. Also, see Durand, *Les Structures anthropologiques*, pp. 301–45.

5. Colin Cherry, *On Human Communication*, 2nd ed. (Cambridge, Mass., 1966), pp. 3–19.

6. Lewis Mumford, *The Myth of the Machine* (London, 1967), especially Ch. 4, pp. 72–97.

7. Marshall McLuhan, *Understanding Media: The Extensions of Man* (New York, 1964).

8. Other techniques or "devices" associated with oral speech which do not happen to be physical objects should be included: chants, song, poetry, prayers, curses etc.

9. By the mid-1960s, educators in America, Great Britain and some Western European countries had noted earlier and more advanced development of verbal skills in pre-school and primary school children, a trend that was explained by the child's exposure to television. Word recognition, vocabulary size, sentence formation and ability to count were among the skills attributed to this experience. By the late 1960s, surveys and standardised aptitude tests (such as the College Entrance Examination Board tests in the U.S.) began to indicate an overall decline in verbal abilities for teenagers, compared to the previous decade. From its earliest use, television has been the subject of debate as to its effects upon vision, the emotions and human behaviour, and clinical studies have produced conflicting findings with regard to correlations between program content and attitudinal or behavioral responses. Although no research has been done on the subject, it may be noteworthy that voter turnouts in national presidential elections in the United States have steadily declined since the 1950s, when television first came to be used for "saturation" coverage of political campaigns. The influence of television is discussed in the following works. R.D. Hess and J.V. Torney, *The Development of Political Attitudes in Children* (Chicago, 1967), pp. 23ff.; 93–115; S. Feshbach and R.D. Singer, *Television and Aggression* (San Francisco, 1971); R.K. Baker and S.J. Ball, "Violence and the Media", a staff report to the U.S. National Commission on the Causes and Prevention of Violence, *Commission Report* (U.S. Govt. Printing Office, 1968); W. Schramm and Parker, *Television in the Lives of*

Our Children (Stanford, Calif., 1961); James J. Best, *Public Opinion: Micro and Macro* (New York, 1973), pp. 129–36; J.D. Holloran *et al., Television and Delinquency* (New York, 1970); Fred Friendly, *Due to Circumstances Beyond Our Control* (New York, 1967); R. Stavins, ed., *T.V. Today: The End of Communications and the Death of Community* (Washington, 1971).

10. The use of the term "technology" here is not to suggest that the present study accepts either a materialist or a mechanistic epistemology as to the nature of language performance. Rather, we shall incorporate the sense of this term's Greek root, *technē*: an artful or creative skill. In any case, the present investigation has to do with the social function of language, and not with the establishment of objective categories.

11. Some writers would appear to lead their readers to this conclusion, especially McLuhan, in *Understanding Media*, and his earlier work, *The Gutenberg Galaxy* (Toronto, 1963). See also Walter J. Ong, *Rhetoric, Romance, and Technology* (Ithaca, N.Y., 1971), pp. 23ff.

12. Jean Baptiste Beck, *Les Chansonniers des troubadours et des trouvères* (Paris, 1927). Also see Gustave Reese, *Music in the Renaissance* (London, 1954).

2

Oral Culture and Early Literacy

> In the beginning was the Word, and the Word was with God,
> and the Word was God.
>
> *The Gospel according to John*

The purpose of this book is to comprehend political language, and in particular modern political language, as a form of social expression. In pursuit of this task, it is impossible to avoid an historical consideration of language, although this is necessarily a secondary and indirect undertaking. Consequently, the reader must forbear regarding the present study as a "history" of language or communication. The narrow focus upon the forms and functions of political discourse will rely upon only very brief presentations of historical materials relevant to the subject, a shortcoming that will be acknowledged in an effort to guide the reader to these materials through numerous bibliographical references.[1] Apart from this confession of omission, it is sincerely hoped that the reader's sympathy will be regained, at least in part, by advancing an argument more swiftly than would be possible if careful and "exhaustive" historical evidence were adduced at each turn. It is abundantly clear, of course, that the use of such terms as "oral culture" or "early literacy" are synthetic terms, in both the good and bad sense of that adjective. Much care is required in avoiding the facile argument founded upon sweeping generalisations; but it is equally important, if we are to understand significant features of the past and the present, to shun the arid reductionism that prevents us from establishing intelligible relationships and identities in the world around us. Thus, when the following pages are sprinkled with references to "eras" of communication, and cultural settings are outlined in broad and sketchy brush-strokes, the reader is asked to remember what this book purports to do: establish the transformations that have taken place in the forms and social function of political discourse that can only be perceived when these aspects are delineated in successive historical manifestations.

In the first chapter it was observed that language and society are coincident phenomena. It makes little sense to think of one without the other, or one preceding the other. If we are to take this as an *a priori* condition of human society, we can follow in the traditional path of least resistance trod by Hobbes, Locke, Rousseau and Marx in avoiding the question of origins: i.e., what was language like in "the state of nature" before the emergence of civil society? We shall presume the existence of some form of oral communication in the very earliest social arrangements. This presumption does not exempt us from considering, however, the forms of expressions themselves and the social functions such communications performed. We shall refer to these earliest social groupings as "oral society" in recognition of the fact that the primary, if not the sole, language technique available to them was that of the oral utterance.[2]

For the present argument, there is no reason why we must become involved in absolute determinations of what constitutes a "purely" oral society. Nor is there any intention of establishing an evolutionary scale upon which oral society must be taken as the most "primitive". Our interest in "oral society" stems more from what is *not* available in language technology than what is present. We are interested, in short, in the functions of language in a social setting that does not have such techniques as a standard ideography or calligraphy, a phonetic alphabet, books, and so forth. We do not want to become entangled in the very arguable proposition that, perhaps oral society never existed, that such things as clothing and ornamentation, face painting, bracelets, knife handles, the shape of housing and other such objects served a communicative function of a quite standardised form apart from oral speech; that, for example, a notch in a tree or a knotted branch was an abstract symbol serving as a "written" token of a particular event. Notwithstanding these theoretically important objections, it is sufficiently evident that oral society is that which has evolved oral speech as its most common medium of communication. It is a language of *parole*, with the complexities of the *langue* (such as rules of grammar, syntax or orthography) either undeveloped or simply not articulated as such. In this society, "language" and speech are subsumed within the single act of oral utterance. Language (and in this sense, language communication) is present only in the spoken word; it is an "event". The form of this technique is thus discrete and easily determined.

What is to be said about the function of language in oral society, especially what we might call its peculiarly public functions? Clearly, even the most mundane uses of language would have a public dimension, such as the communications attendant upon eating, hunting, working and playing. But the spoken word would also be the medium of expressing and maintaining tribal identity: totems, gods, seasons, personal names, life forces, among a host of other things. The identity or "names" of such things, however, would exist only in speech. The name evoked the thing itself, was a part of it—a notion that is hard to conceptualise from a point of view that takes dictionaries and personal signatures for granted.[3]

Although it is ultimately impossible to have knowledge of, much less to describe, all the functions of speech in oral culture, we can suggest general categories of effects that are peculiar to such societies. Rather than try to banish from our minds the technological innovations in language and communication that separate us from this society, we may appreciate the profound differences if we actually keep them in mind. Malinowski[4] discusses four patterns of language usage in his study of primitive society: 1. a mode of behaviour assisting the performance of practical activities, such as fishing; 2. the telling of stories and entertaining narratives; 3. free and spontaneous social intercourse, as in greetings; and 4. a ritual word magic in the casting of spells, curses and prayers.

The second and forth of these language patterns are undoubtedly of the greatest interest for present purposes. With no other medium or "container"[5] for the expression of the past knowledge and experience of the tribe than the body itself, we can appreciate the importance of speech, song and dance. The very identity of tribal culture, the knowledge it had of the world, and the relationship between tribe and natural or supernatural powers: all this "information" had to be stored in oral expressions. The limitations of this technique demanded that speech be both the repository and the method of performance, and consequently it is not surprising that special status was attached to the language of myth and power. The telling and re-telling of tribal myths was precisely a form of social or political discourse. In no other way could the society retain (or build upon) its cultural identity nor engender a knowledge of this information in successive generations. It is no wonder that oral societies heightened the impact of these performances by such embellishments as dance, drums, costumes, song and other dramatic elements.

The language of power in oral society was the language of invocation. Simply to name the deities, magic incantations, or spiritual forces was to invoke their powers. From the political point of view, it is not surprising that rites of initiation and special status attached to the possession and use of this kind of knowledge.[6] Once again it is worth remembering that, to the mind in oral culture that is utterly unencumbered with the image of a word as a "word" in abstract or symbolic form, a taboo, a curse, or the formula of a spell was inextricably bound up in speech itself. The utterance contained the power, the spoken sound was the magic power. Because this was true, the speaking of these sounds had to be restricted to certain settings, occasions and appropriate speakers. There had to be "formal" circumstances for their utterance, and authorised speakers to perform them.

What is particularly noteworthy about these uses of language is that they assume specific forms that are common to a great diversity of oral cultures.[7] At a technological level in which there are no other devices for retaining, storing or ordering information, devices of speech, per se, must be invented. Hence the prevalence of, generically speaking, formulaic speech. We could include in this category rhymed or free verse, songs, addages or proverbs, oaths, slogans, stories and jokes. To complement these patterns of language, adding to their dramatic effect as well as facilitating accurate and easy retrieval, are forms of performance such as accompanying ritualised ceremony (providing "structure" much as would the formal organization of speech in a later form, literate rhetoric), repetitive chanting and dancing. The ritual aspect of speech performance is especially important when it is considered that the "magical" function of language emphasized precise conditions under which curses, prayers and incantations might be given voice. Not only did this ceremony reinforce the status of the speaker and protect his privilege, but it provided protection to both speaker and the "spirit" against inadvertent or erroneous invocations "in vain".

There are specifically "political" functions of language in oral culture. Leaving aside the public discourse of practical operations and informal social intercourse, the cultural and political effects are clear. Culturally, forms of speech are used to retain and transmit information that is essential to the preservation of society. This would include the substance of metaphysical conceptions; the origins of the tribe; the proper relationships to natural and supernatural powers; the ethical and social mores regulating sexes, families, and generations; and even the peculiar specializations in arts, crafts and vocation. Politically, forms of speech are used to establish and maintain divisions of status and to distribute sanctions and rewards. The exercise of power is reserved to those who have the position and the knowledge to perform "the words". Such knowledge, which leads to the appropriate acts of speech, can even be defined as the formation and administration of political policy if the analogies are correctly interpreted: the sanctioning of certain persons or behaviour related to the breaking of sexual or dietary taboos; the naming of enemies or outcasts by the curse; the legitimization of persons or acts through the invocation of natural principles or supernatural powers; the affirmation of duties and obligations through ceremonial ritual. Some of these speech performances would be actual public discourse—the common property of stories, songs, myths, proverbs and common ritual observance. Language of a more specialized nature—containing perhaps elaborate and even systematic information, or knowledge of a traditionally "sacred" nature—would be reserved to special groups or persons of particular station who were initiated into the legends, astrology, genealogies, mnemonic devices or intricate formulae required for such performances.

Numerous examples to illustrate these aspects of oral culture could be cited. Although images spring to mind from the anthropological literature on the "primitive" cultures of New Guinea or South America, there are analogous cultures within early Western civilization. Early Judaic tribes can be taken as classical examples of a vital and durable oral culture. It is well known that the Pentateuch and the Talmud are only written recensions of genealogies, myths, laws and legends passed down orally for many centuries. Clearly, these texts show how formulaic language was used precisely for the cultural functions which have been mentioned above, namely, the retention and transmission of tribal identity, history, metaphysical conceptions and social mores. It is also clear that this culture had a remarkably elaborate division of labour in the use of language, including a distribution of status and power in terms of privileges attached to the performance of certain categories of speech. Prophets, priests, and scholars had their special functions defined precisely in terms of their relationship to language, delineations that were strongly reinforced with the introduction of actual written texts which themselves became holy, were secreted in elaborate arks, and were accessible to only very privileged persons with the authority to read and chant the words contained therein.

Of special note here are the sanctions imposed upon the name of God in the Judaic culture. The sacred character of this divinity was protected from any possible form of human impingement, whether in the form of objectification as a physical image or even in the form of a name to be written or spoken. Only specially sanctified priests were empowered with the privilege to call upon their God; extreme penalties were provided for those who took His name in vain. The name of this God of the tribes of Judea has come down to us as "Jahweh", although this is misleading. This name is actually a transliteration and Romanization of the Hebrew. In fact, Jahweh in its original form was an inscription that was literally "the unspeakable": a tetragramaton composed of four Hebrew consonants that were not susceptible of pronunciation.[8]

It will be noted that the forms of expression to which we have referred in oral culture have not been "political" in the contemporary secular and institutional sense. Rather, we have considered examples of language that would now be called religious, superstitious or occult. Our discussion has shown, nevertheless, that the use of these linguistic performances was coincident with the aims and effects of public discourse in any age: the retention and communication of cultural identity, the preservation and application of special information, the assignment of privilege and status and the exercise of power. Thus is it entirely appropriate to regard the forms and functions of language in oral society as a manifestation of political language. That these forms were necessarily ritualized in character and associated with formal ceremony, communal custom, the observance of holidays and sacred occasions and the recognition of higher powers makes it all the more exact to identify them as a species of public discourse antecedent to political rhetoric of a more self-conscious variety. This is only to reaffirm the common historical and anthropological proposition that early civilizations did not have the institutional distinctions between what we have come to call political, religious and scientific authorities.

A final point should be made about speech in oral society. It is important to re-emphasize the fact that in pre-literate society the performance of language cannot fail to have been remarkable in a way that is virtually incomprehensible to the sensibilities of succeeding cultures. Something of the uniqueness and joyful character of speech can perhaps be grasped if we try, in our imaginations, to divest ourselves of the skills, powers, opportunities for self-esteem and other benefits accruing from the abilities to write, read, record our experiences and ideas and immerse ourselves in the literary and visual horizons available to modern man. Taking all these powers away, we may begin to appreciate how the spoken word was an amazing facility for man in oral society, enabling him to conduct practical daily activities, plan for the future and retain and make use of the past. This latter ability, indeed, was a prime distinction between the powers of expression of man and animal,[9] and is the foundation of culture itself.

In a world without writing, or even an ideographic set of symbols that paralleled speech, speech could not fail to have a quality of magic or mystery that attaches to anything conjured into existence by the will, only to disappear again with the disappearance of the sound. If the cries of animals and birds in the forest were the expressions of spirits and deities, there was no reason why the cries of men were not equally so.

If oral communication had its sacred dimension, so must it have had the profane, which is to say the spirit of entertainment, in the broad sense of that word.[10] Except, perhaps, for special traditions and taboos, there could be no clear distinction between the telling of myths—or performing them in mime, dance and song—for spiritual or for social benefit. We know, in fact, that the telling of stories was refined into a dramatic art in oral society (only to be gradually lost with the expansion of literacy), and that its power was appreciated by young and old. Even for the amateur in this art, however, the telling of stories, jokes and half-fictional accounts of tribal exploits must have been a source of much amusement. It was, in short, a popular entertainment reliant upon the state of the "art" (or technology) of communication just as there has been popular entertainment in all subsequent generations.

Taking these points into consideration, it is easy to see that "oral" culture was precisely that; a society suffused with the sound of the human voice in chant, song, rhyme, laughing, mimicking the cries of animals and the telling of stories. The utterance was not only an object of self-assertion and entertainment, but was also, as discussed on earlier pages, a serious business. Special things had to be learned; rites and recitations were mandatory obligations for social position; certain language was proscribed altogether, or restricted, upon pain of death, to appropriate persons and places. Not illogically, silence, as an illusive companion to the sound of the voice, at times had special significance attached to it and became an important force in the social order.[11] This thorough participation of speech in oral culture is essential to understand if we are to appreciate the differences that separate oral from literate society. Oral society was not simply "illiterate" and "lacking" techniques of language communication that were to be subsequently developed. That is a retrospective point of view only, and one that entirely mistakes the function of human expression in oral society. Rather it was a positively *oral* culture, imbued with levels of sensibilities, skills of expression, forms of imagination, powers of retention and commitments to symbolic orders that were unique to it. Many of these features are denied to other cultures, either because they cannot be adroitly performed, or because cultures with other forms of expression cannot discover their value. This is not to say that all forms of oral culture have been lost, but it is to perceive the process of change in the proper perspective. That is, oral society developed a complex and unique reality of its own, most of which has perhaps been lost due to the character of its expression and to that of succeeding cultures. But oral culture was a fully expressive and fully human reality, and not simply the "lack" or absence of objective linguistic techniques. It had the latter in abundance.

The second linguistically distinct cultural period to be considered is "early literacy". This period is of particular importance to this study because it is associated with the development of a form of public discourse—classical rhetoric—that has come to be a kind of standard of comparison in the field of formal political language. Early literacy, either as a cultural form or an historical period, is as resistant to absolute definition as oral society. Just as pre-literate orality as a social stereotype is available to the objections based upon the difficulty of distinguishing between "writing" and such symbolic forms as ornamentation, carved forms or signs, early literacy is a term that actually invites, as a relative category, criticism. *How* early? This difficulty, it is admitted, has no satisfactory solution. Indeed, early literacy must be taken as a description of cultural forms, rather than the identification of a type or model of society. As a cultural description, it is arbitrary simply because it emphasizes language techniques as a central line of discrimination. But if it is arbitrary, this is not to say that it is without interest or meaning.

The crucial distinction is between orality and literacy. The former, which we have discussed at length, is characterized by the use of oral language as the primary form of communication—in a theoretical sense the only form of communication. Such a technique implies a number of things about how a society will handle important information—that is, how it will be retained, transmitted and actively performed—and how the use of this information will lead to cultural forms, distinctions of authority and ultimately the exercise of power.[12] In oral society, we have noted that speech, the oral act, is called upon as the primary or sole source for the communication of this information. In literate society, another technique is introduced, the technique of writing. We will use the term "literacy" here simply to avoid the use of jargon and to refer to its implicit reference to the use of letters, that is, a form of writing which we commonly understand as a technique of using signs or characters which can be read (by one so skilled) as a set of words which are familiar as oral speech. (Care must be observed in defining "written language" because some forms of writing— e.g., some species of ideographs and hieroglyphs—are not in any syntactical way parallel to the syntax and grammar of the speaker within the society producing such glyphs.[13]) Such a definition of literacy narrows our field considerably, simply because it restricts literacy to a type of language technique that is, historically speaking, relatively late and advanced. This restriction is particularly clear if we insist upon writing techniques which use, in the common sense of the term, "letters", because this virtually rules out systems of writing—such as ideographic or pictographic— that have not developed an "alphabet", by which is meant a set of signs which are purely abstract—referring not to things or ideas, but merely to sounds—and can be manipulated into strings which the reader recognizes as a "word token" signifying a "word event" that is recognized as an item within the vocabulary of that speaker of the language.[14]

It would be unnecessary to make these difficult and confusing (to the uninitiated in the field of linguistics) distinctions here if it were not for the fact that they have great significance in analyzing the social functions of written language. Literacy as a technique that is parallel to and supportive of the spoken language has clear implications for the investigation of political language. It is clear for example, that a writing technique based upon a standard character set (and especially a small, abstract, and phonetically based one) will expand the use of such language because of its impersonal accessibility, its relative stability, and its susceptibility to standard reproduction. So our primary focus upon what we might call "modern languages" is nothing more nor less than the recognition that some language techniques have been more powerful than others, and have had more of an impact upon public discourse.[15]

By literacy, then, we mean a technique of writing that has a driect relationship to speech. Thus we may identify speech and writing as two techniques of the same language. The one technique is the skilful use of the body in the production of sounds which, when controlled to certain patterns and disciplines, can be taken as signs which express ideas or refer to things, and in this way can be understood as a form of communication. The second technique, writing or calligraphy, is the skilful production or reading of signs which compose word-signs or word-tokens into certain patterns and sequences such that they are recognised as references to words and phrases within the given language. Thus we can say that a person "writes down" what he would like to say, or what some other person said. We may "read" in the paper what a person said the day before. Literacy is a technique of setting down and picking up language (as in the writing and reading of a speech manuscript) in a fashion that is adaptable and more or less compatible with oral performance.[16]

We can assume that a literate society would have, in addition to oral speech, persons skilled in the use of a standard calligraphy. This assumes the existence of what we will simply call an alphabet, and a more or less standard orthography, that is, a way of composing (with the calligraphic skills available) the alphabetic characters into meaningful words and phrases of the language. There are, of course, other presuppositions implied by the existence of standardized writing, which will be noted here only in passing. These include such technical aspects as the development of writing materials—pens, inks, paper, parchment—as well as the existence of institutional settings for the propagation of reading and writing skills.[17]

We now turn to the question of "early" literacy. The intention of using this qualification is not to establish chronological boundaries or a time period, but rather to make a qualitative distinction. By early literacy, we mean a stage of society in which the presence of this new language technique—literacy—is confined to a small minority of the (oral) users of language, and, in addition, has not effected a cultural impact sufficient to replace every vestige of oral culture. This is obviously an extremely ambiguous definition of early literacy, and yet it is not wholly implausible. We are simply referring to societies in which there is a growing tradition of literacy —but a tradition, be it noted, that is indigenous in the sense that the literate facility is an organic evolution from the particular oral language[18] rather than an artificial transplantation resulting from external conquest or penetration of foreign cultural and religious influences. Accompanying features would be a population that was largely illiterate, such that communication between the lettered and the unlettered would be, perforce, oral, if at all. Finally, we shall include in this definition the condition that the technique of writing be the most technologically advanced form of communication available, thus permitting our analysis to be undertaken on an assumption that the literacy and illiteracy in question exist in a culture unaffected by, e.g., mechanical printing or radio.

In the present study, we are primarily interested in early Greek and Roman societies. Philological scholarship informs us that a period of "early literacy" as we have defined it existed in a number of different parts of the Middle East, Southern Europe and Eastern Africa, representing in greater and lesser degrees cultures which evolved standard calligraphies, bodies of literature and groups of "literati".[19] Our concern with Greek and Roman culture is a choice based upon an element within these traditions that seems to show an important connection between the spoken and the written word precisely in the area of public discourse and political language: political rhetoric. Before we give direct consideration to this form of language, however, several other aspects of early literacy should be mentioned.

Within a society which we would call early literate, it is easy to imagine that this advanced technique of communication would seem to have little cultural impact, and very few manifestations that would even bring it to the attention of more than a few. Let us, hypothetically, suppose that we take the Greek city-states during the life-time of Socrates (about 470 to 399 B.C.) as an example of an early literate society. We know enough about Athenian society, as well as the larger Hellene culture of which it was a part, to make a few generalizations about the role of language in this era.[20] We know, for example, that the oral heritage was still very strong. Greek "learning" was by and large equivalent to the corpus of poetry and mythology. The poetry of Homer and Hesiod represents a cultural tradition that was only beginning to transfer this heritage from its oral medium to the newly emerging texts. For the most part, the oral tradition was still the channel for conveying information about the heroic and divine past, and this was reinforced by the ritual observance of festivals, worship of a constellation of deities, and the presence within the common idiom of oaths and wise sayings from the folk-loric tradition. It cannot be accidental that the central image of divine wisdom in this period was a voice—the oracle.

Certainly the majority of people in fifth century Athens were illiterate, which is to say that they did not bother themselves about acquiring the curious habit of writing and arguing about tiny figures inscribed on wax tablets or sheets of papyrus. Children learned what they needed to know by word of mouth, the seasons were properly observed by the passing of feast days, and one learned about and appreciated the world's mysteries from the powerfully expressed wisdom of "the poets". In large part, then, the life of the individual was fashioned by the received oral culture. This extended, indeed, to common entertainment, including song, poetry and dramatic presentations.

Within this oral tradition, a new technique of communication was being asserted. The change can have no more profound representation than the fact that Socrates was, although certainly literate, dependent solely upon speech, while Plato, his disciple and amanuensis, was faithfully committed to setting down in writing the ideas and conversations of the master. The children, especially male children, of Athenian citizens[21] were beginning to receive tuition in reading and writing, although this did not replace the cultivation of the fine arts (poetry and music), the practical arts and physical culture. Some of these pupils came under the influence of masters, like Plato and Aristotle, who attracted some attention due to their interest in learned authorities[22] whose ideas were beginning to accumulate in texts, letters and notes from these figures and their disciples. Not the least of this attention was based upon disagreement, inquiry and controversy with regard to popular notions embedded in the Homeric tradition. As these controversies grew, partisan feelings led to the establishment of schools, which only solidified the trend toward the writing and exchange of texts and the building up of bodies of literature. Plato's writing and distributing of the Socratic dialogues were early tendencies in this direction. Aristotle's writings are explicit evidence that Plato's works were read, glossed, debated and made the object of lectures and essays.

There can be little doubt that only a small minority of Athenians was involved in lyceum and academy, and that the portion of the population which was literate was also small. And yet it is equally clear that writing was beginning to have a broad social influence. Scribes may have been useful in the ordinary course of events for writing letters, preparing public documents and composing correspondence between the seat of government and the armies in the field of battle. And yet the great attention paid to legislation and constitutions in Plato's *The Laws* or, especially, Aristotle's *Politics* and *Constitution of Athens* indicates that there already existed a corpus of texts of great social importance, and that this was accumulating outside the poetic and academic traditions. This must be taken as evidence that the written page was coming to be an important medium for the presentation of ideas and information affecting public policy and the population at large. If this is true, it is probably also true that the participants in these deliberations increasingly felt the pressure of literacy, and that the actual deed of composition could no longer be left to a mere scribe.

It is possible to continue to speculate as to the relationship between advancing literacy and the evolution of a large, organized and active city-state. Although we are not especially concerned with establishing patterns of causality between literacy and political expansion, it is enough to take note of the parallels that do exist. Certainly, the society that develops specialized institutions is creating the conditions for frequent and reliable records and avenues of communications. Armies that venture farther from the city become increasingly reliant upon directives, just as the city becomes reliant upon communiqués from camp and field of battle. Deputations for trade or other interests to foreign States create a need for exact records and explicit correspondence. Legislative bodies or courts of law, by the nature of their recurring meetings, stimulate a demand for a definitive record of proposals, suits, factual and technical information, past decisions and the like. The increasing diversity and complexity of public affairs, in short, create a need for effective ways of accumulating, exchanging and storing large amounts of information. So it is not surprising to note that there is a coincidence between the growth of literacy and the appearance of special political institutions.

The importance of literacy in this period is a matter of emphasis. Recognising the prevalence of the oral tradition among the common people, the general illiteracy, and so forth, it is possible to conclude that writing and textual communication were of minor importance. The masters of schools, as well as their young disciples, were few in number and seem to have been held in low esteem. Aristophanes, we know, capitalized on the philosophers in his plays—the very performance of which was a part of oral culture—by ridiculing their intense interest in apparently trivial questions, by casting doubts on their fidelity to the gods and by scorning their obvious satisfaction in endless dialogues.[23] On the other hand, the case can be made that the few manifestations of literate culture—the very appearance of writing as a standard technique, the growing corpus of learned and legal texts, the new schools of philosophy and rhetoric—were evidence that the new form of communication had established itself and was already a major cultural and political force. Our purpose here will be served simply in the appreciation that the role of literacy in this period, of whatever magnitude, exists. In any case, it is possible to see that literacy was a new force whose power even then was seen as having great potential, even if it was not possible to know what new cultural forms were to be created.

An interesting argument in respect of the new role of literacy has been advanced as an interpretation of Plato's *Republic*.[24] Professor Havelock's view is that, properly understood, the *Republic* amounts to an attack upon poetry and the Greek poetic tradition. "It questions the Greek tradition as such and the foundations on which it has been built."[25] The *Republic*, then, is not a utopian political treatise, but a straightforward critique of the Greek system of education in which "the younger generation is continually indoctrinated in the view that what is vital is not so much morality as social prestige and material reward which may flow from a moral reputation whether or not this is deserved".[26] To replace the poetic curriculum with a new one, then, is the chief strategy of the *Republic*. The aim of this revolution is to supplant the cynical conventional morality with an absolute morality of the true philosopher.[27] Mimesis, the poet's method of rendering an account of reality, is found by Plato to be illusionism at the second remove from reality. This method must be replaced with a new one designed to cultivate *episteme*—knowledge, or, rendered as an equivalent, science—in education. Thus the need in Plato's Academy for a curriculum founded in mathematics, geometry and logic, a method that will enable the graduate to "define the aims of human life in scientific terms and carry them out in a society which has been reorganised upon scientific lines".[28]

For the present study, it is important to consider Havelock's reasoning in explaining Plato's harsh and sweeping critique of mimesis and the poets. Havelock's interpretation suggests that the structure, as well as the intensity, of Plato's attack can be understood only if we assume on Plato's behalf "the astonishing presumption that poetry was conceived and intended to be a kind of social encyclopedia. If it was so designed, it was obviously by Plato's day doing a very poor job. It could not carry out the task according to the standards which Plato required in the Academy".[29] What this amounts to is an assertion that Plato was very much aware of the substance of what has come to be called "socialization theory" as well as the idea of oral traditions embodying and transmitting traditional culture. Hence Plato's only apparent confusion when his critique of mimesis as an approach to reality indicts the poet, the actor, the dramatists, the student in the traditional classroom and the adult in festive recreation.[30] The fact that mimesis carries with it a power which grips both actor and audience in pathos and catharsis of identification with the poetic figures only makes this method a more dangerous enemy of knowledge, because it is a "way of reliving experience in memory instead of analysing and understanding it".[31] In brief, then, Plato's new Republic can be regarded as a new order, indeed—a republic of letters and literacy, a reading culture to replace an oral culture.

> . . . just as poetry itself, as long as it reigned supreme, constituted the chief obstacle to the achievement of effective prose, so there was a state of mind which we shall conveniently label the "poetic" or "Homeric" or "oral" state of mind, which constituted the chief obstacle to scientific rationalism, to the use of analysis, to the classification of experience, to its rearrangement in sequence of cause and effect. That is why the poetic state of mind is for Plato the arch-enemy and it is easy to see why he considered this enemy so formidable. He is entering the lists against centuries of habituation in rhythmic memorised experience. He asks of men that instead they should examine this experience and rearrange it, that they should think about what they say, instead of just saying it. And they should separate themselves from it instead of identifying with it; they themselves should become the "subject" who stands apart from the "object" and reconsiders it and analyses it and evaluates it, instead of just "imitating" it.[32]

It must be remembered that the *Republic*, written about 375 B.C., is not the first argument to be made against the oral tradition, nor the only treatment of the topic by Plato. The Athens of this period, under the influence of the development of literacy mentioned earlier, was no longer under the full sway of the poetic tradition. The dialogues of Socrates, as recorded by Plato, demonstrate that there was a new force in society distinct from, and properly regarded as a successor to, the culture based upon epic and tragic poetry. This new force was embodied in a group of "schools" of philosophy and rhetoric headed by what Plato chose to call "sophists". The *Gorgias* is one of the most important dialogues in communicating the role played by the Sophists in Athenian higher education and the respective Platonic critique of it.

Without setting forth what would necessarily be an extended analysis of Plato's critique of rhetoric and sophistry, and the tradition of "ethical imitation"[33] on which they are based (which thereby relates the sophistic method to the poetic method of mimesis),we must briefly examine the connection between rising literacy and the appearance of "academic philosophy" as embodied in these early institutions of advanced learning.

In *Protagoras*, *Gorgias* and *Sophist*, as in others of the Socratic dialogues, Plato makes it quite clear that the Sophists are without a true vocation.[34] The Sophist, especially as epitomized by Gorgias —and as he is pictured in the dialogue named after him, is the heir of an oral culture. As a master of rhetoric, Gorgias is devoted to the art of persuasion through oral discourse. Furthermore, it is apparent that the rhetorician achieves success according to skills which depend upon an acceptance of the conventions of morality conceived solely in terms of mimetic appearance. A primary method of this art, of course, is to use all of the poetic and dramatic resources at the command of the skilled speaker: pathos, empathy, pride, fear or whatever other emotional predisposition is required to gain the conviction of the audience. In this sense, the Sophist is an enemy of truth and an accomplice of the oral tradition. In recognition of this, Plato says of the Sophists that they follow, rather than lead, public opinion.[35] This is a most serious charge when it is considered that by "public opinion", Plato means the common people's views which are steeped in the oral tradition. But what is equally deserving of recognition is the way in which the group of "wise men" in pre-Socratic Greek philosophy known as the Sophists are actually collaborators in an evolution in education of which Socrates and Plato are the creators.[36] As we have indicated above, there was a tradition of scholarship dating back to the seventh century B.C. which concerned itself with questions about the world, nature, reality, being and non-being that increasingly required a new mode of discourse and involved modes of thought that were alien to the Homeric tradition. Not coincidentally, we should claim, the use of a standard alphabet and written texts only dates to the eighth century B.C.[37]

The role played by the Sophists in the Greek "enlightenment" need not be dealt with at length here, but it is enough to suggest their contribution to the growing literate culture by quoting a brief summary of their work.

> The Greek Enlightenment was characterized by a spirit of independent reflection and criticism. The leaders in this movement, the Sophists, substituted the right of private judgement for the authority of existing institutions, which latter they regarded as contracts between the mutually selfish or as dominance of the weak by the strong.[38] . . . The Sophists based their ethical theory upon an epistemological relativism in which, according to Protagoras, man becomes the measure of everything. This relativism easily became a skepticism, excused by Protagoras in the theological field by "the obscurity of the question and the shortness of human life."
>
> Gorgias, another eminent representative, is credited with this gem of agnosticism, not to say of nihilism: "First, nothing exists; second, if anything did exist we could never know it; third, if perchance a man should come to know it, it would remain a secret, he would be unable to describe it to his fellow-men."[39]

As a vivid illustration of the way in which the Sophists were an integral part of the early literate culture, the quotation by

Protagoras above—which begins "As to the gods, I have no means of knowing either that they exist or that they do not exist."—is taken from his preface to his book *On the Gods*, the public reading of which led to his explusion from Athens. The Athenians then "burnt his works in the market-place, after sending around a herald to collect them from all who had copies in their possession".[40]

Clearly, the Sophists cannot be understood apart from the other pre-Socratic schools; the Milesians (Thales, Anaximander, Anaximenes); Heraclitus and Cratylus; The Eleatics (Xenophanes, Parmenides, Zeno, Melissus); Empedocles and Anaxagoras, the pluralist metaphysicians; the Atomists (Leucippus and Democritus); Pythagoras and his followers. The Sophists had nothing to contribute, epistemologically, to the understanding of reality or the accumulation of knowledge, and they were as bold to flaunt this as Socrates was sarcastic in condemning them for it. But they did establish man as an autonomous subject free of the claims of nature or tradition and, most importantly for our present concern, they contributed to the formation of prose as a medium of discourse and theoretical debate. As a rhetorician, a Gorgias might make the bold claim that his good students could put all the poets at their disposal in the most skilful fashion—either to invoke divine authority or to use the dramatic techniques as a a means of gaining emotive sympathy—but this method was hardly aimed at the faithful survival of the poetic tradition. In sum, the Sophists can be seen as participants in an evolution of three centuries' duration in which Greek culture was constructing ways to question tradition, examine man, nature and the universe, and speculate as to the character and limitations of human knowledge. To carry out these kinds of activities, a new medium of communication and a new way of storing and preserving information were required. These requirements were supplied by the ever-growing use of a system of writing that was able to express thoughts and information in a new way, preserving them easily and accurately for other eyes and other generations. No longer was it necessary (or possible) to express ideas as poetic or narrative recensions of an existing oral tradition. One could simply use or not use poetic forms (the former alternative being chosen by most pre-Socratics), not having to worry about relying upon the largely ephemeral survival of ideas by emendations of the oral tradition. One's work would survive, others could read it and successive generations could criticize it as will, simply because texts or critical glosses would be available. Thus it is possible to say that part of the creative energy of Greek philosophy, even before the time of Plato, was due to a technological condition. A new medium made possible new contents, and it is not an accident that one of the visual parodies of philosophers in Aristophanes' plays is the appearance of the Sophists identified by their carrying manuscripts with them wherever they went.

It is even possible to carry out the idea of technological impact by applying the interpretation to the poetic tradition, itself. It is well-established that the "later" poets actually produced their materials with the assistance of written texts, even when they were almost exclusively intended for oral performances. The general public, of course, could not read and were thus introduced to such works in dramatic recitations and plays. The existence of such texts introduced a revolutionary impact upon the poetic tradition simply because the method of preservation was crucially upset. "New " works did not undergo the test of time, in which formerly the limitations of the oral medium would select some works and others would be lost. Also, "new" works did not have to appear in the form of revisions of old ones in the hope of incorporation. Thus, from generation to generation, the sheer volume of poetic and dramatic productions overwhelmed the capacity of the oral medium to preserve and communicate them. Works ceased to be eventually either forgotten all together, or retained in poetic anonymity within the traditional culture. Rather, they were retained, subject to criticism for their authenticity, identified with a particular personnage, and increasingly regarded as elements in a new, literate tradition. From the point of view of the oral tradition, we can see that the poetic culture was simply drowned in the stream of new materials. From the point of view of the Greek "writer", we can see that his expressions no longer had to be so formed as to appeal to the oral medium for performance and survival. Thus it became possible to address new questions with different language. Instead of addressing cosmic problems in terms of heroic allegory and struggles between divine images, it was now possible to perform the disparate tasks of examining physical nature, the nature of human experiences and the activity of abstract reason. In turn, as such texts were produced, they could not help but produce questions of heresy, highly subjective introspection and a highly diverse creative freedom which are characteristic of an intellectual revolution. The same forces could produce reaction. It may have been this concern that prompted Plato to attack the Sophists' heady skepticism and set down the great corpus of Socratic dialogues as a model of the new language which assaulted the poetic tradition, placed heavy emphasis upon re-moulding public opinion, and proposed the image of the philosopher-king as the product of a system of education which was grounded in a cultivation of logic, abstract reasoning, love of knowledge, and the application of these to human experience.

The new technique of communication, literacy, placed an unbearable burden upon the old, oral technique. On the one hand, literacy was able to appropriate much of the old technique's powerful features (as boasted by the Sophists' claim of competence with poetic images and technique). Literacy's greater efficiency in production and preservation overwhelmed the respective faculties of oral culture, and in the process effectively challenged its claim to be the encyclopedia of culture and the means of transmitting that culture. And apart from that, written language simply made possible new forms of expression: criticism, examination of textual accuracy, and highly detailed organization due to the ability to perceive and physically rearrange information; the presentation of great and expandable (and revisable) quantities of information; the exposition of abstract subjects and the discussion of analytical processes without recourse to metaphor or anthropomorphisms; the impetus to standardizing words and meanings through the use of visual word-tokens; the clarification and correction of ideas, stories or arguments which could not previously be accomplished due to the lack of tangible comparisons in spoken language.

The period of early literacy was a time of technological innovation. The transition from Semitic to Greek alphabets which may have occurred as late as 700 B.C., but certainly in the eighth century,[41] produced a technique of language communication that was to have enormous social consequences. Our survey of some of these consequences has indicated that even when illiteracy was the public norm and oral culture the dominant mode of communication it was possible to perceive the seeds of change. The ability to write, read and preserve language texts generated a pressure from within oral culture that would have, on its own, altered the character of oral preservation and communication. But these same abilities also stimulated the beginning of a new tradition, what we would now call a literary, philosophical and scientific tradition, that was in an essential way alien and opposed to oral culture. This opposition was profoundly stated in the writings of Plato, as we have indicated, but it is also clear that several literacy-based traditions, as exemplified by the Sophists, were emerging as revolutionary critiques of the existing cultural foundations, and were engaged in the formation of methods of inquiry and political action that could not fail to bring into being a form of public discourse—that is to say, a technique of language communication—effecting both the general public and the pursuit of higher learning. It is to this new form of discourse—rhetoric—that we now turn.

Notes

1. A massive literature exists on the subject of language. However, the treatment of this subject has been so wide-ranging, and from so many different fields of research , that it is impossible to name a standard compendium on the origins of language. In the footnotes throughout this book, this literature will be reviewed and placed into several more or less distinct categories of scholarship, e.g., anthropology, philosophy of language, writing, technology and philology. For a general introduction, see Otto Jespersen, *Language: Its Nature, Development and Origins* (New York, 1922) or Mario Pei, *The Story of Language* (Philadelphia, 1949). A more ambitious work is Ernst Cassirer's *The Philosophy of Symbolic Forms, Vol I*, "Language" (New Haven, 1953).

   A treatment of the "history of communication" is a different matter, especially because this subject has never been satisfactorily defined as a field of study. "Communication" has been the subject of interest to psychologists, phenomenologists, theologians and, by way of negation, existentialist ethicists. Generally speaking, the *relationship* between speaker and listener, or writer and reader, has not been susceptible of historical research. On the other hand, "communications" is notable as a recent and rapidly growing area of study. This involves an emphasis upon "media technology", information theory and the relationship between social groups and the structures (political, economic, cultural etc.) which control the communication networks. See C. Cherry, *On Human Communication*, 2nd ed. (Cambridge, Mass., 1966) and Karl Deutsch, *The Nerves of Government* (New York, 1963). It is noteworthy that "communications" has become in the past decade an academic discipline in many universities, where presumably students not only acquire knowledge of the history of their field, but also develop skills necessary to use certain of the recent technologies of communication.

2. See W.J. Ong, *Rhetoric, Romance and Technology* (Ithaca, N.Y., 1971), Chs. 1 and 2; Eric A. Havelock, *Preface to Plato* (Oxford, 1963), Ch. VII; André Varagnac, ed., *L'Homme avant l'écriture* (Paris, 1959); R.J. Pumphrey. *The Origins of Language: An Inaugural Lecture* (Liverpool, 1951); and especially, G. Révész, *The Origins and Prehistory of Language* (New York, 1956).

3. The importance of the "named" object may be partially appreciated if it is compared with the significance attached to a "signature" of a legal document in literate society. The spoken name carried this irreplaceable power that is, today, associated with a written sign.

4. Cited in Stuart Chase, *The Tyranny of Words* (London, 1938), pp. 40–44, quoting Malinowski from an essay in C.K. Ogden and I.A. Richards, *The Meaning of Meaning* (London, 1936).

5. L. Mumford, *The Myth of the Machine* (London, 1967), pp. 4, 74ff.

6. See Arnold van Gennep, *Les Rites de passage* (Paris, 1909); A.R. Radcliffe–Brown, *Structure and Function in Primitive Society: Essays and Addresses* (Glencoe, Ill., 1952); also J.G. Frazer, *The Golden Bough*, Part II (London, 1911) Ch. I, "The Burden of Royalty", which discusses the privileges and penalties attached to the observance of sacred rituals.

7. See Ernst Cassirer, *Language and Myth* (New York, 1946) and J. Donovan, "The Festal Origin of Human Speech", *Mind* (Oct. 1891 to July 1892). The use of chants, prayer cycles, poems and maxims as a store of information and a set of customary rules can be seen in such diverse cultures as ancient Hebrew, Confucian, early Greek and New Guinea.

8. The Hebrew language does not have symbols corresponding to vowels. The Tetrgrammaton—translating literally from the Greek, a "four-letter word"—is usually transliterated as YHWH or JHVH and represents, in symbolic form, the ineffable name of God.

9. Numerous scholars have noted that a distinction between man and other animals is man's ability to recover, in various ways, the past. Language, clearly, is a primary instrument in this retentive function. See Cherry, *Human Communication* pp. 18f; also Suzanne K. Langer, *Philosophy in a New Key: A Study in the Symbolism of Reason, Rite, and Art*, 3rd ed. (Cambridge, Mass., 1957). Karl Popper makes the point that language amounts to a line of division in biological evolution. See Popper's *Conjectures and Refutations: the Growth of Scientific Knowledge* (London, 1963) and *Objective Knowledge: An Evolutionary Approach* (London, 1972). A brief summary of Popper's position on this subject is given in Bryan Magee, *Popper* (London, 1973), Ch. 4.

10. *entretenir*, in the French, "to keep up, to maintain, to keep in touch with, to have dealings with, to keep alive . . . " *Larousse Modern French–English Dictionary* (Paris, 1960)

11. The imposition of silence, either upon certain words and phrases, or upon a person or group of persons, has been used as an instrument of authority. See Frazer, *The Golden Bough*, Ch. VI, for extensive documentation of tabooed words. A more comprehensive use of silence can be seen in the imposition of absolute silence for varying lengths of time in certain monastic orders.

12. This is really nothing more than a re-statement and application of the idea that "knowledge is power". It is interesting that this phrase can be traced to Francis Bacon (1561–1626), founder of a new method of communication himself: *"Nam et ipsa scientia potestas est"*, in his *Religious Meditations*.

13. This was true of the early hieroglyphic scripts of Mediterranean civilizations, as well as the Incas, Mayas and Aztecs of the Americas. See Cherry, *Human Communication* p. 33. Also, F. Bodmer, *The Loom of Language* (London, 1944).

14. We are following Cherry's use of linguistic terminology here, p. 11. The technical terms of linguistics and linguistic philosophy can be enormously confusing and will be avoided wherever possible.

15. An example of the relative impact upon society of a language technique: it is obvious that "literacy" and "illiteracy" are very different concepts in one culture having a chirography based upon 10,000 ideographs and another having it based upon twenty-six phonetic symbols.

16. This is not to suggest that there are not significant differences—in vocabulary, syntax, grammar, etc.—between written and spoken language as they are actually performed, especially by various social groups.

17. This passing reference is not to suggest that the technical and institutional accompaniments are inconsiderable. Their treatment is more appropriate to an historical account of the subject. The importance of schools and academies concerning the promotion of literacy will be discussed in subsequent chapters.

18. This qualification might be regarded as severely restricting the category, since it would tend to exclude societies with a "learned" language significantly different from the vernacular. This is a problem which requires a separate and

detailed treatment. For an account of the emergence of the French language from its vernacular status as *rustica romana lingua* in Latin culture, see Peter Rickard, *A History of the French Language* (London, 1974).

19. For example Franz Bopp, *On the Conjugational System of the Sanskrit Language in Comparison with that of the Greek, Latin, Persian and Germanic Languages* (orig. 1816). Also, Franz Bopp, *Comparative Grammar of the Sanskrit, Zend, Greek, Latin, Lithuanian, Gothic, German and Slavonic Languages*, 3rd ed., E.B. Eastwick trans., 3 vols. (London, 1862). For other studies in this field, see Edward Sapir, *Language* (New York, 1921), esp. Ch. IX; Bodmer, *The Loom of Language*, Ch. II; Holger Pedersen, *The Discovery of Language: Linguistic Study in the Nineteenth Century*, J.W. Spargo trans. (Bloomington, Ind., U.S.A., 1962); and a good introductory survey, Winfred Lehmann, *Historical Linguistics*, 2nd ed. (New York, 1973).

20. H.I. Marrou, *Histoire de l'éducation dans l'antiquité* (Paris, 1950); D.L. Clark, *Rhetoric in Greco–Roman Education* (New York, 1957); L.H. Jeffrey, *The Local Scripts of Archaic Greece* (Oxford, 1961); W. Mure, *A Critical History of the Language and Literature of Ancient Greece* (London, 1850).

21. Citizens were a relatively small proportion of the city-state's population. See Havelock, *Preface to Plato* pp. 38–40, 47–48 and bibliographical notes to Ch. 2. Also Marrou, *Histoire de l'éducation*, pp. 200–22.

22. Writings have been attributed to such pre-Socratics as Thales, Anaximander, Zeno, Xenophanes, Parmenides, Melissus, Empedocles, Anaxagoras, Democritus and many others. See text fragments from these figures in T.V. Smith, ed., *From Thales to Plato* (Chicago, 1965).

23. Aristophanes (c. 450–385 B.C.) probably produced about thirty plays, of which eleven survive. *Clouds*, dating from before 416–18, is the play ridiculing Socrates as a corrupt rhetorician.

24. Havelock, *Preface to Plato*.

25. Ibid., pp. 12–13.

26. Ibid.

27. Ibid., p. 14.

28. Ibid., pp. 30–31.

29. Ibid.

30. Ibid., p. 44.

31. Ibid., p. 45.

32. Ibid., pp. 46–47.

33. "Ethical imitation" as a guide to conduct or appearance is to be found in Euripides, Herodotus, Thucydides and Democritus. See n. 22. ibid., pp. 57–60.

34. Benjamin Jowett, *The Dialogues of Plato*, 3rd ed. (London, 1931)., Vol. IV, *Sophist*, pp. 342ff.

35. Ibid., "Introduction", p. 287, citing a reference to *Republic*, vi, 492.

36. This argument is made in fine detail in Havelock's final chapter, pp. 299–305.

37. For a discussion of the arguments surrounding this dating and a summary of the relevant literature, see Havelock, n. 4, pp. 49–52. Also, see references in footnote 20, *supra*.

38. Here, of course, the Sophists are simply accepting the cynical and immoral conventionalism that Socrates condemns.

39. Smith, *From Thales to Plato*, introduction, p. 59.

40. Ibid., p. 61.

41. Jeffery, *The Local Scripts of Archaic Greece*. Also, Havelock, *Preface to Plato*, pp. 49–52.

3

Classical Rhetoric

> For there is nothing of which our great politicians are so fond
> as of writing speeches and bequeathing them to posterity.
> Socrates, *Phaedrus*, 258.

The coexistence of a culture based upon oral communication and
a rising sub-culture whose identity is grounded in new methods of
literate communication is the significant feature of the era to which
we now turn our attention. The intellectual and social tensions
surrounding the introduction of a new language technique lead us
to propose that rhetoric, in its classical conception, is the paradigm
of political language for society in the period of early literacy. As
with any enlightenment period, perhaps, the distinguishing characteristic between the new and the old is not so much a new way
of seeing things as it is a new way of saying things. The latter
implies the former.

On first glance, it may seem paradoxical to state that rhetoric,
presumably a form of *oral* discourse, is the paradigm of communication in a period distinctive for its construction of writing and reading
techniques, that is, *literacy*. This paradox dissolves quite thoroughly
upon the briefest examination, for we know that even the earliest
descriptions of formal rhetoric assumed the technique of writing
in the careful organisation, divisions, and elaborations of the
argument. The very fact that memory (*mnēme*) was an elementary
part of rhetoric suggests that the skilful orator's oral effort
(*pronuntiatio, actio*) was based upon a manuscript.[1] In fact, the
oral delivery of a speech was not emphasized by the Greeks as much
as it was much later by the Roman rhetoricians.[2] The Sophists,
whose reputation was in large part due to the skill with which they
could both prove or disprove anything, framed their arguments in
written texts. Phaedrus tells Socrates that Lysias, the great orator,
has only recently been abused by an Athenian politician, who

"called him a 'speech-writer' again and again. So that a feeling of pride may probably induce him to give up writing speeches". Again, Phaedrus observes that "the greatest and most influential statesmen are ashamed of writing speeches and leaving them in a written form, lest they should be called Sophists by posterity".[3] Socrates, not particularly sympathetically, responds with the passage quoted at the beginning of this chapter. What is clear, then, is the existence of an intrinsic relationship between written texts and formal, or classical, rhetoric. This is not to say that early rhetoricians did not emphasize the importance of the spoken word. This is understandable in a society which remained generally unlettered. In a later passage in the *Phaedrus*, Socrates actually states his preference for knowledge that is present within the mind or is available to speech, rather than merely set forth in writing. "He would be a very simple person . . . who should leave in writing or receive in writing any art under the idea that the written word would be intelligible or certain; or who deemed that writing was at all better than knowledge and recollection of the same matters".[4]

We have discussed in the previous chapter how Socrates was both an enemy of and a collaborator with the Sophists and rhetoricians in establishing a new form of communication. Plato, in expressing the views of Socrates, makes it abundantly clear that the use of writing and speech texts was already an ordinary and accepted practice, even if Socrates is given the opportunity to express his bias—which he undoubtedly shared with others—against the public orator's reliance upon a text to express ideas and to use flourishing manners that belie the speaker's defective understanding. This is not the appropriate place to illustrate Socrates' antipathy to the political and Sophist rhetoricians of the day, which had more to do with his philosophical position than with a mere distaste for orators who are lost without a manuscript and are artless with it.[5] It is clear, however, that in the fourth century, B.C., a direct connection could be seen between the preparation of a written manuscript and formal discourse.

> Until a man knows the truth of the several particulars of which he is writing or speaking, and is able to define them as they are, and having defined them again to divide them until they can be no longer divided, and until in like manner he is able to discern the nature of the soul, and discover the different modes of discourse which are adapted to different natures, and to arrange and dispose them in such a way that the simple form of speech may be addressed to the simpler nature, and the complex and composite to the more complex nature—until he has accomplished all this, he will be unable to handle arguments according to rules of art . . . either for the purpose of teaching or persuading.[6]

The idea that there is a logical connection, rather than a paradoxical one, between literacy and oral rhetoric is only to reaffirm the contention that the period of early literacy coincides with the formation of prose technique. The very tools and capacities of writing made it possible to use language in very different ways from the oral tradition. Complex structure, topical organization, proofs and arguments (syllogisms, factual information and use of testimony) and rearrangement, among others were all due to the exploitation of written texts. But for these new techniques to serve as acts of communication, except within very limited circles of literacy, the medium of oral performance was still essential.

Our contention that rhetoric is the paradigm of language in early literacy is not simply a statement of coincidence, although that is itself a matter of some interest. Beyond the simple discovery of rhetoric as a primary language method in the Greek and Roman period of early literacy it will be argued that 1) rhetoric was the particular expression of that new technology; 2) its emergence reflects the transfer of the communication function[7] to a new language technique; and 3) the use of this new technique (rhetoric) defines social status and articulates the exercise of power. Tracing these lines of argument will, it is hoped, lend support to the major thesis of the book, namely, that successively developed language technologies give rise to dominant forms of expression and hence to a transformation in the forms of political communication, in the broad sense of that term which we have so far used.

What is "rhetoric"? There is fortunately no dearth of answers to this question. The problem may be the over-abundance of definitions and schemas for the conduct of rhetoric. Surely, no single "definition" of rhetoric is required for the instant tasks, although it may be helpful to suggest several—in addition to the one already offered by Plato on behalf of Socrates—as an indication of the range of thought on the subject. Similarly, it will not be necessary to burden these pages with a history of rhetoric, showing the contrasts and continuities in the writings of Aristotle, Cicero, Quintilian, lesser Roman lawyers, as well as the modern heirs of these figures in the Renaissance and Enlightenment period. We shall have occasion to make periodic reference to these ideas and figures, and otherwise indicate their importance in bibliographical citations.[8]

The term "classical rhetoric" is meant to refer to the early writings on rhetorical method from the fifth century, B.C., to the second century, A.D., in Greece and Rome, especially those containing systematic organizational schemes for rhetoric. At its most general level, there is no difficulty in defining rhetoric. It is the art of persuasion. Agreement quickly breaks down at any other level of specification. What is meant by "art"? Must the persuasion be oral or can it also be written? Is persuasion confined to language, or can it also encompass gesture, quality of delivery or even the physical settings and the use of objects, symbols, banners and music? Must the audience be of a certain size, composition or proximity? These questions are representative of the diversity of viewpoints available to notions about rhetoric. A lack of conceptual precision, however, need not prevent us from viewing the technique of rhetoric—as we shall call it here in recognition of its theoretical as well as its active social nature—as a persistent intellectual problem and an objective social force. Even the origins of rhetoric indicate the inherently political character of rhetoric. According to Cicero,[9] rhetoric as a distinct art was born among the Greek inhabitants of Sicily during the fifth century B.C. "At that time landowners and others who had suffered under the recently expelled tyrants began civil proceedings to recover their rights. The Sicilians, reputedly a sharp-witted people and not averse to controversy, enlisted the help of Corax and Tisias in presenting their case. These two men were the first to 'put together some theoretical precepts'; before this time, 'while many had taken pains to speak with care and with orderly arrangement, no one had followed a definite method or art' ".[10] The very term "rhetor" was used to recognise one who was skilled in the art of persuasion and was called upon to address legislative, judicial and administrative issues. In fact, the term was virtually a synonym for "sophist", referring to the teacher of rhetoric as well as to the actual orator.[11] The tradition holds that Tisias was the master of Gorgias.[12]

What we need to know about classical rhetoric for present purposes may be taken from Aristotle's *Rhetorica*. This is not meant to diminish in any way the work of his successors, especially Cicero and Quintilian, in whose works may be found remarkably elaborate codifications of formal techniques as well as psychological insight. The importance of Aristotle's work rests upon his efforts to re-direct the "art" of rhetoric and establish it as, in effect, a science. This claim recognizes that Aristotle, unlike any of his predecessors, namely, the Sophists and Plato, had established a connection between rhetoric and "dialectics". Dialectics was a term used commonly by Sophists, Socrates and Plato referring to logical proof, that is, a methodical procedure for discovering that which was true and rejecting that which was false. In this way, rhetoric was no longer simply an "art" of persuasion dependent upon an appeal to emotional dispositions. In Aristotle's exposition, rhetoric becomes a systematic method, incorporating what was then understood to be the science of knowledge, logic.[13] Thus rhetoric lays claim to being a demonstrative science with its own standards of proof. This was the reason why subsequent exemplars of rhetoric, such as Cicero, developed exhaustive variations upon the enthymene, and regarded the application of rhetoric in philosophical discourse, law, morals and even the observation of natural phenomena as an essential method in the acquisition of knowledge.

The significance of the introduction of logic into rhetoric by Aristotle, even if perhaps prefigured by Plato,[14] cannot be over-emphasized. This change elevated oral discourse from its prior status as "merely" a method of securing the persuasion of an audience by the mastery of eloquent speech, understood as a mimetic skill relying upon heroic models, an art that was accorded the status of a human excellence even in the epics of Homer.[15] Logic was the new method (*metho-dos*, a path, a way of going) for the pursuit of knowledge in all phases of human endeavour, including the discourse of law, morals and politics. If logic and rhetoric could be combined in a single method, the result could only be an all-encompassing theory of learned and public communication. This method, in a way that Gorgias had not fully appreciated, truly had the whole world for its frame of reference and potential application. It is easy to see how this new language technique—combining the power of artful eloquence and the organizational and truth testing methods of logic (e.g. division, composition, syllogism and inference)—possessed such enormous potential for the performance of that social function which we have called "communication": the preservation, elaboration, and transmission of information (knowledge) essential to social life. Aristotle, himself, it must be admitted, made a distinction between the science of dialectics as "a method [a scientific systematic procedure] by which we shall be able to draw logical conclusions on any question proposed to us from *probable* materials [or premises]", "which was the method of logic available to rhetoric, and "apodictics", or scientific demonstration, "that is, demonstration when the syllogism consists of certain and primary principles".[16] Nevertheless, Aristotle set forth a rhetorical method which seized upon the idea that oral discourse, when grounded in the careful organization and stable meanings afforded by literacy, could be a medium for the composing and persuasive articulation of ideas, the organization of complex materials, the presentation of convincing arguments on questions supported by conflicting or insufficient information, and the testing and clarification of knowledge.[17]

In his *Rhetorica*, Aristotle states that "Rhetoric is the counterpart of dialectic". He makes quite plain that there is both a distinction and a close connection between dialectic—meaning with virtual synonymity logic, philosophy or science—and rhetoric. Dialectic deals with certainties: first principles, axioms and logical divisions. Thus dialectic is able to proceed according to methodologically sound syllogism. (This, of course, accepts an Aristotelian epistemology for present purposes of argument.) Rhetoric, on the other hand, has at its disposal the enthyeme. This method of proof, although similar in so many ways to dialectical syllogism, particularly as to structure and arrangement, is different in the crucial respect that the information upon which its propositions are based are probabilities, rather than matters of fact or evident principle.[19] This is not to say that political rhetoric, among other forms, does not require knowledge and certainty, because these it must take for granted, to the extent that they are available.[20] The difference between rhetoric and dialectic, therefore, arises from the particular subject matter the orator treats.[21]

> There are few facts of the "necessary" type that can form the basis of rhetorical syllogisms (i.e., enthymemes). Most of the things about which we make decisions, and into which we therefore inquire, present us with alternate possibilities. For it is about our actions that we deliberate and inquire, and all our actions have a contingent character; hardly any of them are determined by necessity. Again, conclusions that state what is merely usual or possible must be drawn from premises that do the same, just as "necessary" conclusions must be drawn from "necessary" premises; this too is clear from the [*Prior*] *Analytics*. It is evident, therefore, that the propositions forming the basis of enthymemes, though some of them may be "necessary",[22] will most of them be only usually true.[23]

The kind of "specialized information" that Aristotle's political orator must have is further defined by the kind of audience that is addressed and by the dimension of time. Of the three divisions Aristotle makes, we shall be immediately concerned with only one, but it is important to see in the philosopher's own words how the proper subject matter for the political orator is indicated.

> Rhetoric falls into three divisions, determined by the three classes of listeners to speeches. For of the three elements in speechmaking—speaker, subject, and person addressed—it is the last one, the hearer, that determines the speech's end and object. The hearer must be either a judge, with a decision to make about things past or future, or an observer.[24] From this it follows that there are three divisions of oratory —(1) political, (2) forensic, and (3) the ceremonial oratory of display.[25]

Aristotle goes on to show that these three kinds of oratory really "refer to three different kinds of time".

> The political orator is concerned with the future: it is about things to be done hereafter that he advises, for or against. The party in a case at law (the forensic) is concerned with the past; one man accuses the other, and the other defends himself, with reference to things already done. The ceremonial orator is, properly speaking, concerned with the present, since all men praise or blame in view of the state of things existing at the time. . . .[26]

Aristotle goes into considerable detail concerning the subjects which are treated by the political orator, "the subjects of public business".[27] Specifically, they are five in number: "ways and means (food supply, revenues (*et cetera*), war and peace, national defence, imports and exports, and legislation".[28] Obviously, then, Aristotle expects political rhetoric to treat subjects about which actual information—times, dates, quantities, places and events—is normally available and directly relevant. This point, although seemingly obvious, will gain considerable significance in a later chapter, when the subject matter of contemporary political speech comes under scrutiny. Aristotle's emphasis upon what the political orator must know is significant. Besides the knowledge of these five general subjects, the possession of which will make him a learned man about the present and past state of his own society, he must know about other societies as well.

> He must, therefore, know how many different forms of constitution there are; under what conditions each of these will prosper and by what internal developments or external attacks each of them tends to be destroyed. . . .
> It is useful, in framing laws, not only to study the past of one's own country, in order to understand which constitution is desirable for it now, but also to have a knowledge of the constitutions of other nations, and so to learn for what kinds of nation the various constitutions are suited. From this we can see that books of travel are useful aids of legislation, since from these we may learn the laws and customs of different races. The political speaker will also find the researches of historians useful.[29]

In passages such as this, we cannot miss the impact of literacy upon the conception of classical rhetoric, and in particular, classical political rhetoric. Aristotle's political orator is, clearly, a literate man. His political rhetoric is a form of expression—a medium of communication—which is precisely to effect persuasion by the use of proofs and demonstrations which are grounded in actual knowledge. Consequently, when Aristotle defines rhetoric "as the faculty of observing in any given case the available means of persuasion",[30] he is proposing rhetoric as a method of comprehending social reality —with a view to acting upon it. The orator's resources must include all the knowledge available to the "political scientist",[31] as we have just noted. Indeed, the true orator must examine and have knowledge concerning virtue, individual happiness and the common good so that he may declaim with regard to the future, not only as to time, but concerning the common good. Aristotle is typically straightforward[32] in requiring the orator to know his people, to know their past and present estate, all with an eye to exercising ethical judgement that will promote and preserve the common good. This assumes a comprehension that will lead to wise choices concerning policy and courses of action, as well as the possession of the wisdom to identify the common aims and directions of the community. This, of course, is a perspective that one would assume on behalf of Aristotle as a representative of the classical mind. To know a thing was to know its purpose, its aim, its tendency: the *tēlos*.

The Aristotelian political rhetorician is more than a clever master of eloquent self-ingratiation. He is, rather, a man of singular learning whose task is to use this knowledge to urge a course of future action that is conducive to the common good of the *polis*. It is interesting and very important to take note of the fact that Aristotle's exposition of *political* (as opposed to forensic and ceremonial) rhetoric begins with an examination of the goods and aims of individual life—e.g., what it is to be happy—and extends this analysis, unbroken, into a systematic consideration of the four forms of the State[33] and their respective ends.[34] Thus Aristotle's conception of political rhetoric was one that emphasized empirical, practical and historical knowledge, but precisely with a view to communicating the kinds of deliberate advice required for the ethical and spiritual well-being of the community. So it is proper to conclude that Aristotle regarded the political rhetorician as possessing special knowledge, and thus to be a type of expert, in his chosen field of study. The possession of this special information was merely a pre-condition for putting it to use for the good of society, and, significantly, rhetoric was this very application, both as to the capacity of rhetoric to order, clarify, construe and prove matters of fact and probability, and as to the communication of this knowledge to the community. The *Politics*, therefore, confirmed that political science was the master science. The orator who would become such a master was not simply a demagogue holding sway with the magic of the spoken word; was not, as Aristotle said, the monarch or a powerful office holder;[35] was not merely a man of noble birth and becoming demeanor; was not, finally, an oligarchic power whose word commanded obedience. The classical rhetorician was a man of superior knowledge and experience, perhaps not unlike Plato's statesman or recurring "stranger"[36]—a *theoros* (spectator) —or Aristotle's *spoudaios*, the mature citizen, full of years, full of experience, full of wisdom.[37]

Guided by Aristotle, we are able to discover a coincidence between political rhetoric, as a paradigm of political language, and the more general conception of rhetoric as an innovative technique in communication during the period of early literacy. The political orator, in the Aristotelian frame, is presumed to have a special command of a body of knowledge. Political rhetoric was conceived as a method of special competence in arranging, testing and refining broad areas of information, all with a view to articulating this information as an argument on behalf of policies and actions contributing to the public good. So bold is this claim, it is not to be wondered at the scorn, and even violence, heaped upon those who dared to advise politicians who possessed more power than wisdom. In recognising the rhetorician as the possessor of special knowledge, we are likewise introducing the problem of differentiation in authority and status. If this implies intellectual, social and political divisions—and it does—this is only a recognition that the clarification and application of human knowledge is a difficult and dynamic process. It is, as well, an appreciation that a culture is not advanced or refined (or even preserved *in situ*) by superficial and confused perceptions of the moment, and that nature does not reveal her secrets to the unprepared and inattentive mind. Finally, then, we have depicted a paradigm of "classical rhetoric" and the characteristics of the person skilled in this art, the orator or rhetorician.

In the discussion of pre-literate oral society, a case was made for the political significance of language performance. A similar case for rhetoric would seem to be superfluous, considering the obvious relationship between this form of discourse and the exercise of political power. To the extent that rhetoric is, in fact, a form of "communication", we expect it to perform many of the functions carried out by oral performance in pre-literate society. However, as rhetoric is a technique of communication that has essential differences compared with pre-literate orality, we must expect that literate orality will produce substantially new effects within the political community.

Pre-literate society made no clear distinction between *magis-*

tratus and *mysteria*. Precisely this distinction, between the political and the supernatural, occurs with the emergence of literacy. This is illustrated in the secular prose of the Sophists as well as in the creation of formal rhetoric and dialectic. In oral society, a conflict among individuals might be articulated in the form of curses or formulaic exorcisms. Such uses of language are "received", in the sense that their form and content do not depend upon a speaker or author. The language—the word—itself is magic. In early literate society, a technique of articulating conflict develops that recognizes the speaker's own composition of speech. Rhetoric, of course, retains much that is formulaic, and emphasis is placed upon formal structure, but the substance of a rhetorical performance is, by definition, determined by the writer–speaker to meet the peculiar demands of the occasion. Rhetoric is created by a skilful—that is, literate—user of language.

The emergence of rhetoric as a public act, produced according to identifiable and complex "rules" of expression by the speaker himself, is a concomitant of the separation of the political and the sacred in society. The "ritual" of speech is retained in formal rhetoric, but the structures and patterns of rhetorical composition are largely independent of the subject matter that is being addressed. Rhetoric, then, as a public performance, is no longer a sacred incantation, but an argument. Rather than being an invocation and reinforcement of sacred powers, rhetoric is an articulation of conflict over power.

The complexity of rhetorical theory as set forth by Aristotle, Cicero and others is testimony to the effect of literacy upon the form and content of public oratory. The formal rules of logic admit the introduction of new types of information and new forms of proof. The eloquence exemplified in Homeric poetry, with its use of heroic allusion, ancient authorities and maxims of received wisdom, now yields pride of place to logic: to the examination of rational premises, known facts, probabilities and the rigors of syllogism. Thus rhetoric becomes complex, strives for intrinsic persuasiveness, and is increasingly independent of legendary wisdom, spiritual invocation or ritual incantation.

If there is a greater freedom for the speaker to provide his own subject matter and proofs, it is true, on the contrary, that turning one's back upon received wisdom and divine or legendary authority greatly increases the speaker's burden. The rhetorician must direct public attention to ideas and propositions the truth or value of which are not indicated by the collective wisdom of the ages. He will need more than chants and curses to advance his particular case.

Classical rhetoricians responded to this challenge with microscopic attention to the multitude of logical arguments (and fallacies), demonstrations and expositions that were available to the accomplished orator.

The greater "burden of proof" experienced by the classical rhetorician implied a comparable burden for the audience. In the paradigmatic audience of an oral culture, the response to oaths, curses and ritual incantations is obvious: the listener either believes in the powers thus invoked, or he is outside the tribal identity—the "magic circle"—and is a proper object of condemnation by the guardians of that culture. The auditor of rhetorical speech has a more onerous task, if not so threatening a fate. The response to classical rhetoric depends upon the availability of a more extensive and permutative vocabulary than that required for ritual and chant. The listener will need a more precise understanding of the meaning of words, an independence of mind that facilitates the acceptance of new information and the consideration of new ideas, and an ability to comprehend the structure, organization and transitions of the rhetorical demonstration with a view to forming an opinion of its persuasiveness. Classical argument, then, places the audience in the role of judge, instead of invoking an unquestioned authority. Power does not come, magically, in the spoken utterance, but from what the audience makes of the words. Most significantly, the element of persuasion appears in the relationship that the spoken words and phrases bear to each other, and not simply by virtue of the fact that they were spoken at all. This marks the difference between an oral culture and a literate culture, precisely because it points up the crucial function of the speaker speaking, on the one hand, and the word spoken, on the other. In the literate setting, as embodied in rhetorical performance, both the speaker and the audience are obliged not just to recognize the "word",[38] but to make sense of words and phrases as tokens of available or acceptable ideas and information which are presented in an intelligibly structured sequence that leads to comprehension. In sum, the listener must understand, not merely recognize.

The classical setting conferred a status upon the rhetorician as the possessor of special skills, but it also conferred on him the obligation to hold the attention of his audience. Without this skill, the speaker's efforts might well be repaid with boredom and scorn. If the setting accorded a subordinate position to the relatively illiterate audience, the orator's superiority did not guarantee the interest or conviction of the audience unless his rhetorical skills could command and win them.

The possibilities of psychological gratification in such a setting are numerous. An effective speaker has the opportunity to enjoy the success of his persuasive skills, as well as the happiness of finding a broader acceptance for his special knowledge. The distance between himself and the uninitiated in the audience may also be a source of gratification as he sees himself—as we might well credit to a speaker's ego—lifting them up, broadening their vision and ameliorating their ignorance. The possible regret in having to "popularize" one's information or "lower" the level at which it should properly be understood is balanced by the reward of succeeding in his rhetorical performance.

The audience is not without its claim to self-gratification. To be addressed by a speaker who wins you over, persuading you clearly of the good and true position, is in itself gratifying. Doubt, hesitation, ignorance or ill-confidence are happily laid to rest. To fall under the sway of a learned and convincing orator is gratifying simply because of the coincidence of interest between oneself and the speaker, who manifestly desires what you have to give: your attention and applause. The distance between oneself and the enlightened orator is no cause for pain, because in the very act of listening this gap is narrowed, and a community of interest expanded. It is gratifying, moreover, just to be the object of concern for the superior intellect, especially when one stands only to gain by it. Finally, it is highly rewarding to be, as an audience, with the strength of numbers and in a position to judge and evaluate the man of learning. It is not humiliating to fall under the sway of the orator, precisely because of the element of choice. If he were unconvincing, he could be ignored.

To say that the audience response to rhetoric is linguistically more demanding than in oral culture is not to say that the audience is necessarily literate in any advanced degree. We are talking about the use of language as a technology, and the prime focus is upon the developer and user of that technology, rather than the extent to which it proliferates in society as a whole. The technical complexity of rhetoric certainly does not operate independently of affective and charismatic features of language performance. As all students of rhetoric, both ancient and modern, have recognized, the power of rhetoric is precisely due to the combination of cognitive and affective impact upon the audience.[39] The magical component of eloquent speech is never fully replaced, especially for those who participate relatively less skilfully in literacy. For these reasons, it is clear why rhetoric has always concerned itself with its dual powers, and has preserved this symbolically in the image of the dual metaphor of *logica* as a clenched fist and *eloquentia* as an open hand. Borrowed from Zeno (of Citium, c. 340–265 B.C.), reintroduced by Cicero and Quintilian, and often used in the rhetorical works of the English Renaissance,[40] this metaphor expresses the point that Aristotle makes[41] when he admits the wide compass of the rhetorical method, and the independently powerful avenues to persuasion, dialectic (logic) and oratorical eloquence. Thus it is possible to appreciate the "artful" character of rhetoric —the lyrical appeal of the open hand—as a literary tribute to the oral past. Indeed, Zeno and Aristotle, as well as the tradition after them, often refer to "the rhetorical arts", by which they mean rhetoric as the "art of public speaking" and dialectic as the "art of logical expression". Zeno's metaphor is evoked by a sixteenth-scholar scholar, Peter Carter, with the equivalent distinction: "Dialectic is the art of disputing, rhetoric the art of speaking, the latter being more copious, the former, more compressed".[42]

This duality of rhetorical method, what we might call a philosophical reluctance on the part of literati to pay a full measure of esteem to the spoken word, is nothing other than the process of linguistic "retrenchment" discussed in an earlier chapter. The *new* (to early literate culture) method of dialectical disputation— an art whose development was seen to depend upon an emerging literate class—has rendered old forms of discourse technologically obsolete, and in the construction of a "rhetorical method"[43] undertakes the transformation of the old technology. Public oratory gains a new lease on life as "rhetoric", but does so only in the process of appropriation by, and on the terms of, the new technique, dialectical logic. Hence "oral discourse" undergoes a transformation as to its social effects. But to say that literacy has rendered oral discourse obsolete, causing it to be transformed or retrenched, does not imply that oral speech withdraws as a social force. Such evolutionary terms are used only to convey the idea that there is a dynamic—one might as well say a symbiotic or parasitic— relationship between an old and a new technique of communication.

The entrenchment of a new technique, in the present case the emergence of a literate tradition, involves the retrenchment of the old as to the formalities of its retention and appropriate use as a means of communication. This is illustrated by the insistence of classical rhetorical theorists upon a careful distinction between logic and the "art of public speaking". The aim of this art, to marshall the passions as a means of persuasion, was necessary so long as there were illiterate audiences, but this admission was qualified with open distaste at the idea of bodily emotions being used to perform the function rightly reserved for dispassionate intellection. The importance of such a distinction was confirmed for the classical rhetorician by the extravagant and wildly mannered *declamatio*, a fashionable form of entertainment in the Roman Republic. This oratorical throwback to the worst excesses of heroic "eloquence" and sophistic skepticism reaped the scorn of the learned, notably the Elder Seneca, Tacitus, Petronius and Quintilian, who regarded it as an enemy of reason and the true rhetorical method.[44]

Logic or "dialectic", therefore, emerged as a direct expression of literacy as a technique to communicate with those who participate in its skills, and artfully to persuade those who do not and who must be carried along with eloquence, the residue—as they are—of oral culture. Consequently rhetoric (combining dialectic and eloquence) has the capacity to reach a diverse audience and cover a broad range of topics, a capacity which amounts to a genuine "technological advance" in communication. Eloquence, the residue of the pre-literate past, is always there as an underlayer of language and culture, but it has been transformed. (In pre-literate culture, we might argue that dance and song are the residual layers of communicative expression for emerging linguality and orality.) Now, in literate society, the emotional use of language is seen as a specious and inferior mode of speech, to be characterized with opprobrium. Affective speech is inflammatory, self-indulgent, a mark of incivility and lack of education and a vulgar resort for those incapable of marshalling the forces of logic. Eloquence, if it relies simply upon heroic and poetic figures and expresses itself in commonplace wisdom, becomes archaic and merely quaint. Thus affective speech in all the forms characteristic of oral culture finds itself relegated to its now more appropriate place outside the significant channels of public discourse: demagoguery, religious rituals and creeds, poetry and song. Emotional language loses its authority in literate society. Its use discredits both those who resort to it and those who allow themselves to "come under its spell".

As the outmoded "language" becomes an anachronism in the new, literate society,[45] a sub-culture identified with it may acknowledge and defend its essentially transformed character. This may secure survival and a degree of cultural significance for the old forms by developing them into specific institutional identities: for example, religious ceremony, spiritual societies, folk-song and literature, dramatic forms and slang speech. Such institutionalization is, in a certain sense, reactionary, especially from the point of view of those with a vested interest in the new medium of communication. On the other hand, this process is an integral part of the cultural sedimentation of any society. Alternatively, the outmoded form of expression may be used as a countervailing force opposed to literate rhetoric and the segments of society interested in its consolidation as the new mode of communication. In this way, the old form may be a potentially revolutionary force as a medium of communication to the vast portion of society for whom literate and logical discourse is not an available instrument, and who may be brought to see it as a tool of oppression.

Notes

1. The use of written texts, including notes, outlines, etc., to prepare speeches certainly dates to the period of early literacy. This practice is assumed, for example, in a number of the dialogues of Plato. See *Phaedrus* at p. 464, B. Jowett ed., 3rd ed. (London, 1931), Vol. I.
2. A. Craig Baird, *Rhetoric: A Philosophical Inquiry* (New York, 1965), p. 15. The reader is referred to Baird's bibliography for primary and secondary materials on Greek and Roman rhetoric. A good general work on the subject is Donald L. Clark's *Rhetoric in Greco–Roman Education* (New York, 1957). Aristotle's *Rhetoric*, Cicero's *De Oratore* and Quintilian's *Institutio Oratoria* are the major classical sources.
3. *Phaedrus*, 258, pp. 464–65. The number preceding the page reference represents the pagination of the octavo edition of Stallbaum's Greek text of the Platonic corpus. It is used by Jowett, as it is here, to assist textual location in a variety of editions of Plato's works.
4. *Phaedrus*, 276, p. 485.
5. For the Socratic objection to the rhetorician, understood to be a Sophist, whose "art" has no proper sphere of activity or *telos*, see the *Gorgias* (Jowett, ed., Vol. II), esp. pp. 325–48 and 447–67; and *Phaedrus*, 258–79, pp. 464–89.
6. *Phaedrus*, 277, p. 487.
7. That is, the linguistic function by which society preserves, transmits and elaborates (perhaps adding to) information essential to the survival of its culture.
8. Besides A.C. Baird's general bibliography, Clark, *Rhetoric in Greco–Roman Education*, provides an extensive bibliography of primary and secondary sources for the classical period. Also see George Kennedy, *The Art of Persuasion in Greece* (London, 1963). Renaissance rhetoric is treated in D.L. Clark, *Rhetoric and Poetry in the Renaissance* (New York, 1963) and W.S. Howell, *Logic and Rhetoric in England 1500–1700* (Princeton, 1956); also N.W. Gilbert, *Renaissance Concepts of Method* (New York, 1960) and L.A. Sonnino, *A Handbook to Sixteenth-Century Rhetoric* (London, 1968).
9. Cicero, *Brutus*, trans. G.L. Hendrickson. Loeb Classical Lib. ed. (London, 1962), p. 46.
10. Peter Dixon, *Rhetoric* (London, 1971), pp. 7–8. This book contains a concise general bibliography on rhetoric, pp. 78–85.
11. Baird, *Rhetoric*, p. 5.
12. An excellent essay on classical rhetoric, including the forerunners of Aristotle, Aristotle himself and his Roman followers is E.M. Cope's *An Introduction to Aristotle's Rhetoric* (London, 1867). This work is a monument of scholar-

ship, and will be useful for any reader interested in pursuing special problems of etymology and translation from the Greek.

13. W.D. Ross ed., W.R. Roberts trans. *The Works of Aristotle*, Vol. XI, *Rhetorica* (Oxford, 1924). No single commentary can substitute for the immediacy and clarity of Aristotle's own exposition of this subject, especially Book I, 1354–1357. References to this edition of *Rhetorica* are the same Arabic numerals used by Ross (whose edition does not use page numbers) to correspond with Roemer's recension of the Greek text, second edition, 1898.

14. Cope, *Aristotle's Rhetoric*, p. 7, n. 1. See also pp. 6–14 and 67ff. for his discussion of the "science of logic".

15. Dixon, *Rhetoric*, p. 7. For an extremely valuable discussion of ancient conceptions of "method" and "logic", see Chs. I and II of Gilbert, *Renaissance Concepts of Method*.

16. Cope, *Aristotle's Rhetoric*, p. 74, translating from the *Topics*, 1c.

17. These assertions are precisely confirmed by Aristotle, esp. in *Rhetorica*, Book I, 1355[a], 1356[b] and 1359[b]. W.S. Howell, *Eighteenth-Century British Logic and Rhetoric* (Princeton, 1971), p. 262. Professor Howell has pointed out the distinction between consistency or coherence as a criterion of truth, and the criterion of factual observation. This illustrates a critical difference in a society's possession of knowledge, the former attitude (coherence) stressing *retention,* the latter emphasizing the *extension* of knowledge. Although it is clear to the modern mind that logic is appropriate for retention and clarification, and perhaps little else, it was seen by the Greeks precisely as a way to admit new content into man's understanding, in contrast to an adherence to the poetic tradition. See the related discussion with regard to E.A. Havelock's argument, *supra*, Chapter II.

18. *Rhetorica*, 1354[a].

19. Ibid, 1357[a]. Also, 1356[b].

20. Ibid. Aristotle mentions this specifically: "For if any of these propositions is a familiar fact, there is no need even to mention it; the hearer adds it himself". (1357[a])

21. Ibid., 1358[a].

22. I.e., matters of well-known fact.

23. Ibid., 1357[b].

24. Aristotle's word for observer is *theoros*, "spectator".

25. Ibid., 1358[a].

26. Ibid., 1358[b].

27. Ibid., c. 4, 1359[b].

28. Ibid.

29. Ibid., 1360[a]–1360[b]. See also passage at c. 8, 1365[b].

30. Ibid., 1355[b]. Note that Aristotle makes a precise distinction between persuasion and teaching (or "instruction"), 1355[a], since "there are people whom one cannot instruct. . . ." But even these may be persuaded by the non-dialectical features of rhetoric.

31. Ibid., 1360[b].

32. Ibid., 1359[a]–1360[a].

33. Democracy, oligarchy, aristocracy and monarchy.

34. Ibid., 1362–1366 *et seq.*

35. *The Politics*, Ernest Barker, ed. and trans. (New York, 1962), p. 1; also p. 231.

36. Plato's *Seventh Letter*, written late in life, is a sad reminiscence about his youth and the political turmoil in Athens in the late years of the fifth century. The young Plato confesses a longing for the wisdom of earlier ages and older men

which was at that time unheeded by his young and ambitious friends entering public life. See "Introduction" to *The Republic of Plato*, F.M. Cornford ed. (New York and London, 1941), p. xvii.

37. For an interesting discussion of Aristotle's conception of the man of superior wisdom, see Eric Voegelin, *Order and History*, Vol. III, *Plato and Aristotle* (Baton Rouge, U.S.A., 1957), pp. 299ff.

38. In the form of myth, ancient maxim, curse, etc.

39. See *Rhetorica*, Bk. II, 1378–1379, and Bk. III, 1404.

40. Wilbur S. Howell, *Logic and Rhetoric in England, 1500–1700*, p. 4. Also, see title page of this volume for an excellent reproduction of this symbol.

41. *Rhetorica*, 1354[a].

42. Howell, *Logic and Rhetoric*, p. 51. Carter's work, *Dialectica Ionnais Setoni Cantabrigiensis, annotationibis Petri Cartieri* (1572) popularized the work of another Cambridge scholar, John Seton (d. 1567). Translated by Howell.

43. As directly embodied in Aristotle's works: *Prior and Posterior Analytics, Topics* and *Rhetoric*.

44. See S.F. Bonner, *Roman Declamation in the Late Republic and Early Empire* (Liverpool, 1949). For a brief summary of this "debasement" of rhetorical method, see essay on "Rhetoric" in the *Oxford Classical Dictionary*, 2nd ed., pp. 316–17.

45. It must be remembered that this change is *evolutionary* in character, taking generations to manifest itself.

4

Literacy and Communication in the Age of Printing

> The art of printing is a commendable one, as it were the final trumpet-call of the world. It is the finest jewel of the German territory.
>
> *Martin Luther*

We have now to turn to another major innovation in the techniques man has used to communicate through the general medium of language. The technique that especially concerns us here is mechanical printing. This facility will be discussed with particular reference to the consequences borne within mechanical printing—as we shall argue—for public discourse and one of its particular elements, political rhetoric. From the outset, of course, we shall have to invoke the appropriate disclaimers to justify our precipitate and selective method of analysis. There is, surely, not a swift and direct connection between classical rhetoric as a scholastic method and the fifteen-century letterpress. Between these landmarks are several major scholastic, intellectual and technological heritages, each worth several volumes merely to record their history. Thus we can only give credit in passing to the accounts that have been written about the amazing durability of rhetoric in European history as a pedagogical tradition, as a formal influence upon philosophical inquiry, *belles lettres* and theological discourse, and as a guide to the shapes and sounds of oral discourse.[1]

If we have emphasized only the early development and effects of rhetoric as a form of language expression in Greek and Roman society, this is not to suggest that this technique, dating from early literacy, did not produce an effect in literate communication carrying over to later periods. As a brief illustration of this influence, it is quite obvious that rhetoric as a "technique" of handling information (organizing, clarifying, re-arranging, synthesizing, disposing of facts through proof or rejection) was particularly suitable to the Christian Church's doctrinal, ceremonial and liturgical needs and to the defence of its hierarchical structure.

It is equally true that the history of printing is a voluminous subject, and that any discussion of fifteenth and sixteenth century printing must take for granted the background of a rich and varied tradition of techniques by which graphic reproduction came to fruition.[2] Again, our present interest is not in tracing this evolution, but in identifying the peculiar effects upon political discourse that are the result of the appearance of mechanical printing. Thus if we do not extend our analysis to the task of establishing the successive transformations in the use of rhetoric throughout a period longer than the middle ages, and if we also cannot encompass the actual history of printing and early publication, we do claim as our immediate interest the process by which printing, as a form of expression for language, led to important changes in what we have generally called public discourse. These changes included, as we shall see, certain transformations in the form and function of rhetoric—defined as systematic oral expression—and in the very kinds of information that served as the content of learned and public discourse.

Marshall McLuhan has given a colourful slogan—"the Gutenberg galaxy"—to the period of civilization achieved, articulated and defined in terms of the improving technology of printing. This age is characterized by McLuhan as "linear", by virtue of the form in which printed texts are composed, as on this page, in many lines of language text which have to be read sequentially, as if they were a single, continuous line. This, of course, is not a rare insight, and would not deserve special notice if it were not for the suspicion that there are numerous implications to such an efficient, compact and relatively confining form of handling language.[3] McLuhan, himself, does not hesitate to suggest that the development of printing actually extended to the creation of a "linear culture".

From the point of view of language technique, the age of printing obviously presents us with a qualitatively different potential for expression. In earlier chapters we identified the purely oral technique by which language is directly produced as a phonic performance, and the chirographic or written technique, by which signs or representative tokens for sound images are "written down" and "spoken back". Now we are faced with assessing the effects of a mechanical printing technique, the chief significance[4] of which is the aspect of virtually unlimited replication of an identical text. This presents us with the direct paradox that a technique whose notable characteristic—among, albeit, many other important ones —is quantitative has produced qualitative differences. This result, which is not really such a puzzle, will be discussed at some length.

The advance in "communication" associated popularly with Johannes Gutenberg (Mainz, c.1400–1468), namely, the printing of books from a press using cast metal moveable types, certainly coincides with what we regard as the "modern" world. And yet from the viewpoint of the literate tradition pre-dating this technology, we must appreciate the fact that "linear" communication extends to much earlier times, including the earliest developments in chirography: stone engraving, wall paintings, wax tablets, papyrus scrolls and many others. So we cannot regard the appearance of mechanically printed books as an absolutely new technical phenomenon producing unprecedented cultural effects. Consequently, we will have to take care in settling upon the features of political language and rhetoric that are peculiarly associated with the rise of mechanical printing. "Books", as a class of cultural objects, were around and making important contributions to society long before moveable types, so we shall have to attempt to separate the one influence from the other—but with a view, in the present chapter, to establishing the unique effects of printing. We postulated an era of classical rhetoric that coincided with early literacy, i.e., the technique of writing. In doing so, we noted how the ability to read and write, especially with the skill of a Sophist or dialectician, contributed to the process of superseding the ancient oral culture; and we credited this process with significant social implications, recognizing that literacy was (like a sacred ritual before it) a powerful technology available to the few as a perquisite of power, status and the control of knowledge. Now our task is to see if we are able to discover a characteristic form or tradition in (political) language expression that coincides with the efflorescence of mechanical printing and its attendant effect of widely distributed texts, and at the same time to understand the political ramifications of the products, use and cultural integration (that is, control) of this new technology.

As we have noted already, this study will make no attempt to trace a continuous evolution of political language and rhetoric as inter-related articulations of advancing literacy and progressively refined printing technology. If we avoid that arduous task, we cannot ignore the distinct appearance of transformations in social communication that do emerge, slow and imperceptible though that process may be. Thus it is our present concern to determine the character of political rhetoric, broadly considered, when linear (printing) technology had established itself as the dominant technique of language expression. Specifically, what was the impact of printing upon public discourse generally, and upon "rhetoric" as an identifiable form of oral expression in particular?

It may be initially observed that such an approach begs an embarrassing historical question. When, after all, was there such an "age" of printing? The very idea of a proto-typical moment or era, indeed, mistakes the fact that any technological evolution— as for example in the development of the Phonecian alphabet— is dynamic and continuous. So, in this sense, the idea of an acme is a hopeless over-simplification. Similarly, it would be misleading to select a single date or generation in European history, and then survey the "evidence" of our subject (printing techniques, speech texts, books in print and other records) as if we were peering at a photograph—a "snapshot"—through a magnifying glass.[5] It will be the wiser course, as opposed to arguing for an archetype of "linear culture",[6] to set broad criteria for this presumed new age of communication. The criteria which distinguish such a period are likely to describe a broad span of time and place, and thus facilitate our examination of public discourse, rather than narrow down the scope of analysis to trivializing periodization. In fact, the difficulties of evidence and methodology are likely to dissolve as we move from the abstract to the direct investigation of the applications and effects of printing with respect to public discourse.

It must be conceded that we imply a degree of technological determinism when we speak of a "linear culture" or an "age of printing". Put more simply, language communication and public discourse will be viewed here as problems of technique rather than, say, of meaning and intention. To admit this as the focus of the present inquiry is certainly not to introduce an argument on behalf of a form versus content dualism, especially if we accept the classical Greek understanding of the relationship between creativity (*technē*) and culture. Surely it is apparent by this time that our entire investigation is grounded upon an assumption that the forms or techniques of linguistic performance are elemental components of speech, in its production and its meaningful reception. So let us move to the task of establishing the criteria defining the culture within which printing is a crucial determinant.

As we have noted, printing by mechanical means dates to a very early period. The first printed "books" appeared in Japan as early as the eighth century, A.D., although these were not produced with moveable types, an innovation that was vastly more prodigious than the process of printing by page plates.[7] We can confidently assume that "linear culture" did not appear so early, especially within civilizations whose chirography was pictorial or ideographic in character. So we must pass by ancient civilizations altogether, however elaborate their silks, scrolls and tablets; pass by the first Western books, scarce and laboriously created as they were; pass by even the first "editions" of books painstakingly crafted by teams of skilled copyists in Medieval monasteries. We shall even have to continue somewhat past Gutenberg himself, whose achievement represents the work of other printers and was historic in the sense that his work finally released the powers of the phonetically-based (as opposed to ideo- or pictographically-based) Roman alphabet through the use of moveable types. If we are to arrive at a culture in which the printed word has made a deep impression—legally, politically, aesthetically, intellectually and psychologically—it is apparent that we cannot settle for a period of time when books, even though produced on a mechanical press, were still virtually sacred in character. It was not until the sixteenth century that books and other printed texts first became a "mass" medium. Although books remained scarce and highly prized for centuries after this, it is astonishing how many thousands of books were printed in the first century's experience of this medium.[8] Pamphlets, tracts, manifests, journals and documentary materials were among many other texts that arose with indebtedness to the same technology, and it is clear that these artifacts were significant contributions to the substance of public discourse. The identifying feature of a linear culture, therefore, would simply be the broad availability of printed materials. An obvious corollary to this is that these materials would have a broad usage, ranging, perhaps, from popular consumption (whether as entertainment or, e.g., public notices) to special roles in official— political, religious and commercial—transactions. With these stipulations taken for granted, we should expect that the "linear age" which we are trying to evoke must post-date the times when the Bible appeared chained to altars, and when other books were enormously expensive and served as the playthings or status symbols of youthful nobility.[9]

Linear culture is identified by the presence of a mechanical or technological facility to produce books and other printed texts, not by the dozens or hundreds, but by the thousands and tens of thousands. This is not to ignore or underestimate the importance of the features which underlay the plain mechanical fact, such as the emergence of entirely new subjects of discourse about which to write (science and secular approaches to such subjects as Renaissance school curricula, manners, travel diaries and politics); the growth of universities; the expansion of literacy, and the expression of religious reformation across the continent. The conditions for widespread circulation of books and other printed materials existed as early as the sixteenth century in London, Paris, Heidelberg, Amsterdam, Brussels and many other centres of learning, which were not just coincidentally also centres of political administration. It is astonishing how the period beginning in 1440, with the appearance of Gutenberg's first Bible, and ending in 1600 encompasses a bibliography running to the tens of thousands and total volumes amounting to tens of millions.[10] Even more impressive is the display of books and authors that have come to be recognized as epitomes of Western civilization, all manifesting themselves within the first century and a half of printing. The list is virtually endless: Erasmus, Luther, Thomas More, Jean Bodin, Guillaume Budé, the Italian Bartolus of Sassoferrato,[11] Hughues Doneau, Peter Ramus, François Hotman, Machiavelli, Bacon and scores of others. Speaking only of the first sixty years of printing, one study makes the following estimate of the sheer volume of printed material: "Most specialists agree that the presses produced during the XVth century about 40,000 titles (books and broadsides); even at the low average of 250 copies per title, this amounts to an impressive total, 10,000,000 pieces, of which the great majority was produced during the last quarter of the XVth century".[12]

The distribution of this material is noteworthy, because it serves as a clear indication of the service to which this new technique of communication was devoted. The study already cited, which discusses early printing from the practical point of view as a business venture as well as a craft, offers an interesting analysis of the uses, and users, of early printed matter, before its "proliferation in the middle 1460s":

> Once printing had been invented its ultimate success was inevitable, but its early development and spread depended upon the willingness and ability of readers to absorb the production coming off the presses in sufficient quantities to support and encourage the printers and their financial backers. It is useful to examine the production before the proliferation in the middle 1460s; this, in turn, permits us to define the groups of consumers which by their purchases supported the new art. We note mainly the following groups: sacred and liturgical texts, law codes, a dictionary (*Catholicon* of Balbus), school books, calenders, indulgences (concerned with the proposed crusade against the Turks), broadsides serving political controversy, literary works of a moralizing character written in German. From this list we conclude that the earliest customers were mostly clergymen (the Church had been the prime user of books throughout the Middle Ages), teachers and students, and an undefined medley of townspeople; church and secular government had already begun to employ the press for their own aims.[13]

It is remarkable how the circulation of books achieved in the first two decades of printing set the pattern for the centuries to come. This trend is even more firmly established by virtue of the fact that during this same period early printers were producing works with illustrations, with texts in the vernacular. One printer in Bamberg, Albrecht Pfister, issued eight illustrated volumes, seven of them with German texts, and three of them were sufficiently popular to require reprintings.[14] Even a brief review of the categories of books appearing at this time demonstrates what is crucial to the present study. Printing was quickly, and predominantly, seized upon by the two primary centers of authority—Church and secular government—as a medium of communication and as a crucial supplement to previous modes of expression (*viz.*, oral performance and handwritten texts) in the form of liturgical books, homiletic aids, law codes, official and polemical broadsides, journals and dictionaries. Moreover, it is clear that printing gave expression, from its inception, to material of a secular, vernacular and (in a broad sense) literary dimension. In the area of education, which is particularly important in our consideration of the relationship between printing and rhetoric, we find that the mechanical presses of the earliest date were instrumental in providing texts in the special subjects of law, philosophy, rhetoric and science. The appearance of "text books" was even more significant, and far greater in magnitude, in the sixteenth century and beyond.

A more accurate impression of the subject matter and probable readership of the books of the fifteenth century is provided by J.M. Lenhart's exhaustive survey of the publications of that period.[15] Although his findings may be subject to the limitations endemic to such an undertaking,[16] the results illustrate the existence of major classifications by subject matter (and probable readership) and the presence of printed matter for broader sections of society outside the literate classes. The general tabulation for books printed to the year 1500, by subject matter, is as follows:

	%
Theology	44.5
Literature and Philosophy	36.1
Law	10.9
Science and "Pseudo-science"	8.5

Lenhart also reports that among these books and pamphlets, approximately nineteen per cent were clearly intended for broader readerships than the literate or intellectual élite.

	%
Romances, tales, facetiae	3.8
Poetry	4.3
Plays, orations, letters	4.1
History, biography	3.4
Virgin Mary	1.4
Calendars	.7
Witchcraft	.3
Occult	.9

It is also worth noting that Lenhart's analysis of more than 24,000 incunabula—books and pamphlets pre-dating 1500—showed that 77.4% of them were printed in Latin, 7.4% were in Italian, 5.8% in German, 4.6% in French, 2.1% in Dutch or Flemish, 1.3% in Spanish, and 0.66% (162 incunabula) in English. Hirsch criticizes Lenhart's conclusion from these figures that the vernacular tongues were held in general dis-esteem. By accounting, not for the percentages of total production, but for the "percentage of titles of each national tongue in its own language area", Hirsch concludes that the following percentages of books were printed in the vernacular tongue of the country of origin:[17]

	%
Italian	17.5
German	19.7
Flemish or Dutch	24.4
French	29.3
English	55.0
Spanish or Catalan	51.9

With Leon Battista Alberti (1402–1472) as an early defender of the mother tongue, followed by Dante's *De vulgari eloquentia* and Pietro Bembo's *Prose della lingua vulgare*,[18] the sixteenth century was to give evidence of an even greater use of the vulgar tongue in books and pamphlets. Latin had ceased to be the sole language of the learned and lettered class, and was used exclusively thereafter only by the Catholic clergy, among small groups of professionals and what might be called an intellectual élite in the universities and literary circles. The importance of the vernacular in early printing is noteworthy, but this need not be taken as an indication that Latin had somehow lost its pre-eminence as the language of the official and learned classes, even as late as the seventeenth century. Descartes' raillery against the clergy and university faculties, using Latin as a kind of symbol of their rigid backwardness, made this clear in his *Discours de la méthode*.[19] For present purposes, it is not necessary to enter into the dispute about the relative importance of Latin and the vernacular tongues during the growth of printing in the fifteenth and sixteenth centuries. It is sufficient to appreciate that printing greatly expanded reading and the production of language texts in whatever tongue, and that the rise in use of the vernacular was an indication of the expansionary force of this medium of communication.

Here it should be remembered that Latin had been, in an important sense, the "vulgar" tongue throughout the Middle Ages. Although *vulgaris* had, in Cicero's Rome, a rather negative association with "plebian" and the "mean" or "common people", as early as the fourth century A.D., the word "vulgate" was attached to St. Jerome's translation of the Bible, deriving its meaning from *vulgātus* (common, popular) and *vulgāre* (to make commonly known). Thus Latin, as a "technique" of language, was used to expand and facilitate biblical literacy for those who were not competent to read the scriptures in Aramaic, Hebrew and Greek. The fact that Latin became, in an age of printing, a restrictive language of special orders and élites only serves as further evidence of the evolutionary tendencies of language techniques, and how their appearance in successive ages is not only obsolete, but actually contradictory to the original communicative function. With the gradual impact of Latin-speaking culture on Europe, first under the Empire and subsequently with the expansion of the "Holy" Roman Empire, it is not surprising that this literate culture (in the actual sense of having a standard alphabet, orthography and grammar in classical Latin, including both a pre-Christian and Christian corpus of literature) would eventually stimulate the development of vernacular literacy.[20] Clearly, the evidence of fifteenth-century printing illustrates that a vernacular literacy had emerged, even in the face of Latin as the standard language for Church, State and school.

One must assume that the emergence of vernacular literacy and printing were symbiotic phenomena. It would, certainly, be futile to engage in debate over which was the stronger, or initiating, influence. We know that the use of vernacular languages in letter, song, oath and treaty pre-date the earliest letterpress printing,[21] but on the other hand it is equally certain that the use of printing influenced these languages by way of serving as a force for increased usage, standardized orthography and grammatical consistency. Yet the first books were in Latin, and one might even say that it was the users of Latin who first needed, and profited from, the facilities of printing. Thus it would be unfair to say that the development of printing was simply the effect of vernacular literacy's causal force. Without becoming entangled in a debate over printing's stronger association with Latin or vernacular, the wiser course would seem to be to follow the argument that the growth of literacy, generally, was the condition[22] in which printing was a plausible, necessary and apparently profitable enterprise.[23]

We are presently concerned with new and distinct phenomena which appear in the age of printing, and not simply with the increase or expansion of older phenomena associated with literacy, *per se*. Surely, the sudden acceptance of French, Italian, German and Spanish in literary works in the fifteenth and sixteenth centuries would be numbered among these new effects. A number of other uses of language which can be said to have emerged as consequences of printing are the printed broadside or broadsheet; school "textbooks"; periodical publications; a wide variety of collections, compendia and compilations; the standard "reference" books, which might be regarded as libraries in microcosm. The various roles of these products will be discussed in some detail below, but it is important to note that, together, they serve two intimately related functions: 1) communication at an extensive or public level, in the sense of transmitting and conveying information, and 2) the convenient (i.e., compact, standardized and easily retrievable) storage of information.

We may take for granted that any society—indeed, any civilization—which makes extensive use of printed materials, including the categories mentioned above, will be by definition "literate". By using this term, we do not intend to imply that such a society is qualitatively or intellectually superior to any other, or that the term recognizes "progress" over any other dominate mode of communication. Rather, we simply indicate that literate society relies upon language techniques for transmitting and storing information that are epitomized by the skills associated with producing and using widely distributed language texts. This is really only an overly cautious way of saying that literate society is capable of both publishing and using books and other printed texts. It is necessary to stress this fairly obvious point simply because of the social and political perspective of this study, and because of the many large assumptions that must be made on behalf of this perspective when it is taken for granted that extensive communication—that is, the transmission of information to large and remote groups, classes, or "publics"—can be accomplished by a medium which requires a popular skill, reading, that has not existed for the greatest part of human history. From the social perspective, then, what conditions are required to engender literate skills, and what will be the political consequences of having succeeded?

Before attending to these questions, we should distinguish between the meaning of "extensive literacy" as it is used here and the possibly misleading sense of such terms as "mass literacy". Extensive literacy and mass literacy are both essentially relative terms, and require specific information and standards of comparison to give them meaning. With the latter term is associated all of the ambiguities of the word "mass", leading to semantic connections with the notions of universal literacy, demographic indices and sociological jargon. By extensive literacy, we mean a social condition in which the availability of printed material, the means of printing and the ability to read and "use" the materials are not restricted to one or even a small number of groups. This definition does not solve the problem of relativity, but since we are not examining a single society or establishing a theoretical social model there is no need to set absolute definitions. In short, extensive literacy is a condition in which the printed word can be used by a number of groups, treating a number of different subjects, for entirely or largely different purposes. This is, in a sense, a pluralistic literacy in which the printed word serves a number of different and even conflicting interests, as opposed to early literacy, where reading and writing were the virtual monopoly of one or two distinctly élite groups.

The idea of extensive literacy exempts us from thinking about literate skills from the deceptive viewpoint of pseudo-objectivity which may perceive literacy to be simply a scarce economic commodity, a social or intellectual caste discriminant, or an arbitrary proportion of a given population. "Mass literacy" as a social characteristic is particularly ambiguous when it is considered that any society is bound to have an uneven use of language techniques. In urban centres, which we may characterize as amalgamations of many special associations—cultural, commercial, educational, religious and administrative—we are bound to discover literacy in its most intense employment. These centres always exist amidst vast expanses of provincial, agrarian culture, where language use is less specialized, and technically less "proficient" in terms of the most advanced modes of communication. Thus it is not surprising that provincial areas outlying the centres of culture and commerce will less faithfully reflect the dominant culture. This is true in any age, as it was in the early years of printing. The important feature of literacy for present purposes, then, is that the very existence of this skill among great numbers of people is evidence that society had responded, both technologically and institutionally, to a new form of language communication. This response is not only in the evolution of actual techniques of printing and its attendant phenomena—the craft of printing, paper making, type design and casting, sales and legal regulation—but in the development of schools and the production of books aimed at engendering the skills of reading and writing (among other subjects) on a scale never before possible or necessary.

This conclusion, holding that literacy and printing are essentially dependent phenomena, can be elaborated from any number of points of view: as history (of technology or education), *belles lettres,* sociology or even Hegelian or Marxian dialectics, to name only a few. But it may also be regarded as simply quite obvious and not very helpful. To explain extensive literacy, with a view to under-standing the implications for particular forms of public discourse, as merely a by-product of printing does not advance our argument very far. Much more may be learned about the growth of literacy, and its implications, by an approach which does not exclude the importance of technological innovation, but merely takes it for granted while investigating social and literary phenomena that tell us much more about literate discourse. This approach directs our attention to literacy itself, and the activities characteristic of this use of language in numerous social realms. These "activities" would include pedagogy; the use of language in science; public oratory of various kinds (religious, political and dramatic); and "reading" of any extensive type, including sacred texts, novels and newspapers as important examples. Among these activities—particularly related to pedagogy and public oratory—can be discovered "rhetoric", and because of the special emphasis this study places upon political discourse, we shall have occasion to examine this venerable class of language as it is manifested in literate culture.

Before turning to the characteristics of literate communication, particularly those features closely related to political discourse, we must settle a question as to the historical reference for what has been called literate society and culture, or the "age" of printing. Fortunately, we can date the origins of this period with an unusual degree of precision and confidence. As we have noted, letterpress printing was first used in the middle years of the fifteenth century, and spread rapidly thereafter. The production of books and other publications has steadily grown as printing technology has de-veloped: steam and electrical energy for mechanical operation at faster speeds, chemical and photographic processes for versatility and more recently the use of electronic computers for phototypesetting. However, if we are to examine the specific impact of printing upon public discourse, it is important to place a reasonable limitation upon the breadth of reference. The most obvious way to do this, of course, is to delineate a boundary at which it would be safe to say that printing was no longer an unrivalled medium of communication in terms of its ability to reach and convey information to extensive, diverse and potentially massive groups of people. Thus it is possible to establish the near boundary of the age of printing as coinciding with the emergence and proliferation of techniques of communication which have in common the use of electric transmission. Inventors were experimenting with the transmission of electric signals through wire conductors in the middle of the eighteenth century. W. Watson sent signals over two miles of wire in 1746. Within a few years, others were experimenting with coded signals.[24] Within a century, this technique was developed to a point of practical application with the needle telegraph of Cooke and Wheatstone, which was granted a patent in 1836. Samuel F.B. Morse's telegraph was patented in 1840. The invention of the telephone is credited to Alexander Graham Bell, in whose name a patent was granted in 1876. Improvements upon the invention of wireless transmission by Guglielmo Marconi led to the first successful "radio" transmissions in 1895, with a transmission across the English Channel in 1898. This list is only the briefest illustration of the rapid growth of electric communications, but it serves well enough as an indication that a technological transformation was underway in the history of language communication by the middle of the nineteenth century.[25] It is certainly appropriate, therefore, to establish this milestone as a terminal boundary for a consideration of the unique contributions of printing to political culture and political discourse. For analytical purposes, we shall assume that the "age of printing" as an historical epoch encompasses a period from the middle fifteenth to the middle nineteenth centuries, and that this term refers broadly to the use of printed texts as the dominant technique of communication, and not simply to the ability to read. The literate person—the man of letters— is not someone merely capable of reading, but is rather a person whose character is actually formed by his relation to books, be it as an author or a scholar. We shall assume this same sense of "literate" and "literacy" on behalf of Western culture in the period to which we have referred.

We cannot hope to trace the history of printing, book and periodical publishing, educational theory and practice, or even the history of political and religious oratory for the period 1440–1850. No single volume will be able to account for such a vast amount of material. Yet each of these subjects is important to our present interests, and will have to be within the scope of reference as we inquire into the character of political language and discourse during this period. We may be able to support such a broad inquiry if we keep carefully in mind that our essential task is to trace the changes appearing throughout the period in the forms and functions of political discourse, if such changes can be perceived at all. Because of the underlying proposition of this study that language communication—by whatever technique—has social and political implications (see Chapter I) with respect to the preservation, elaboration and administration[26] of the political culture, our investigation is as likely to touch upon the grammar school textbook, the novel or the scientific treatise as it is the speech in parliament or election campaign rhetoric.

An important aspect of a print-based literate culture is its cumulative nature. It is, quite simply though crudely put, a form of expression or communication that does not go away. Whereas in oral culture one of the primary efforts is to devise methods of retaining and preserving the elusive and ephemeral spoken word, one can observe by contrast how literate culture, even pre-dating the mass production of books, gave birth to its corpus, its opera, simply by failing to destroy or purge its heritage from earlier generations. This aspect is highlighted by the frequent occasions when exceptions were made and books were burned.[27] Even massive proscriptions of books or entire bodies of literature by the Church or certain political régimes can be seen in retrospect as monuments of recognition that such texts represented a powerful cultural presence. Consequently, we are compelled to add the dimension of time to our earlier definition of printing as a form of extensive communication. Books have somehow never managed to lose their sacred identity, and their preservation has taken on the character of a positive moral and cultural duty among many groups of people. The great libraries of the world are indeed monuments, and their costly maintenance by society reflects the importance placed upon their status as a tie to the past. The *opera omnia* of Western civilization place more than a financial burden upon contemporary society, however, and in later chapters we shall discuss the relationship between society's accumulated literature and the special status conferred upon those closely related to it. Here we merely need mention that the cumulative effect of surviving texts (in great numbers and sometimes "standard" editions) due to the quality of the printed object has important implications for other forms of language expression. In one sense, communication through printed texts "automatically" takes care of one of the primary functions of language—storage or preservation of information—and enormously simplifies another—access or retrieval. Finally, the extensive and cumulative availability of information[28] in printed texts cannot help but be a force leading away from the employment of other less powerful devices for preserving information and for symbolizing the authority associated with a source of valued information.

Another aspect of the period under consideration is the growth of literacy, in the general sense of that term. By the nineteenth century, with vernacular language firmly established as the medium for learned discourse, societies were bold enough to conceive for the first time public programmes aimed at imparting at least rudimentary skills of reading, writing and other subjects to every individual in the population. But there is some evidence to suggest that the ability to read was spread among "the common people" as early as the fifteenth century. Certainly by the sixteenth century we can infer from the great volume of books produced, the trend toward the vernacular, and the treatment and subject matter of these texts, that reading was becoming an extensive social phenomenon.[29] Sixteenth-century authors obviously addressed some books to people outside the learned and clerical classes, and produced kinds of books and pamphlets that could only have appealed to persons occupying secular and relatively mundane stations in life. A book which had originally been written, possibly by Guy de Roye, in Latin in 1388, *Doctrinal de sapience*, was published in a total of 21 editions in the fifteenth century after its first publication in French in 1478. The translator explained the purpose of rendering the book into the common tongue: "transcrit . . . pour le salut de son âme et des âmes de tout de son peuple et . . . especialement des simple gens laïques . . . "[30] *Danse macabre,* appearing in Paris in 1486, recommended itself as "Salutaire pour toutes gens et de tous estats". Lanzkranna introduced his *Himmelstrasse* (1484) in this way: "I have put this book into concise form and I have used simple words to show how men should live; I have done so for the sake of the poor and the ignorant, the intemperate and the lazy, the forgetful and the simple."[31] Geiler von Keysersberg translated Gerson's *Opusculum tripartitum* (*c.* 1510) into German with the following explanation: "prepared for the ignorant and simple priest and clergyman, for uneducated laymen and churchmen, for children and the young, and for those who take care of the sick".[32]

The Protestant Reformation is well known for the impetus it provided for popular education, particularly with regard to its emphasis upon the pious responsibility to read and study the holy scriptures. But Martin Luther's advocacy of popular education must also be understood as a protest against a tendency to undervalue the importance of formal schooling among parishioners, who apparently saw less reason to supply tuition to their children now that the Bible could be read in German and Latin was no longer a clerical language. In his *An die Ratsherrn* (1524), Luther reacted to this tendency:

> People say, why educate children, no longer chosen to become priests, monks or nuns. . . . Gentlemen, you spend each year a good deal for firearms, roads, bridges, dams and many more such facilities, to insure peace and a pleasant life to the people in town. Why not spend more, or at least as much, for the needy youth. . . . It is worse to neglect a student than to corrupt a virgin. . . . There is good reason to establish the best schools everywhere. . . . because we need trained men and women, men to govern, and women to attend house, children and servants.[33]

Apart from the revolutionary emergence of vernacular tongues in Renaissance and Reformation literature, and the effect this was to have on popular education and literacy, it is also noteworthy that Latin as a medium of learned discourse and formal education continued to play a great role in the general expansion of literacy. This role is indicated not only by the great preponderance of Latin texts, estimated at more than 77% of the total volumes produced,[34] in the early generations of printing, but also by the way in which early book publishing enabled for the first time widespread use of Latin grammar and other schoolbooks. Indeed, the growing importance of the vernacular in the fifteenth and sixteenth centuries certainly led to a clearer understanding on the part of the learned groups of the function of Latin as a universal language and to its defense as a crucial instrument for scholarly communication. This was all the more essential for the humanists of the sixteenth century, epitomized by Erasmus, whose interest lay not only in reaching back to the learning of Greece and Rome but also in maintaining a universal language for men of common endeavours located in lands of many different tongues. If this humanist concern gradually assumed an anachronistic character in European and English classical education in the seventeenth and eighteenth centuries, it is still accurate to conclude that Latin remained the language of school and university throughout this period.[35] An illustration of the importance of textbooks printed in Latin and of the inevitable contribution this use of printing made to the general increase of literacy is the large number of Latin textbooks on the subject of rhetoric. One bibliography lists no fewer than ninety rhetoric textbooks in Latin used in sixteenth-century schools and universities.[36] The same study lists thirteen treatises on rhetoric written in English, many of them having gone through several editions.[37]

There can be no doubt that the development of printing, and its consequent impetus for the widespread trade in books, had a great deal to do with the expansion of literacy. Although it is clear that this trend was uneven in some respects,[38] a general impression can be formed that the ability to read and the actual use of that skill grew steadily and massively in the period under consideration. From a cultural point of view, we may conclude that this trend was associated with a proportional impact upon public discourse, simply because literacy for all intents and purposes served as a new and relatively distinct medium of discourse apart from political oratory. This phenomenon is evident not only in the use of printing for the establishment of official journals and government records, but even more importantly in the evolution of newspapers, quarterlies, reviews and *pièces d'occasion* of frankly political treatment such as tracts, pamphlets and book length apologias. It is especially noteworthy that political journalism in the broadest sense, encompassing texts ranging from the broadsheet to the book, relied upon common literacy and the vernacular for its very existence. Latin was simply not an appropriate medium for this genre, and only a few scholarly journals ever appeared in the classical language.[39]

Printing was a medium for active political controversy. Tracts and pamphlets were the channels of communication for the doctrinal and political disputes of the Reformation, and the fame of such figures as Luther, Calvin, Zwingli and Erasmus owed much to the opportunity provided by the press. The pamphlet had a number of advantages for one who chose to contribute to public discourse. The writer could remain anonymous; the size, distribution and composition of his readership could be more or less controlled; the cost was relatively modest; an edition could be produced with speed; and the offering of a printed text made possible the presentation of an elaborate argument and the assumption of a clever literary style. The corpus of religious and political pamphleteering from the sixteenth to the nineteenth century is enormous,[40] and is best suggested by several outstanding examples. Apart from the work of the Protestants and their Catholic respondents, John Milton's *Areopagitica* is especially noteworthy because it was actually devoted to the defence of freedom of the press for controversial literature against a Bill before Parliament in 1643 proposing the licencing and censoring of all books, pamphlets and papers.[41] Thomas Hobbes and John Locke are also notable in this tradition. Locke especially availed himself of occasional anonymous little publications on religious and political issues which greatly concerned him. Without the opportunity to publish his view in this manner, his fame garnered from his philosophical works (and influential political ties) would actually have served to inhibit his participation in controversial public discourse.[42]

We have thus far established several characteristic features of the "age of printing" that, as we shall subsequently argue, led to significant changes in the form and function of political discourse. To review these features by way of summary, they are:
(1) the constant accumulation of language texts;
(2) the creation of bibliographical skills and instruments for the use of such materials;
(3) the growth of "extensive" literacy;
(4) the emergence of vernacular languages in literature and education; and
(5) the appearance of "political" publications and official and popular media—taking on the character of direct (printed) contributions to public discourse—based on vernacular literacy.

Notes

1. Chapter V, *infra*, discusses rhetoric and logic in some detail for this period. In addition to the two excellent monographs by W.S. Howell, *Logic and Rhetoric in England 1500–1700* (Princeton, 1956) and *Eighteenth-Century British Logic and Rhetoric* (Princeton, 1971), see his "Renaissance Rhetoric and Modern Rhetoric: A Study in Change", in *The Rhetorical Idiom: Essays in Rhetoric, Oratory, Language, and Drama*, D.C. Bryant, ed. (New York, 1966), pp. 53–70. A good general survey of the rhetorical tradition from Classical times is Donald L. Clark, *Rhetoric and Poetry in the Renaissance* (New York, 1963). A provocative and fresh analysis of this subject is Walter J. Ong, *Rhetoric, Romance, and Technology* (Ithaca, 1971); his other books on the tradition of Petrus Ramus (1958, 1967; ed., 1969, 1970) are also worth consulting. For a guide to rhetorical literature in the Middle Ages, see James J. Murphy, *Medieval Rhetoric: A Select Bibliography* (Toronto, 1971); illustrations of this tradition are given in a volume by the same author, *Three Medieval Rhetorical Arts* (Berkeley and London, 1971).
2. A number of comprehensive studies of the history of printing and publishing are available. A good reference work is W.T. Berry and H.E. Poole, *Annals*

of Printing, A Chronological Encyclopaedia from the Earliest Times to 1950
(London, 1966). This volume contains a good general bibliography. Henri
Bouchot, *The Book: Its Printers, Illustrators and Binders from Gutenberg to
the Present Time* (London, 1890) is superbly illustrated and retains its general
appeal. Also of interest are Warren Chappell, *A Short History of the Printed
Word* (New York, 1970), T.M. MacRobert, *Printed Books: A Short Introduction to Fine Typography* (London, 1957), which includes excellent plates of
early printed works, and John Carter and Percy H. Hunter, eds., *Printing and
the Mind of Man* (Cambridge, 1967). A carefully documented account of the
first century of printing is Rudolf Hirsch's *Printing, Selling and Reading,
1450–1550* (Wiesbaden, 1967). A beautifully prepared and richly illustrated
account of early printing and the graphic arts by Elisabeth Geck bears the
unfortunate title, *Johannes Gutenberg, From Lead Letter to the Computer* (Bad
Godesberg, 1968).

3. Marshall McLuhan, *The Gutenberg Galaxy: The Making of Typographic Man*
(Toronto, 1963). Also see McLuhan's *Understanding Media: The Extensions
of Man* (New York, 1964).

4. There are, of course, many other effects: the standardization of orthography,
the move from graphic to typographic illustration, the introduction and
standardization of punctuation etc. See *infra*.

5. It is enough to observe that the very idea of a "moment in time" is a logical
and conceptual fallacy. Clearly, then, historical precision is also unavoidably
extensive, contextual and relative as to "periods" of time.

6. As some have done. See McLuhan's books (1963 and 1964) and W.J. Ong
(1971).

7. Chappell, *Short History* (1970), pp. 3–12.

8. "An inventory of the physical and material progress of printing until the year
1500 would reveal more than 1,100 shops in 200 cities, in which some
12,000,000 books, in 35,000 editions, had been produced." Ibid., p. 84. These
figures are disputed by other sources, but appear to be of a reliable magnitude.
For example, the *Encyclopedia Britannica* (14th ed.) reports there were 40,000
editions of books between 1440 and 1500, yielding 15–20,000,000 volumes. This
source also cites the existence, by 1500, of 1,700 presses in nearly 300 cities
and towns in Europe.

9. See Charles H. Haskin's entertaining description of books in 13th century
university libraries and the care medieval students took in collecting an
impressive library of texts they may not have managed to read for their degree,
The Rise of Universities (Ithaca, 1957), pp. 37ff; 62ff.

10. See footnote 8, *supra*. Actually, throughout the sixteenth century, it is possible
to recognize printing as an essential feature of European culture, not only as
a medium of exchange in the Reformation debates, but also in education,
humanist scholarship and in the growing profession of the law, an accompani-
ment to the emergence of independent secular government. See Julian H.
Franklin, *Jean Bodin and the Sixteenth-Century Revolution in the Methodology of Law and History* (New York, 1963) for an account of the growth
of legal and historical literature in the 16th century.

11. The works of Bodin, Budé and Sassoferrato are discussed in J.H. Franklin,
ibid., Part I.

12. Hirsch, *Printing, Selling and Reading*, p. 15, n. 9.

13. Ibid., pp. 15–16. Hirsch bases these estimations upon Seymour de Ricci's
Catalogue raisonné, an *oeuvre* catalogue of the early printers in Mainz, and
Konrad Burger, *The Printers and Publishers of the XVth Century* (London,
1902). Hirsch reports that printing was an exclusive pursuit of the German

Rhineland until the 1470s, and notes that German printers predominated even in the several other European countries during the remainder of the 15th century. See Konrad Haebler, *Die deutchen Buchdrucker des XV. Jahrhunderts im Auslande*, (Munich, 1924).

14. Hirsch, *Printing, Selling and Reading*, p. 16, n. 11

15. J.M. Lenhart, *Pre-Reformation Printed Books* (New York, 1935). The figures in the following tables are taken from pp. 68–70, and are rounded to the nearest tenth of a per cent.

16. See Hirsch, *Printing, Selling and Reading*, pp. 125–26, n. 2.

17. Lenhart, *Pre-Reformation Books*, pp. 133–34.

18. Hirsch notes that a discussion of this movement appears in Vernon Hall, *Renaissance Literary Criticism* (New York, 1945). Hirsch, pp. 132–33.

19. The *Discours* first appeared, in French, in 1637. See Paul E. Corcoran "Descartes' Method of Humour", *The Dalhousie Review*, LII, 2, 1972, pp. 281f, for a discussion of Descartes' attack upon the scholastic tradition.

20. Peter Rickard, *A History of the French Language* (London, 1974), pp. 22–66.

21. Rickard, ibid., dates the earliest French text to the Strausbourg Oaths taken by Charles the Bald and Louis the German, sons of the successor to Charlemagne, on 14 February 942, pp. 29f. The first record of French serving as an officially sanctioned spoken language was recognized by the Council of Tours in 813, where "it was agreed by the French bishops that priests were to preach in the Romance or German vernacular, called respectively the *rustica romana lingua* and *theotisca lingua* 'so that all may understand what is said' ". (27)

22. Readers of a more Heglian persuasion may wish to establish this evolution more firmly by using the term "pre-condition".

23. See Hirsch, *Printing, Selling and Reading* at pp. 27ff and 63ff.

24. Colin Cherry, *On Human Communication*, 2nd ed. (Cambridge, Mass., 1966), p. 42. The entry under *telegraphy* in the *Encyclopedia Britannica* provides a historical summary of early developments in this field.

25. Not only did the telegraph and telephone play an important communication role in World War I, but as early as the American Civil War (1861–65) the telegraph was in daily use for communications to and from the battlefields, and for the transmission of newspaper reports.

26. By "administration" we mean the effective power to confer privilege and social status, and the determination of policy and social resources.

27. It is an interesting, if unanswerable, historical question as to whether more authors were condemned to death than there were books successfully censored and burned.

28. The availability is enhanced by the accumulation of books and other texts in libraries and other specilaized institutions; by the development of a special literature having to do with access: reference works, bibliographies, dictionaries and encyclopaedia; and, of course, by the gradual spread of literacy (in the sense of reading ability). By "information", we mean the encompassing definition as set forth in Chapter I, i.e., the very substance of the political culture as expressed in its language, ideas, and "specialized knowledge".

29. Hirsch, *Printing, Selling and Reading*, pp. 147–53.

30. Ibid., p. 149.

31. Ibid., p. 150. Hirsch provides other instances of authors addressing themselves to the "rude" man in French and German literature, pp. 149–53. Studies devoted to early readers, and what their authors thought of them, are rare. See H. Hajdu, *Lesen and Schreiben im Spätmittelalter* (Pécs, 1931), and H.S. Bennett, *English Books and Readers, 1475–1557* (Cambridge, 1952).

32. Ibid., pp. 150–51. G. von Keysersberg was a renowned preacher of the early sixteenth century.
33. Ibid., p. 151. Hirsch trans.
34. Lenhart, *Pre-Reformation Books*, pp. 36ff.
35. The accounts—and bitter complaints—of Latin and Greek pedagogy in European and English education are numerous. A feeling for the student's view of this tradition can be gained from the critiques by Hobbes, Descartes and Locke in their seventeenth and eighteenth-century writings.
36. Lee A. Sonnino, *A Handbook to Sixteenth-Century Rhetoric* (London, 1968), pp. 233–38.
37. Ibid., pp. 238–40.
38. It is an interesting feature of early printing and sixteenth-century humanism that Italy was the most important source of important classical texts and original humanist literature. See Hirsch, *Printing, Selling and Reading* pp. 137–43. Also Konrad Burdach, *Reformation, Renaissance, Humanismus* (Berlin, 1919), Part 2. At the same time, it is clear that Italy lagged far behind the North in popular literacy. This is suggested by the almost total absence of fifteenth-century examples of broadsheets, books on crafts and other forms of "popular" literature. Hirsch, p. 149. Also, H.S. Bennett, *English Books and Readers, 1475–1557* (Cambridge, 1952), esp. Chs. II, V and VI.
39. Although Latin was still the appropriate language for scientific treatises through the seventeenth century (a situation illustrated by the exception of Descartes' original edition of *Discours de la méthode* in the vernacular, later translated into Latin), Hirsch makes the point that the vernacular was often used in fifteenth-century incunabula to disseminate to a wide audience information of a scientific, pseudo-scientific and medicinal nature. Hirsch, p. 146. This argument is made in greater detail in Leonardo Olschki, *Bildung und Wissenschaft im Zeitalter de Renaissance in Italien* (Florence, 1922). An example of a vernacular treatise on science is Antonio Francesco Doni's *Marmi* (1552) which discusses the findings Copernicus reported in *De revolutionibus* (1543). See also, R. Hirsch, "The Invention of Printing and the Diffusion of Alchemical and Chemical Knowledge", *Chymia* (III, 1950), pp. 115–41. An interesting commentary on the supposed difference between the Continent and England regarding Latin literacy can be found in the title of a pamphlet that appeared in 1649, anonymously (George Bate), *A Short Narrative of the Late Troubles in England, First Written in Latin by an Anonymus for the Information of Forreners, and Now Don into English for the Behoof and Pleasure of our Countrymen*, London, 1649. (Fac. ed., London, 1902).
40. A number of collections of tracts and pamphlets have been published. One of these is by George Orwell and Reginald Reynolds, *British Pamphleteers*, 2 vols. (London, 1949–1951), which contains good surveys of the tradition by George Orwell (Vol. I, pp. 7–16) and A.J.P. Taylor (Vol. II, pp. 7–15). Also, a new and excellent study with facsimile title pages by Leona Rostenberg, *Literary, Political, Scientific, Religious & Legal Publishing, Printing & Bookselling in England, 1571–1700*, 2 vols. (New York, 1965).
41. Another of Milton's important political pamphlets was *The Tenure of Kings and Magistrates* (1649). See Chappell, *Short History*, pp. 111–13, and R.F. Howes ed., *Historical Studies of Rhetoric and Rhetoricians* (Ithaca, 1961), for W.E. Gilman, "Milton's Rhetoric on the Tyranny of Kings", pp. 239ff. For a discussion of the question of licensing, censorship and the role in England of The Stationer's Company, see L. Rostenberg, *op. cit.*, Denis B. Woodfield, *Surreptitious Printing in England, 1550–1640* (New York, 1973), and Roderick Cave, *The Private Press* (London, 1971).

42. Cave, *The Private Press*, presents a broad survey of the English press down to the present day, and provides a good introduction to the many interests which this medium has served. Also see Colin Franklin, *The Private Press* (London, 1969). Locke's *A Letter Concerning Toleration* (1689) is a case in point of a pamphlet serving as a mediation between learned and public discourse. The *Letter* appeared originally in Latin in Holland, was translated first into Dutch and French, and then appeared in London in an English translation (William Popple) the same year. A compilation of less well known works of the 17th and 18th century is available, Mabel D. Allardyce, *Aberdeen University Library: A Catalogue of Books, Pamphlets, Broadsides, Portraits, etc, in the Stuart and Jacobite Collection gathered together by W.M. MacBean* (Aberdeen, 1949).

5

Rhetoric, Logic and Scientific Inquiry

> The invention of printing is the greatest event in history. It is the mother of all revolution, a renewal of human means of expression from its very basis. Printed thoughts are everlasting, provided with wings, intangible and indestructible. They soar like a flock of birds, spread in all four directions and are everywhere at the same time.
>
> Victor Hugo

It is no small task, as the reader will appreciate, to bear all of the features of literacy in mind as we survey the social dimensions of language in post-Renaissance civilization. To make this task easier, we will turn to a consideration of rhetoric as it appears in the intellectual tradition of this epoch. As we have noted more than once, public discourse is a far more encompassing subject than rhetoric, and it is true that the former rather than the latter is the object of primary interest. Still, if we look at rhetoric in the period roughly described between 1440 and 1850, we will be able to establish a more concrete examination of one stream of discourse, and this may in turn serve as a point of reference as other, more broadly ranging, forms of discourse are examined. By way of foreshadowing one conclusion, it may be expected that the experience of one particular language technique—including formal structure, specific spheres of address (as to audience and subject matter), and social roles—will illustrate in a general sense the fate of other forms of discourse.

In an age of printing, with gradually accumulating stores of information recorded on the printed page, increasing literacy among the common people and the power of this technique to communicate with extensive and even massive readerships, what is the fate of rhetoric? Chapter III indicated that the rhetorical method was closely related to the early developments of literacy, and although it retained its identity as a form of oratory and its aim of popular persuasion, it was nevertheless firmly grounded in a technical effort to elucidate and give order to new kinds of information.[1] As a technique of public discourse, rhetoric attempted to persuade, but it accomplished this task through the application of reason (*logos*), a process which made a distinct contribution to knowledge simply because logic required division and discrimination among different classes of information, tests for the reliability and consistency of one item in relation to others, and rules or limits of propriety according to which the certainty of knowledge could be enhanced. Now, with our immediate interest turned to the role of public discourse in an age of extensive literacy, we are interested in discovering significant differences in both the conception of rhetoric as a "method" of (in the broad sense) handling information and as a technique of persuasive communication in this later period. We may anticipate addressing the following questions: What are the public and political functions of rhetoric in the age of printing and extensive literacy? What is the relationship between rhetoric and science, i.e., how are they similar or dissimilar methods of ordering and communicating information? Is rhetoric still an art of persuasion? In what sense is rhetoric a form of political language?

Even a brief survey of the rhetorical tradition from the sixteenth to the nineteenth century illustrates the profound transformation in the conceptions of rhetoric as a method of communication. We shall attempt only a rough schema of this tradition in the following pages, but it is important to touch upon several significant transitions which affected the role of rhetoric in education, in the pursuit of scientific knowledge and in public oratory. The central idea that we shall attempt to develop in this discussion is that rhetoric, from the sixteenth century onwards, underwent a transformation in the school curriculum and in philosophical circles that separated it from dialectical logic (and hence the substance of arguments); separated it from grammar (and hence the structure of speech), and relegated it to the status of an "art" of elegant and mannered speaking. At the same time, the elevated status of logic, resulting from educational methods which assigned to logic all responsibility for the accumulation and disposition of knowledge, was gradually lost when the influence of scientific experimentation promised a method of inquiry and discovery as compared with logic's association with disputation and deduction.

Although it is impossible to avoid simplification and overgeneralization, we can identify several relatively coherent conceptions of rhetoric in the medieval school curriculum. While appearing eccentric to contemporary views of education, especially at the primary level, rhetoric was an integral part of the school curriculum. Why this was true had to do with classical conceptions of rhetoric as a method incorporating the discipline of logic by which to arrange information, construct sound arguments and communicate them persuasively. Thus rhetoric, grammar and dialectic (or logic) were the "three roads" of the *trivium*. Upon this foundation, a student in the middle ages completed his education in the seven "Liberal Arts" by mastering the *quadrivium*: arithmetic, geometry, music and astronomy.

Looking more closely at the medieval background of what we have called the "age of printing", we are able to distinguish four separate traditions of scholastic rhetoric.[2] The first of these—and the one emphasized in earlier chapters—was the Aristotelian conception of rhetoric. This approach was philosophical, and consolidated the idea that the dialectic was an essential element of persuasive discourse. Aristotle's rhetoric "became extremely important in the medieval universities as a base for the Disputation (*disputatio*); Paris and Oxford, for instance, made the *Topics* and *On Sophistical Refutations* required reading for several centuries".[3]

The second tradition was the Ciceronian, and came into medieval education primarily through Cicero's *De inventione*, the Pseudo-Ciceronian *Rhetorica ad Herennium*, and a partial text of Quintilian's *Institutio Oratoria*. These texts could not have been nearly so influential without the aid of many writers, known and unknown, who produced abstracts, compendia, and commentaries of the seminal texts.[4] Ciceronian rhetoric was especially concerned with what might be called legal argumentation—what Aristotle called the forensic function—and can be divided into its five constituent parts: "*inventio* (finding of material), *dispositio* (arranging of it), *elocutio* (putting words to invented material), *pronuntiatio* (physical delivery), and finally *memoria* (retention of ideas, words, and their order)".[5]

The two remaining rhetorical traditions, the Grammatical and the Sophistic,[6] are of less importance to the present study, and were not nearly so influential in the development of the medieval school and university curriculum. The Grammatical tradition, especially in Roman schools, emphasized the importance of individual words, and of using classic poems or speeches as the basis of the student's rewritten (*imitatio*) model. Actually, this tradition introduced grammar as a separate discipline through its emphasis upon words as "parts of speech" and standard syntactical rules, a contribution primarily resulting from the *Ars maior* of Donatus (c. 350 A.D.)

and Priscian's *Ars grammatica* (c. 525 A.D.), which served as a textbook without rival until the thirteenth century.[7] The Sophistic tradition is worthy of note because of its association with "sophistic rhetoric" in the form of *declamatio* and *progymnasmata* which were, respectively, exercises in preparing and delivering fictitious political speeches, and the writing of short compositions.[8]

The importance of rhetoric in the school and university curriculum must be appreciated if we are to recognize the changes that took place in the conception and content of rhetorical study beginning in the sixteenth century. In both the Aristotelian and Ciceronian conceptions of rhetoric, the student's achievement in this discipline required a close familiarity with classical texts and the standard tropes and figures,[9] a mastering of the essentials of grammar and skill in forming proofs according to the rules of logic. The insistence upon the *deiectic* (dialectical or logical construction) method by Aristotle, and the presence of *inventio* (not just "invention" but the accumulation of substantive information bearing upon the argument) in the Ciceronian rhetoric assured the student that his rhetorical studies were inextricably tied to acquiring knowledge in any and every field of learning, along with the skills provided by logic in disputing, testing, clarifying and communicating that knowledge. So long as these traditions prevailed, rhetoric was an essential technique of communication among the learned, and between the learned and those—pupils and the common people —who were not so.

The Ramist Reform

The transformation away from the classical rhetorical tradition is a long and complicated evolution whose beginning may as well be traced to Pierre de la Ramée (1515–1572) as to any other single figure.[10] The truly revolutionary contributions made directly and indirectly by Petrus Ramus—his adopted Latin name—to logic, rhetoric and the liberal arts curriculum are admirably summarized by Wilbur Samuel Howell, and need not be recounted in great detail here.[11] A brief summary of his ideas will, however, convey the significance of Ramus in the transformation of rhetoric from its central role in the medieval curriculum to a greatly diminished status with much more narrowly defined responsibilities on behalf of knowledge and communication.

Ramus established his cause early in his life. At the age of twenty one, having overcome the severe disadvantages of an impoverished provincial childhood, he received his Master of Arts degree for defending a thesis which affirmed in the boldest of terms that the Aristotelian tradition was responsible for a system of education that was artificial, redundant and based upon philosophical claims of authority that could not be upheld. This was an attack upon the scholastic tradition embedded in the universities which was to be revived by other voices over the next century and more, most notably Thomas Hobbes, René Descartes and John Locke. In its essence, Ramus's reform was a proposal to reorganize the liberal arts curriculum. The difficulty, as he saw it, was that the curriculum based upon Aristotelian and Ciceronian divisions was inefficient and, most particularly, redundant. In this sense, we must identify Ramus as a kind of transition figure. As as educational reformer he was concerned with the improvement of the classical curriculum, not with its abolition and replacement—a work for later figures, notably Descartes, whose efforts and vision were firmly grounded in an entirely new method.

What disturbed Ramus was the way in which the Latin *trivium* contained ambiguous and inexact distinctions between fields of study, a confusion which led to duplication of instruction and unnecessary claims on behalf of rhetoric, in particular. As far as Ramus was concerned, the separation between logic and rhetoric in the *trivium* was especially artificial, and required students to learn substantially the same principles and supporting materials for each when actually only one was necessary. An associate of Ramus who participated in 'this reform movement, Audomarus Talaeus (Omer Talon, c. 1510–1562), summarized his efforts in *Institutiones Oratoriae* (1544) with admirable clarity. "Peter Ramus cleaned up the theory of invention, arrangement, and memory, and returned these subjects to logic, where they properly belong."[12]

Ramus had been anticipated in the reform of logic and rhetoric by Rudolphus Agricola (1443–1485) and was actually influenced by his thought through the lectures given by Johannes Sturm, attended by Ramus, at the University of Paris.[13] Agricola contended that dialectic was the proper method for the search for knowledge. Rhetoric was to be limited only to style and delivery. In addition to re-stating this plan, however, Ramus mounted a thorough revision of the liberal arts, the objective of which was to establish the proper methods and subject matter for all the arts, and hence the proper organization of all learning. The Ramian reform is a subject too great in detail, and too well treated in the literature,[14] to be discussed at length in the present study, but it is essential to illuminate the crucial effects of this reform on rhetoric.

It is not an exaggeration to say that Ramus assailed rhetoric in the same spirit as Plato in the *Gorgias*, where Socrates's larger contention is that rhetoric cannot be an art, simply because it does not have its proper and unique subject matter. Ramus does not deny that rhetoric is an art, but he forcefully concludes that its proper subject is style and delivery.[15] This distinction deprives rhetoric of the responsibility to encompass the theories of invention and arrangement, the methods which are the very foundation of the selection and organization of knowledge. And since the "art" of rhetoric has no need for these functions, the school curriculum should faithfully reflect this distinction. On the other hand, logic, or "dialectic, [is] the general art of inventing and judging all things",[16] and hence is charged with the great responsibility of presiding over the pursuit, organization and testing of knowledge. "To Ramus, logic was the center of the programme of liberal studies, and the chief instrument of man in the quest for salvation."[17] Even the art of disputation is subsumed within logical method, and not in rhetoric. Ramus points out that disputing well requires the study of .dialectic

> because it proclaims to us the truth of all argument and as a consequence the falsehood, whether the truth be necessary, as in science, or, as in opinion, contingent. . . . But because of these two species, Aristotle wished to make two logics, one for science [dialectic], and the other for opinion [rhetoric]; in which (saving the honor of so great a master) he has very greatly erred. For although articles of knowledge are on the one hand necessary and scientific, and on the other contingent and matters of opinion, so it is nevertheless that as sight is common in viewing all colours, whether permanent or changeable, so the art of knowing, that is to say, dialectic or logic, is one and the same doctrine in respect of perceiving all things. . . . [18]

Ramus is quite open in his views about the relationship between rhetoric and logic. Rhetoric, in general discourse, disputation or in education, is clearly subordinate and subservient to logic. Ramus identifies arrangement (*dispositio*) with "method", and declares that there are two essential forms, the natural and the prudential.[19] The natural method is equivalent to and appropriate for the organization of scientific discourse, where evidence and propositions can be joined together in logical progression. This, for Ramus, is an "artistic method", "a sort of long chain of gold, such as Homer imagined, in which the links are these degrees depending one from another . . . "[20] The prudential method of arrangement is not so precious a metal. It is necessary because the orator cannot always expect to have an audience capable of following a dialectical argument through the descending levels of generality to certain conclusions, and thus being captivated by the natural method. Rather, Ramus claims that the speaker must accept his audience "as a beast of many heads", and rely upon a captivating delivery to win their attention.

> And in brief all the tropes and figures of style, all the graces of action, which make up the whole of rhetoric, true and distinct from logic, serve no other purpose than to lead this vexatious and mulish auditor, who is postulated by this [i.e., the prudential] method; and have been studied on no other account than that of the failings and perversities of this very one, as Aristotle truly teaches in the third of the *Rhetoric*.[21]

It is very clear that Ramus has reduced the conception of rhetoric to a subordinate status as a theory of communication. As an art, rhetoric is stripped of the substantive tasks of invention and arrangement, and then is further diminished by its appropriation as an inferior concession to the unlearned in the prudential method of arrangement. Ramus has consequently effected an important break with the rhetorical traditions of both Aristotle and Cicero by depriving rhetoric, in its practice by orators as well as in the university curriculum, of the elements essential to learned discourse. Rhetoric had no need of invention and arrangement since these were the proper functions of dialectics in the composition of learned and scientific discourse within and among those conversant with the natural method of logical disputation. Professor Howell summarizes this reform as follows:

> To Aristotle and Cicero, dialectic was the theory of learned communication, rhetoric of popular communication, and thus both arts needed [invention and arrangement], while rhetoric needed [style and delivery] in particular. To Ramus, dialectic was the theory of subject matter and form in communication, rhetoric the theory of stylistic and oral presentation. By his standards, invention and arrangement were the true property of logic, and must be treated only in logic, even if arrangement had to have two aspects, one for the learned auditor and the other for the people. By his standards, style and delivery were the true property of rhetoric, and must therefore be treated only in rhetoric, even if the popular audience which demanded them had to have also a special theory of method that rhetoric was not allowed to mention.[22]

Tracing the changes from classical to Ramist conceptions of rhetoric is an important step in understanding the fate of rhetorical discourse in the age of printing and rising literacy. Of course it is impossible to conclude anything definite about actual political discourse merely by surveying the permutations in theories of rhetoric and the revisions of school and university curricula. If we have shown that the theoretical and educational importance of rhetoric as an academic discipline declined after the sixteenth century—a trend that is adequately demonstrated in the literature, even if it cannot remain the focus of our present interest[23]—this does not bring us very near to an estimation of the social and political roles of oral address in the post-Renaissance period. Nevertheless, it will be readily appreciated that our present argument is not confined to the narrow and untenable position that the ideas published by Agricola, Sturm, Ramus, Talaeus and many others were unrelated to broader social and intellectual conditions. Indeed, Agricola's critique of the liberal arts, Ramus's devotion to separating and subordinating the art of rhetoric, the wider publicity contributed by the writings of Talaeus, and the consequent curricular reforms on the Continent and especially among the Cambridge Ramists were all elements within a larger cultural movement involving the growth of science and the secularization of education and politics.[24]

It is clear that a relationship exists between the essential objective of the Ramist reforms and the emergence of extensive literacy in a society adopting printing as its primary form of communication. Let us review the reasons enabling us to posit such a relationship. To the extent that we do credit rhetorical theory and pedagogical practice with being factors in understanding the place of rhetorical address in society, of course Ramism has to be taken into consideration, even at the theoretical level of that tradition. Moreover, it is abundantly clear that the emergence, extensive distribution and gradual acceptance of Ramist reforms are essentially related to the fact that the guiding ideas were communicated in print. Without the publication of these ideas in books of many editions and many thousands of volumes, it is inconceivable that Ramist reform could have been debated and adopted so widely in learned circles in such a short period of time. From what has already been presented with regard to the association between early printing and the publication of books in vernacular languages, we are still further able to appreciate the impact of printing upon the dissemination of Ramist ideas. This aspect is especially pertinent in view of Ramus's undertaking to have his seminal work translated from Latin into French in 1555 and the re-translation by still another hand in 1576, four years after his death.[25] The earliest record of an Englishman's awareness of Ramus is a letter written by Roger Ascham in 1550. A Cambridge orator, he was writing to a friend in Strasbourg whom he assumes will be familiar with three orations published in Paris by Joachim Périon, a French Benedictine, defending Aristotle and Cicero against the attacks of Peter Ramus.[26] Such is the indisputable effect of printing on learned communication.

Perhaps the most important relationship between Ramist ideas and printing (or literacy) is the very interest in educational reform. Although the concern on the part of Ramus for philosophical integrity and theoretical consistency is undoubtedly genuine, it is hard to explain his enthusiasm for accurate divisions, propriety, clarity and non-duplication in the liberal arts unless this were an expression of the real growth of schooling, the need for efficiency and the express desire for standardization of techniques and "texts" on the range of subjects under instruction.

Taking all of these relationships between Ramus and the effects of printed communications into account, we can immediately detect a line of influence between printing and rhetoric. The capacities and techniques of one constitute a force (at both the theoretical and practical levels) that is imposed on the other. Thus the power and breadth of Ramus's attack is not only due to the printing and publishing of his ideas. This undoubted advantage in printed communication is not to be underestimated, but it is probably less important than another effect of printing, namely, the availability of (printed) techniques of storing, arranging and cross-referencing quantities of information that of themselves made the critique of traditional rhetorical doctrines effective by pointing out how the latter were redundant, confused and inefficient. The Ramist reforms in educational method—broadly viewed as a de-emphasis in the importance of rhetoric and a virtually religious devotion to the method of logic[27]—can therefore be seen as a major step, reaching all the way back to Aristotle's *Rhetoric*, in the gradual replacement of oral discourse by literate techniques. The contribution of Ramus is notable precisely because it is an explicit example of this transformation. The pruning of rhetorical studies and the growth of logic as the primary method of instruction (and specialized communication) occurred in an era of broadened and diversified education and expanding literacy. Most notable of all, this was a time of theological and political upheaval. The formulation and articulation of the lines of debate required, more than artful delivery, a method to perform scriptural exegesis and provide rules for accumulating, organizing and testing the admissibility of information relevant to the major issues dividing ecclesiastical and political authorities.

Ramus died in 1572, but his reform of scholastic logic spread throughout Europe in the late sixteenth and early seventeenth centuries. The Ramist system of educational reform was particularly popular in England, provincial France, Holland, Belgium, Denmark, Switzerland and Germany—in short, virtually the entire world of reformed Protestantism.[28] The opposition to this movement from established scholasticism was considerable. Two schools of resistance can be identified—the Systematics and the Neo-Ciceronians—and these are worthy of mention only to reveal a significant feature of Ramism. The Systematics were a diverse group of counter-reformers who endeavoured to establish a compromise with Ramism while still insisting upon the classical dialectical divisions sacred to Aristotelian scholasticism. The Neo-Ciceronians are more accurately described as those who simply rejected the Ramist reforms, and insisted upon "the Ciceronian position that rhetoric had the duty of providing a machinery for invention, arrangement, and memory, as well as for style and delivery, even though logic might also claim some jurisdiction over the first three . . . "[29] We note the lines of this debate that carried over into the seventeenth century simply to reveal the fact that the reform of logic and rhetoric, however important it was as an educational innovation and a reflection of profound changes in society, was essentially a movement confined to the scholastic tradition. The tenor of Ramus's writings and the reforms issuing from them were refinements and reforms of the scholastic tradition itself. The Ramist reforms of logic did not provide the foundations for what was to become the new, scientific direction of logical method. Thus to complete our picture of the changes which took place in forms of communication during the period of extensive printing and literacy, we must turn to a consideration of the descendants of scholastic theories of communication. This will require an account of a virtual revolution in the methods and application of logic, whereby the rigor of that discipline is transferred to a very different task: experimentation rather than communication, discovery of new information rather than the verification of old. As we enter upon this stage, a guideline may be of assistance. The transitions that we have so far identified —from rhetoric to logic to scientific experimentation—may seem to have taken us far afield of our subject, political discourse. That this seems evident is an illustration of the many ramifications of this subject, and how their pursuit carries us into technological, political and intellectual areas of inquiry. If however, we merely recall our fundamental definitions of political discourse and rhetoric —the communication of socially vital information, and the formal methods of communicating specialized and problemmatical bodies of such information, respectively—it is clear that we must indeed turn our attention to the evolution of a profoundly new method of informed inquiry and the relationship of that method to both learned and public discourse.

The Cartesian Method

To illustrate the evolution of this new method, we need only turn to the experience of René Descartes within the scholastic tradition, and his account of the dissatisfactions which led him to establish a new approach to learning. It is clear from his autobiographical account in Part I of *Discours de la méthode* that Descartes had undergone a classic scholastic education, and yet, delightful as his studies may have been under his Jesuit professors, he was convinced that, with the exception of mathematics, all their learning had "no better foundations than sand and soft shifting ground".[30] In contrast to this, Descartes reports that since terminating his formal study he has developed a new method during the course of his scientific studies that amounts to "a new means of self-instruction".[31] The boldness of this method is actually advertised in the sub-title to the *Discourse*, "for rightly conducting the reason and seeking truth in the sciences".[32] The reader of the first half-dozen pages of the *Discourse* cannot miss the sweeping condemnation of the "exercises" constituting his formal education at the Jesuit *collège* at La Flèsche, described by Descartes as "one of the most celebrated in Europe".[33] His literary strategy seems to be one of damning with faint praise, and at least we can be thankful that his education did not destroy his sense of humour. Ancient classics, therefore, are "fables [that] charm and awaken the mind". Books written by "the finest minds of past ages" are "artfully contrived talk in which they give us none but the best and most select of their thoughts; . . . the writings which treat of morals contain numerous precepts and many exhortations to virtue which are very helpful; . . . philosophy enables us to speak with the appearance of truth on all matters, and secures to us the admiration of the less learned . . . " In short, says Descartes with regard to the exercises he has practiced, "there is no one of them, even of those most abounding in superstition and falsity, the acquaintance with which is not of some utility, if only as enabling us to estimate it at its true value and to guard ourselves against being deceived by it".[34] Appearing in 1636, only three years after Galileo's works were condemned in the Inquisition, the *Discourse* was obviously a self-conscious prolegomena to a new method of scientific inquiry. Yet this work took the form of an aggressive and sardonic attack upon the scholastic curriculum, not as a programme, necessarily, for educational reform, but for the setting forth of a method of scientific inquiry. In this respect, the *Discourse* is a companion piece to the attack upon the scholastic curriculum of the English university by Thomas Hobbes in his *Of Vain Philosophies and Fabulous Traditions*.[35] In one sense, the *Discourse* was a piece of polemical journalism, not even taking the trouble to make use of the customary literary conceit of posing as a private letter to a friend.

It is significant that the *Discourse* appeared in print from a press in Amsterdam, and that the first edition was published anonymously. The availability of the techniques of printed publication is a contributing factor on both counts, considering that the production and distribution of a book could be accomplished at convenient and strategic locations, and in a manner that might circulate a writer's ideas widely without risking an acknowledgement of authorship. Descartes was painfully aware of Galileo's fate in Rome, as he suggests in the *Discourse*,[36] and did his best to delay the appearance of the essay until such time as he could publish his thoughts without inviting martyrdom.[37] This was very likely his reason for having it appear in French, on the assumption that censors might take a "vulgar" work less seriously, with the additional reason that his use of the vernacular reinforced the theme of rejecting the traditional demands of scholasticism.[38] Taking all of these aspects into consideration, one might be forgiven the conclusion that Descartes was an early strategist in the literary (i.e., "book") world who was consciously attempting to accomplish a *succès de scandale* through the appearance of a revolutionary work.

In addition to the importance of the *Discourse* as a literary event, there is even greater significance in this work with regard to the establishing of a method of inquiry that would profoundly affect subsequent conceptions of logic, and by implication, the relationship between knowledge and oral discourse. The fundamental and most revolutionary element in Descartes's method of "rightly conducting the reason" was the idea of learning "to distinguish the true from the false"[39] by ridding himself of both the form and the content of all that he had acquired in school. "In respect . . . of the opinions which I have hitherto been entertaining, I thought that I could not do better than decide on emptying my mind of them one and all, with a view to the replacing of them by others more tenable, or, it may be, to the re-admitting of them, on their being shown to be in conformity with reason."[40]

Although Descartes does not recommend this method to everyone, he is absolutely clear in stating that anyone following this new method must "resolve to strip oneself of all opinions hitherto believed".[41] Descartes does not blink at the radically personal character of his scheme: "My design has all along been limited to the reform of my own thoughts, and to the basing of them on a foundation entirely my own".[42]

What is of especial significance in the present discussion is Descartes's resolve to eliminate from his mind all that he has learned (the "opinions of the Schools") as well as the methods, including philosophy and logic, which supported this knowledge. Henceforth, anything that he will accept as knowledge will have to pass the test of the four rules of his new method,[43] the observance of which will assure its truth "so clearly and so distinctly that I could have no occasion for doubting it".[44] The effect of this method so far as the scholastic curriculum is concerned is revolutionary. For philosophy, logic and grammar alike—in the Ramist mode or otherwise—Descartes was disposing summarily of the elaborate Aristotelian methods and the stores of proofs, functions and "evident truths" which that tradition relied upon as the substance of classical learning. In arguing this case, we see what is the real intent of Descartes's project emerging repeatedly: *the discovery of new knowledge*, not just the sorting, separating and testing of opinions that have been held from ancient times.

> . . . in the case of logic, its syllogisms and the greater part of its other precepts are serviceable more for the explaining to others the things we know (or even . . . for speaking without judgment of the things of which we are ignorant) than for the *discovery* of them; and that while it does indeed yield us many precepts which are very good and true, there are so many others, either harmful or superfluous, mingled with them, that to separate out what is good and true is almost as difficult as to extract a Diana or a Minerva from a rough unshaped marble block.[45]

We discover in this new method an articulation of the great transformation into what has come to be called the "modern world" of thought and practice. Considering the efforts of Copernicus, Galileo, Francis Bacon and others, we cannot say that Descartes alone forged a method of discovery, experimentation and induction. It is, nevertheless, clear that Descartes set forth a clear outline "in the search for truth in the sciences", and that his method expresses as well as any other treatise the tendencies of seventeenth-century scientific activity, and its inherent need for a completely new foundation of epistemology, logic and communication. Thus we see Descartes as a revolutionary writer, so far as the scholastic tradition was concerned. We may observe the radical implications of Descartes's thought simply by assuming the scholastic perspective and suffering the arrows rained upon its philosophical fortress, logic, and its theory of communication, disputation. In addition to the definition of logic in the above quotation, where logic is deemed more useful for the explanation of the known, rather than the discovery of the new, Descartes delivers the following barb. "Nor have I ever observed that previously unknown truth has been discovered by way of the disputations practiced in the Schools. Each participant, striving for victory, is more concerned to dwell on whatever has the appearance of truth than to weigh the reasons for and against: those who have for long been good advocates are not afterwards on that account the better judges."[46]

Not content to charge "the philosophers" in the scholastic tradition with a disputatious method of reviewing received and apparent truths, Descartes suggests that they have in all likelihood lost much of their own heritage.

> I am indeed confident that those who, in these present days, are most insistent in adhering to the teaching of Aristotle would consider themselves fortunate if they had as much knowledge of nature as he possessed, even if this were on the condition that they should never obtain more. They are like the ivy which never strives to rise above the tree which sustains it, and indeed falls backwards after reaching its top. . . . Not content with knowing all that is intelligibly explained in their author, they insist on also finding in him the solution of various difficulties in regard to which he has nothing to say, and of which he has probably never even thought. This manner of philosophizing is well suited to those whose mental powers are of a decidedly mediocre quality.[47]

The final blow is dealt when Descartes likens the scholastic philosopher to a blind man. Invoking the image of Plato's allegorical cave, Descartes states that this is a willful retreat which constitutes an advantage to the blind man over his opponent, whereas the new method seeks to conduct its battle in the light of day, publishing its findings and claims and subjecting them to every possible adversary.[48] "Truth we discover only little by little, on some few issues; and it obliges us, when called upon to speak of other matters, frankly to confess our ignorance of them."[49] The effect of this attack is to replace disputation with experimentation. Instead of basing "learning" upon a method of ordering and clarifying knowledge passed down from the ancients, and trying to solve contemporary problems through a process of rectification with old categories and proofs, Descartes advocates a method of discovery. Reason must not be retained in the rigid service of logical disputation which assumes a solution resting in old notions and received knowledge. Rather, reason must be placed in the service of inquiry, discovery and the accumulation of new knowledge.

The implication of Descartes's new approach is that logic, or "reason", becomes a method of inquiry, shedding not only—as at the hands of the Ramists—rhetoric, but learned dispute, as well. From this it follows that the Cartesian *logos*—reason—is no longer a theory of communication at all, in any traditional sense of public discourse. It is a theory of invention, *tout pur*. It is a theory of knowledge based upon direct human experience, observation, and accumulation of knowledge in unprecedented depth and breadth. Moreover, this method assumes that the essential feature is not communicative or pedagogical, but is, in the modern sense, experimental and "scientific".[50] Indeed, it may properly be said that discovery is the pervasive theme of the *Discourse*, not only because it serves as a preface to "*La Dioptriqve, Les Meteores et La Geometrie, Qui sont des essais de cete Methode*", but because it was actually a work substituting for a larger work, *Le Traité du Monde ou de la Lumière*, containing a fuller account of his discoveries but which was deemed inadvisable for publication considering Galileo's plight at the Inquisition of 1633.[51] In Part I of the *Discourse* Descartes strikes this theme: "For so abundant are the fruits I have already reaped by way of my method in the search after truth, so complete is my satisfaction in the progress I deem myself to have made, that I cannot but continue to entertain corresponding hopes for the future . . . "[52] This theme of discovery, of accumulating new knowledge, actually amounts to a youthful enthusiasm for his scientific studies, which Descartes faithfully records even though the *Discourse* appeared in his forty-first year.

> . . . I have, it seems to me, discovered many truths more useful and more important than all I had previously learned or even hoped to be able to learn.[53]

> As soon . . . as I had acquired some general notions regarding physics, and on beginning to make trial of them in various special difficulties had observed how far they can carry us and how much they differ from the principles hitherto employed, I believed that I could not keep them hidden without grievously sinning against the law which lays us under obligation to promote, as far as in us lies, the general good of all mankind.[54] For they led me to see that it is possible to obtain knowledge highly useful in life, and that in place of speculative philosophy taught in the Schools we can have a practical philosophy, by means of which, knowing the force and the actions of fire, water, air, of the stars, of

the heavens, and of all the bodies that surround us . . . we may in the same fashion employ them in all the uses for which they are suited, thus rendering ourselves the masters and possessors of nature.[55]

. . . I am sure there is no one, even of those engaged in the [medical] profession, who does not admit that all we know is almost nothing in comparison with what remains to be discovered; and that we could be freed from innumerable maladies, both of body and of mind, and even perhaps from the infirmities of age, if we had sufficient knowledge of their causes and of the remedies provided by nature. Intending, therefore, as I do, to devote all my life to the search for this indispensible science [of medicine], and having discovered a path which, as it seems to me, must, if we follow it out, infallibly guide us to our goal, provided we be not hindered by the shortness of life or through lack of empirical data,[56] I judged that there was no better means of overcoming these two impediments than to communicate to the public all the little I have myself found, and to summon those who are well-disposed and suitably equipped to help . . . in the making of the required observations,[57] and in making public all the things each has thereby learned. In this way those who follow will be enabled to begin where their predecessors have left off. By thus uniting the lives and labor of many, we should collectively advance much further than each by himself could contrive to do.[58]

The Cartesian programme, as can be detected from the above passages, is evidently a revolutionary point in the scholastic tradition, and constitutes a transformation in logic that must be linked to the alteration of rhetoric brought about by Ramus. Professor Howell has succinctly summarized three important changes in logical method contained within Descartes's innovations, and these are of special interest for present consideration because these changes are integrally related to the emergence of new methods of accumulating and communicating knowledge. Moreover, these methods can be seen to have significance theoretically, as well as practically and therefore socially, a significance which looms large in any estimation of the character of change within public discourse.

In the first place, Descartes's *Discourse* calls for a logic that will accept experiment rather than disputation as the chief instrument in the quest for truth. The logic of the scholastics and the Ramists had been a logic of learned disputation . . . and its great unwritten assumption was that by conducting disputes man could detect error and establish truth.

In the second place, Descartes's *Discourse* calls for a logic that will be a theory of inquiry rather than a theory of communication. The logic of the scholastics and the Ramists had been formulated as an instrument for the transfer of knowledge from expert to expert. Thus invention was construed, not as the process of discovering what had been hitherto unknown, but as the process of establishing contact with the known, so that the storehouse of ancient wisdom would yield its treasures on demand, and would bring the old truth to bear on the new situation. . . . Once he had established systematic contact between these two sets of realities, the learned man had the materials for communication, and his next problem was to arrange these materials for presentation. This problem was solved by the scholastic and Ramistic theory of method. Method, to these logicians, was not a method of inquiry but a method of organization. Thus Ramus's natural method required that the more general statement should have precedence over the less general whenever ideas were arranged into formal treatises. But how were those general statements found in the first place? Ramus found them in custom and example, but Descartes could not find them there, inasmuch as his original loss of belief occurred because all knowledge found in custom and example seemed to him doubtful or erroneous. . . .

In the third place, Descartes's *Discourse* calls for a logic of practical as distinguished from speculative science. By practical he meant actually usable in life. . . . [He] speaks of the new science of man, and indulges immediately in a minute description of the functioning of the heart and the arteries. A practical science composed of minute descriptions of this sort would postulate induction as the basic logical procedure, and induction was to become the chief intellectual operation as discussed in the new logic.[59]

In view of the hopes Descartes expressed "to communicate to the public all the little I have myself found", Professor Howell's second point—that the new method was not a theory of communication—may seem somewhat at odds with Descartes's own views. The essential point to be considered, however, is that the desire to publish experimental data is an integral part of the theory of inquiry. By doing so, the scientist may offer to others, for their verification or extension, what he has found, thus contributing to the process of inquiry. The "general public" of which Descartes spoke was, no doubt, the small and dispersed community of scholars concerned with experimentation and observation about natural phenomena. This technique of communication, by publishing treatises on experiential findings, retained its specialist character, although it is clear that Descartes anticipated practical applications of these findings which would affect the lives of people generally. In any case, the communicative aspect of the new method was essentially different from scholastic logic's formal appearance as disputation, in which the organization, presentation and validation of knowledge is embodied within a form of discourse. For Descartes, communication amounted simply to publication—"making known" his observations—to others of like mind and abilities. Proofs or conclusions were merely tentative and temporary generalizations based upon these particular observations, and were naturally subject to revision or verification by newly discovered relationships or subsequent observations. Thus, as opposed to logical disputation, there was no point in retaining argumentation, exhaustive proofs or deductive logic as the superstructure for conveying one's discovery to the public. A theory of inquiry does not need a theory of communication as it was understood—invention, arrangement, delivery etc.—by the scholastic tradition.

The Port-Royal Logic

There are two additional events in the evolution of modern logic which bear upon our consideration of public discourse in the period dating from the sixteenth to the nineteenth century. Having surveyed the development and virtual transformation of logic—and by implication, rhetoric—during this era, we shall have arrived at an understanding of the relationship between the respective theories of knowledge (i.e., scientific inquiry) and communication produced in the closing generations of the age which we have identified according to its predominant technique of communication: the age of printing. This survey will not be complete, however, until we have traced the consolidation of logic as a method of scientific inquiry, and consequently, the isolation of rhetoric as a discipline of oratory bearing no relationship whatever to the method of scientific inquiry and publication.

The integration of the Cartesian method into systematic logic, and hence into the school and university curriculum, began with the appearance of what has come to be known as a classical text, *The Port-Royal Logic*. The first edition of this book appeared anonymously in Paris in 1662, only 25 years after Descartes's *Discourse on Method*, under the title *La Logique ou l'Art de Penser; contenant outre les Regles communes plusieurs observations nouvelles, propres à former le jugement*. This book, and the *Grammaire Générale et Raisonnée* (1660), which came to be known as *The Port-Royal Grammar*, were the product of a Jansenist sect of educational reformers attached to the monastery in Port-Royal, just outside Paris. The *Grammar* was written by Claude Lancelot and Antoine Arnauld. The *Logic* was the combined work of Arnauld and Pierre Nicole.[60] Along with Blaise Pascal and other Port-Royalists, these men applied their reforms—exemplified by the content of these two text books—in several "little schools" in the Port Royal district,[61] and conceived their educational theories as an attack upon the Ramist and scholastic methods in use in Jesuit schools and the universities. Imbued with the Jansenist ideas of anti-papalism and the importance of individual experience in spiritual life apart from the mechanical abstractions of scholastic "reason" and formal religious liturgy, this circle and its work were declared to be heretical by the Church. This did not arrest the influence of their writings in France and especially in England, where the books went through frequent editions for a period of more than two centuries.[62] *The Port-Royal Logic* first appeared in French, but had been issued in Latin by 1666, the first of many editions printed in many parts of Europe. Its first appearance in English was in 1674, followed by several other translations and editions turned out at frequent intervals down to the end of the nineteenth century.[63]

The significance of *The Port-Royal Logic* to this study is perhaps best conveyed by the very first sentence of *The Port-Royal Grammar*: "Grammar is the art of speaking".[64] But what must also be appreciated besides the absolute separation of logic and rhetoric —indeed the re-naming or substantial elimination of rhetoric, considering that grammar already had its place among the *trivium* —implied by this first sentence is the Port-Royalist concern in eliminating scholastic rhetoric virtually root and branch. In this sense, they were carrying out reforms in educational method that were implied in the Cartesian method, and this they did with an explicit acknowledgement and a reference to "a celebrated philosopher of this age".[65]

The Port-Royal Logic takes on the systems of logic associated with every notable figure of the scholastic tradition from Aristotle through Cicero and Quintilian, and even Ramus particularly comes under attack. The "places" and categories of classical logic are "of very little use, and not only do not contribute much to form the judgement, which is the end of true logic, but often are very injurious . . . "[66] The scholastic reliance upon standard authorities and arbitrary conventions in arranging arguments amounts to a distraction of the "reason" in its pursuit of a "distinct knowledge of things". Distinguishing between those sciences "treating of things above reason" which ought to "follow another light . . . that of Divine authority", and the proper province of human reason, the *Logic* contends "there is no ground whatever in human sciences, which profess to be founded only on reason, for being enslaved by authority contrary to reason".[67]

With the traditional structure and divisions of scholastic logic disposed of as mere artifice and unhelpful convention, the *Logic* is free to establish a system of logic that is amenable to the four rules of method which Descartes had set forth in his *Discourse*. The *Logic* accomplishes this by arguing that "Logic is the art of directing reason aright, in obtaining the knowledge of things",[68] and that this art consists in attending to "the four principal operations of the mind: conceiving, judging, reasoning, and disposing". Here we have a foundation that is consistent with the Cartesian method, even in tone and choice of language. The *Logic* separates logical method into two parts, analysis and synthesis. "Thus there are two kinds of method, one for discovering truth, which is called analysis, or the method of resolution, and which may also be termed the method of invention; and the other for explaining it to others when we have found it, which is called synthesis, or the method of composition, and which may also be called the method of doctrine".[69]

Under-scoring the turning away from logic as a speculative method for rendering and defending philosophical systems by disputation to a logic of inquiry, the authors conclude the above paragraph with this deceptively off-handed comment: "We do not commonly treat of the entire body of a science by analysis, but employ it to resolve some question", and a footnote to his sentence offers the following acknowledgement: "The greater part of what is said of questions is taken from a MS. of the late M. Descartes, which M. Clercelier had the goodness to lend me".[70] "Questions" may be either of "words or things", and the "things" are clearly of greatest interest to the authors. Merely to list the four principal kinds of these questions illustrates how the *Logic* incorporates the spirit of inquiry and discovery and departs from scholastic method's interest in deductive demonstration. Thus the four kinds of questions of interest to the Port-Royalists:

The first is, *when we seek causes through effects*. We know, for example, the different effects of the loadstone. . . .

The second is, *when we seek effects through causes*. [Mention is made of the difference between the ancients' conception of the effects of wind, and the way wind is harnessed to drive wind mills, "useful to society", "the appropriate result of true physics".]

The third kind of question is, *when through the parts we seek the whole*
. . . .

The fourth is, *when, having the whole and some part, we seek another part*.[71]

It is quite clear from this approach to logic that the Port-

Royalists were indeed deeply indebted to both the method and the spirit of Descartes. Later in the same chapter from which this list is taken, the authors leave no question as to their indebtedness to Descartes, and to their commitment to the practical results and benefits of logical inquiry—or, as they call it, "analysis"—and not to the rigorous adherence to an elaborate system: "This is what may be said generally touching analysis, which consists more in judgement and sagacity of mind than in particular rules. The four following [rules], nevertheless, which M. Descartes proposes in his Method, may be useful for preserving us from error . . . ".[72]

The *Logic* has much less to say about synthesis, which is that part of method concerned with composition and presentation. Nevertheless, it is evident that the Port-Royalists were not sufficiently advanced in their theoretical conception of logic as to deprive it altogether of its presentational obligations. Logic was still required to communicate the discoveries achieved by analysis and inquiry, and thus the Port-Royalists made no sweeping exclusion of this residual responsibility that by then, a large step further removed from the Ramist diminution in the status of rhetoric, could hardly claim to be called the "art of rhetoric". Indeed, rather than relegate "presentation" back to rhetoric, it seems that they were more inclined, as indicated in the sentence quoted from the *Grammar*, to associate this function with grammar itself.[73]

The Port-Royal Logic performed one task that was to have historic importance: the inclusion of induction within a system of logic, with the associated modification of the predominant role of the deductive syllogism.

> When, from the examination of many particular things, we rise to the knowledge of a general truth—this is called induction. . . . It is in this way that all our knowledge begins, since individual things present themselves to us before universals, although, afterward, universals help us to know the individual.
> It is, however, nevertheless true, that induction alone is never a certain means of acquiring perfect knowledge. . . .[74]

The qualification stated in this last phrase is notable not so much for its lack of commitment to the value of induction as for its evocation of a practical, open and admittedly imperfect approach to the discovery of knowledge. In fact, the authors of *The Port-Royal Logic* made it quite clear[75] that logic of all kinds, and the method of syllogism in particular, were likely to mislead one in the pursuit of certain knowledge. The message is clear that one should rely less on *principles* and more on empirical *observation*.

It goes without saying that the *Logic*'s faithful reflection of Descartes's emphasis upon experience of the discrete and particular event as the foundation of the inductive method was a milestone in the history of scientific method. This was true not because observation and induction had never been employed as an experimental method prior to the *Logic*, but because the appearance of this book, and its central role in school and university curricula thereafter, confirmed and established a new method for the acquisition, organization, verification and (now more crucial than ever before) the rejection of knowledge.

Having made this claim on behalf of *The Port-Royal Logic*, we must be fair to the special interests of its authors and recognize that their direct concerns had more to do with religious doctrine and authority than with the "human sciences". The *Logic* was not simply a prolegomena to scientific experimentation by way of an attack upon the scholastic curriculum, although it was indeed both of these in part. Rather, the *Logic* saw that the use of the method advanced by the "celebrated philosopher" was appropriate to the task of fighting rigid authority and false doctrine and advancing the argument in favor of personal experience and discovery as the foundation of spiritual life, educational theory and practical (scientific) knowledge. In this sense, the impetus given to the human sciences and the natural sciences generally by the *Logic* was implicit, if somewhat inadvertent, in the "new logic" that was set forth. This no doubt explains why the *Logic* devotes so much attention to semantics, imperfect reasoning, moral confusions and common and doctrinal fallacies,[76] and yet makes periodic, even casual, references to the effect that this new method of "analysis" happens to be applicable to—or even coincident with—the method propounded by Descartes for the sciences.[77]

The importance of the new logic to the school and university course of study was evident, and the Port-Royalist *Grammar* and *Rhetoric* were to become standard textbooks for generations. Moreover, these works constituted the reform tendencies which finally supplanted the scholastic approach to learning and made way for an educational method susceptible both to the scientific method and to the spirit of inquiry and discovery. The compatibility of the *Logic* of the Port-Royalists to the sweeping changes in education and the advancement of learning implied by Descartes can be appreciated on a number of fronts. Just as Descartes had criticized disputation as a barren approach to knowledge in favor of experimentation, so the *Logic* denies a place for disputation among the four "operations" of the mind and the three "services" of logic.[78]

In fact, the Port-Royalists suggest that "the spirit of debate" can be "a vice very injurious to the mind" due to the tendency of seeking unwise arguments to support one's opinions as well as one's pride.[79]

The Port-Royalists must also be seen as reinforcing the movement away from the conception of logic as a theory of communication —as a method of imparting truth—and toward a logic of inquiry and discovery. It must be granted that the *Logic* retained a vestige of the rhetorical function in its method of synthesis or composition, by which the substance of inquiry may be offered to the public. Yet is it clear that the Port-Royalists' chief concern was the method of "analysis", and the fact that this method is advanced by way of simple incorporation of Descartes's four rules of method is unmistakable evidence that the educational reforms of Port Royal point to the future of scientific inquiry and turn away from the conception and function of logic within the scholastic tradition.

Finally, the Port-Royalists were directly concerned that logic be of practical use and that logic "exists for the very purpose of being an instrument to other sciences".[80] Scholastic logic is criticized because "those who study it are accustomed to find out the nature of propositions or reasonings, only as they follow the order and arrangement according to which they are fashioned in the schools, which is often very different from that according to which they are fashioned in the world and in books—whether of eloquence, or of morals, or of other sciences".[81] Thus, say the Port-Royalists, "experience shows that, of a thousand young men who learn logic, there are not ten who remember anything of it six months after they have finished their course".[82] The concern of the new logic, therefore, was to provide a method according to which knowledge could progress according to a procedure and in actual areas of inquiry suggested by the real needs of society. The old logic, as it were, did not exist apart from the dusty textbooks of scholasticism and the formal rules, schemes and examples contained therein. *The Port-Royal Logic*, then, was a plan to create a useful method of inquiry into subjects the advancement of which would itself guarantee the lively survival of logic. Logic need not be propped up as an artificial method or "art" in abstraction from the practical concerns of men and the content of empirical knowledge produced by seventeenth-century scientific inquiry, which was obviously straining against the confines of scholasticism. Rather, "logic" must be seen as an instrument whose existence is to be found in the service of the practical endeavours of experimental science.

Mill's Scientific Logic

The special interests in educational reform and religious doctrine of the Port-Royalists prevented their *Logic* from serving in any explicit sense as a treatise on scientific inquiry. Nevertheless, *The Port-Royal Logic* pointed the way in articulating a method of scientific investigation and integrating this discipline into the school curriculum, and the book remained a powerful influence into the nineteenth century. We shall conclude this account of the evolution of modern logic as a method of scientific inquiry by identifying the work which finally accomplished the task of translating the Cartesian spirit of inquiry, empirical observation and practical knowledge into a fully developed system of logic. This honour, if it is to be so regarded, surely belongs to John Stuart Mill's *A System of Logic, Ratiocinative and Inductive*, first published in 1843.[83] If ever the sub-title of a book were important to illustrate the intentions of its author and the importance of its contents, here is such a case: *Being a Connected View of the Principles of Evidence and the Methods of Scientific Investigation.*

Mill's *System of Logic* can be said to be a culmination in the tradition of scholastic logic. We think of it as a culmination rather than a point of departure because it finally incorporated the requisites of the Cartesian method of experimentalism and induction into a fully elaborated logical system, and yet this task was accomplished by a mind trained to meet the arguments and perceive the problems of scholastic logic beginning with Aristotle and surviving into the treatises of philosophy and logic of his own day.[84] The primary problem to which Mill drew his attention is precisely the one that is of present interest in this study, namely, the establishment of a logic of inquiry—a system of logic which would finally admit experimentation, inference and empirically-based knowledge into the privileged company of justifiable rational conduct. Furthermore Mill's *Autobiography* makes it clear that this is how he understood and approached the problem.

> In . . . 1837, and in the midst of [other] occupations, I resumed the Logic. I had not touched my pen on the subject for five years, having been stopped and brought to a halt on the threshold of Induction. I had gradually discovered what was mainly wanting, to overcome the difficulties of that branch of the subject, was a comprehensive, and, at the same time, accurate view of the whole circle of physical science, which I feared it would take me a long course of study to acquire. . . . Happily for me, Dr. Whewell,[85] early in this year, published his History of the Inductive Sciences. I read it with eagerness, and found in it a considerable approximation to what I wanted. Much, if not most, of

the philosophy of the work appeared open to objection; but the materials were there, for my own thoughts to work upon . . . .[86]

Mill's *Autobiography* makes it plain that the tendencies voiced by the Port-Royalists on behalf of practical and empirical logic were far from realized in his own day. Mill credits Archbishop Richard Whately's *Elements of Logic* (1831) with having "rehabilitated the name of Logic, and the study of the forms, rules, and fallacies of Ratiocination; and Dr. Whewell's writings had begun to excite an interest in the other part of my subject, the theory of Induction",[87] which Whewell had argued was a method essentially inappropriate to logical method. Mill doubted that his work would be very popular, however, since "students on such subjects were not only (at least in England) few, but addicted chiefly to the opposite school of metaphysics, the ontological and 'innate principles' school".[88] So once again we find a thinker faced with the seemingly irrepressible scholastic tradition and the conception of logic based upon an understanding of human reason which was fundamentally opposed to "knowledge from experience".

I have never indulged the illusion that the [*System of Logic*] had made any considerable impression on philosophical opinion. The German, or *a priori* view of human knowledge, and of the knowing faculties, is likely for some time longer (though it may be hoped in a diminishing degree) to predominate among those who occupy themselves with such inquiries, both here and on the Continent. But the "System of Logic" supplies what was much wanted, a text-book of the opposite doctrine—that which derives all knowledge from experience, and all moral and intellectual qualities principally from the direction given to the associations . . . The notion that truths external to the mind may be known by intuition or consciousness, independently of observation and experience, is, I am persuaded, in these times, the great intellectual support of false doctrines and bad institutions. By the aid of this theory, every inveterate belief and every intense feeling, of which the origin is not remembered, is enabled to dispense with the obligation of justifying itself by reason, and is erected into its own all-sufficient voucher and justification. There never was such an instrument devised for consecrating all deep-seated prejudices. And the chief strength of this false philosophy in morals, politics, and religion, lies in the appeal which it is accustomed to make to the evidence of mathematics and of the cognate branches of physical science. To expel it from these, is to drive it from its stronghold: and because this had never been effectually done, the intuitive school . . . had in appearance, and as far as published writings were concerned, on the whole the best of the argument. In attempting to clear up the real nature of the evidence of mathematical and physical truths, the "System of Logic" met the intuitive philosophers on ground of which they had previously been deemed unassailable; and gave its own explanation, from experience and association, of the particular character of what are called necessary truths, which is adduced as proof that their evidence must come from a deeper source than experience.[89]

This passage is noteworthy particularly because it reveals Mill's understanding of the broader intellectual and political implications of intuitive reason and the innate basis of truth. But what is equally revealing in this passage is the largely transformed conception of what logic *is*. To Mill, logic is no longer one of the liberal arts, nor an autonomous "method", nor even the keystone of the school curriculum in any narrow sense. Although Mill calls his work a "text-book", we are probably correct in reading that description in a figurative sense and as an epitome of the author's considerable modesty in characterizing his work. In short, the *System of Logic* is not a revision for the curriculum so much as it is an exposition, clarification and defense of scientific inquiry, a mode of conduct that was actively present in the nineteenth century, no matter how often "logicians" published books attacking the methods or validity of scientific work. We receive the distinct impression, then, that Mill's work is a final re-definition of logic, not only philosophically and epistemologically but, even more importantly, as to the place and function of logical inquiry in society. Mill was certainly not calling for the elimination of logic, *per se*, from education, but he was identifying logical method with scientific method, logical inquiry with scientific inquiry. Even the syllogism and deduction are regarded by Mill as ultimately inadequate methods of proof.[90] Thus we receive the impression that Mill has delivered logic into the realms of experimental inquiry. Logic, of itself, is not an art, not a science, not a form of communication, not a framework for the educational curriculum. Mill seems to be saying that, to the extent that logic is defined as a method of inquiry, investigation, accumulating evidence and establishing the probabilities and certitude of knowledge, logic is the articulation of the process of human understanding and the pursuit of knowledge. To the extent that logic is conceived as a process or discipline related to arriving at or validating only certain kinds of knowledge—particularly those kinds referred to as innate, *a priori*, or necessary truths—logic is a barren deception that is not only irrelevant to the advancement of human understanding, but is actually inimical to it; and such a conception of logic must be discarded. "Logic, then, is the science of the operations of the understanding which are subservient to the estimation of evidence: both the process itself of advancing from known truths to unknown, and all other intellectual operations in so far as auxiliary to this" [91]

There is never any doubt in the *System of Logic* that Mill's primary intention is to solve the "problem" of induction, that is, to demonstrate that not only is this process properly within the province of systematic logic but that its association with experience and particular knowledge makes it the only fruitful approach to questions of knowledge.

> Whether, therefore, we conform to the practice of those who have made the subject their particular study, or to that of popular writers and common discourse, the province of logic [discussed herein] will include several operations of the intellect not usually considered to fall within the meaning of the terms Reasoning and Argumentation.
>
> These various operations might be brought within the compass of the science, and the additional advantage be obtained of a very simple definition, if, by an extension of the term, sanctioned by high authorities, we were to define logic as the science which treats of the operation of the human understanding in the pursuit of truth.[92]

An adequate appreciation of Mill's "extension" of logic to include induction within the domain of systematic logic is obtained simply by noting how his system places inductive logic at the very heart of his treatise, in Book III, "Of Induction". In turn, the heart of this section is to be found in Chapter VIII, "Of the Four Methods of Experimental Inquiry". These are the words Mill chose to introduce Book III:

> The portion of the present inquiry upon which we are now about to enter, may be considered as the principal, both from its surpassing in intricacy all the other branches [i.e., "names and propositions" and "reason"], and because it relates to a process which has been shown in the preceding Book to be that in which the investigation of nature essentially consists. We have found that all Inference, consequently all Proof, and all discovery of truths not self-evident, consists of inductions, and the interpretation of inductions: that all our knowledge, not intuitive, comes to us exclusively from that source. What Induction is, therefore, and what conditions render it legitimate, cannot but be deemed the main question of the science of logic—the question which includes all others. It is, however, one which professed writers on logic have almost entirely passed over.[93]

The degree to which Mill alters our conception of logic as a formal discipline is measured by his substantial transformation of systematic logic into a method of inquiry fully compatible with Descartes's "method of rightly conducting the reason", the latter having been especially concerned with a method of inquiry, and only indirectly sensible to the adequacy of a systematic logic. In the first place, like Descartes, Mill identifies empirical observation

—the knowledge of particulars—as the paradigm of the search for truth.[94] His lengthy discussion of "The Four Experimental Methods" and the conspicuous absence of any role for disputation illustrate that experimentation is the chief instrument in mankind's search for truth.[95]

The *System of Logic* also discusses logical method as a theory of inquiry, and not a theory of communication. Mill allows the possibility that the principles and operations of which he treats may well be useful to the common man. In any case they describe the operation of the mind prior to the establishment of a science of logic. Yet we have seen Mill's plain assertions that logic has to do with "the pursuit of truth".[96] Mill leaves no doubt about the element which distinctly separates his logic from that of the scholastic tradition, a move which must be considered within the context of logical doctrine from the time of Plato to be appreciated. Mill notes that others have had a more inclusive "conception of the scope and province of our science". "The employment of the word Logic to denote the theory of Argumentation, is derived from the Aristotelian, or, as they are commonly termed, the scholastic, logicians. Yet even with them, in their systematic treatises, Argumentation was the subject only of the third part . . . ."[97] Mill suggests his more restrictive definition of logic by complimenting "the able author of the Port Royal Logic" for defining the subject simply as "the Art of Thinking", and denounces the views held by "popular writers and common discourse" which admit the term "logic" to be applied to speakers with a good "command over premises", with a clever ability to develop refutations and with an amplitude of knowledge in the service of argumentation.

> They may all be regarded as contrivances for enabling a person to know the truths which are needful to him, and to know them at the precise moment at which they are needful. Other purposes, indeed, are also served by these operations; for instance, that of imparting our knowledge to others. But, viewed with regard to this purpose, they have never been considered within the province of the logician. The sole object of Logic is the guidance of one's own thoughts: the communication of those thoughts to others falls under the consideration of Rhetoric, in the large sense in which that art was conceived by the ancients; or of the still more extensive art of Education. Logic takes cognizance of our intellectual operations, only as they conduce to our own knowledge, and to our command over that knowledge for our own uses.[98]

Mill leaves no doubt whatsoever that logic and rhetoric are completely separate endeavours of the intellect, and that it is the part of logic alone to guide the intellect in the pursuit of truth.

The more or less skilful contrivances which enable man to dispose knowledge in clever ways and at needful moments have nothing to do with logic. Imparting knowledge, then, is an entirely separate activity. No matter how laudable certain arts of communication may be on their own merits—in persuasive rhetoric or even more so in education—these merits have nothing to do with the logical methods of inquiry and the formation of particular information into propositions having the merits of truth, certitude and probability. Rhetoric, then, is cut off from any possible epistemological and scientific foundations. Rhetoric is free to obtain its subject matter where it will, in empirical knowledge or otherwise, but more probably, Mill would feel, precisely in those areas peripheral to logical inquiry: intuition, emotion, received ideas, prejudice and speculation.[99] Rhetoric has, *ipso facto*, lost its tie to logic, a point which Mill merely asserts in passing with no apparent interest in rhetoric, obviously a dead issue so far as he was concerned with the advancement of actual knowledge. This point, essential to our present study, marks a major—and in some senses, a final—turning point in the history of rhetoric. Rhetoric may have some connection with knowledge; knowledge, indeed, may well be imparted to others. But if this is so, it is fortuitous and merely coincidental. There is nothing intrinsic to rhetoric that requires its subject matter to derive from, much less depend upon, inquiry and the rigors of logical method. At the same time, there is nothing intrinsic to logic that implies or demands communication. Logic is simply the process of the inquiring intellect; it is both a description and a guideline for inquiry. Nothing is demanded, nothing need be contributed, in respect of communication. In fact, the *System of Logic* manifests less concern for the publication and general dissemination of knowledge than we found in Descartes's *Discourse*, although this point need not be carried too far. We have ample testimony to Mill's interest in the liberal exchange of ideas and information. To suggest that he advocated some form of scientific élitism would be an unfortunate interpretation, even taking into consideration the pessimism of his later years with regard to the chances of improving the general educational and intellectual levels of society.[100]

Finally, and by way of modifying the implication that Mill's logic had no concern for the larger context of scientific inquiry, we take note of the similarity of his expectations to those of Descartes with regard to the practical and useful character of the knowledge produced by inquiry according to the inductive method. Mill speaks easily and often of "the progress of science" and addresses directly "the question, so often agitated, respecting the utility of logic. If a science of logic exists, or is capable of existing, it must be useful".[101] There can be no doubt that he saw in the physical sciences a promise of the better understanding of nature, therefore of human nature, and consequently of the improvement of the whole range of society's material and psychological needs. The very character of empirical knowledge, with its relationship to particular phenomena, illustrates the practicality of the subject matter of scientific experimentation. In this sense, Mill's logic is inevitably more practical than the speculation, intuition and ratiocination of earlier logic. Not unlike the examples offered by Descartes, Mill illustrates the applicability of his four experimental methods by examples from medicine, pathology and biological science.[102] The last two books of the *System of Logic* remove any doubts that Mill did not expect practical benefits to accrue across a broad range of human endeavour from the growth of scientific inquiry and a proper use of logic. Book V, "On Fallacies", suggests how many types of faulty thinking may be exposed by attention to logical principles. Book VI, "On the Logic of the Moral Sciences", is a large, concluding treatise on the applicability of the inductive method in areas many of which were not commonly considered susceptible of scientific investigation: moral science, human nature, psychology, ethology, the social sciences and history, *inter alia*. So it must be concluded that, apart from a requirement of a theory of presentation or communication, Mill's logic was generously and even originally concerned with the practical relationships between logical inquiry and the needs of society. The extent of this concern —that logic be a method of empirical inquiry—is fully appreciated when it is considered that, echoing the themes of Descartes again, Mill refused to see the reform of logic as purely a philosophical question, or even as a problem of educational reform. Rejecting this scholastic horizon, Mill saw the acceptance of his logic as a question of knowledge, *per se*, which carried through and beyond the schoolroom to the laboratory, the treatment room, industry and to the clarity of the popular understanding on the broadest questions of culture. Modern logic, then, was not primarily concerned with providing a text and convenient exercises for the student; was largely unrelated to the elaborate resorts of disputatious professors in the university; had nothing to do with the spirit which sought ancient categories and wisdom to contain and test current experience, or to pronounce the importance or lack of importance of questions having no precedent in received wisdom; and, finally, modern logic had virtually nothing whatsoever to do with rhetorical presentation and persuasive oral discourse.

Logic and Public Discourse

This excursion into the history of logic has temporarily removed our attention from political language and public discourse, but it is important to recognize that this primary interest is served by a brief reprise of these landmarks in logical and scientific method. The reader will be well aware by now that a systematic treatment of language and discourse must account for the techniques of communication—the means which are available to discourse—as well as the experience and content of discourse peculiar to the period in question. This requirement has led us, in this chapter and the one preceding it, to consider phenomena which are not precisely components of public discourse, and yet which are inextricably linked to it and make it what it is: printing, educational techniques and practice, literacy, logic and rhetoric.

This chapter has devoted considerable attention to evolving conceptions of logic and rhetoric, with regard to their place in education and particularly the transmutation in logic involving its assumption to a status essentially independent of education in the classical arts and coincident with a new method of discovery and inductive reasoning in modern science. We have, consequently, noted the theoretical separation of logic and rhetoric and the demotion in status thus entailed for rhetoric. At least this was true from the classical perspective, where rhetoric was provided with methods appropriate to the task of handling complex information, and was thus competent to share in all endeavours to communicate human knowledge and understanding. The reader may well ask what the promotion of logic (to an experimental method responsible for the progress and validity of human knowledge) and the demotion of rhetoric (to an "art" of eloquent oratory, alone) has to do with the actual experience of public discourse during the centuries we have defined as the age of printing. What, in other words, is the importance of coming, as we have, to the conclusion that rhetoric is cut off from invention, proof and inquiry; that logic has been transformed into a method of inquiry, and no longer shares any responsibility as a theory of communication? It is granted, of course, that when we speak of "theories of communication" and "conceptions" or "systems" of logic and rhetoric, we are not directly addressing the form and substance of political discourse in speeches, tracts, debates and other attempts at political dialogue. Any attempt to address the subject of public discourse by a consideration of method and theory, without reference to the appropriate examples, is clearly and seriously limited. On the other hand, it must be admitted that very little can be said by way of comprehension and instructive generalization with regard to a field of discourse simply by reviewing specific uses of language unless we have a theoretical framework within which speech and language have a known role and communication is a form of (social) activity having a theoretical identity. Fortunately, we have acknowledged such a theoretical framework. We have argued, and subsequently assumed, that language and communication have an inherently social character. Communication is not simply a fortuitous device, but is actually a social function which is realised—through changing techniques —in the disposition[103] of special information required for the maintenance and elaboration of the political culture.

The reader is reminded of this perspective, with apologies, simply to clarify the relationship between logical and rhetorical method —which on its own may appear to be nothing more than esoteric academic dispute—and actual public discourse. From our first consideration of classical rhetoric, we noted the way in which such a language technique, actually a technical innovation, not only appeared in terms of its superior capacity to articulate special information, but even substantially new and highly specialized information *vis-à-vis* the traditional oral culture. Thus we must anticipate significant changes in the substance of public discourse if we are to establish that, indeed, a new method is developed for the production and disposition of specialized knowledge. This is particularly important when it is considered that the inductive or scientific method advocated by Descartes was, as we have demonstrated, not merely a question of "abstract theory", but was actually the articulation and consolidation of re-directed intellectual efforts in the creation of vast fields of new knowledge.

From this point of view, the fate of logic and rhetoric is anything but indifferent to our larger interest in the character of public discourse. Moreover, the changes in theory on behalf of logic and rhetoric do not simply amount to an intellectual battle between scientific and scholastic epistemology. The re-direction of the boundaries and scope of rhetoric and logic, dating back to the work of Ramus, was a reflection of emerging techniques of learned communication, printing significantly among them, which in turn reflected the new methods and accomplishments of highly specialized areas of knowledge. In this way, we find an intimate connection between communication techniques (e.g., oral disputation, printing, periodical literature) and methods of learning and inquiry. Further, we begin to see the practical relationships between the individual, and perhaps apparently unrelated, subjects of this and the previous chapter: printing, literacy, reform of the scholastic curriculum, the rise of the scientific method, the re-definition of logic, and the discharge of rhetoric from the methods associated with specialized knowledge. As we shall argue in a later chapter, the fate of rhetoric may be its total exclusion from informed or specialized discourse.

One cannot avoid the conclusion that there is a direct relationship between, on the one hand, a powerful technique such as printing, in conjunction with the methods of scientific discovery in the expansion of human knowledge and, on the other hand, the decline and disestablishment of rhetoric as a method responsible for what we have called in its broadest sense, the social function of communication. Thus the tendency of *The Port-Royal Logic*, finally confirmed in Mill's *System of Logic*, to restrict the scope of rhetoric was simply the recognition of the unsuitability of rhetorical method to the experimental tasks of science. This was not a move to restrict or cut off "communication" at the level of the public—although such an effect may well have occurred—but merely a consequence of the requirements of the scientific method itself: doubt, direct observation, accumulating masses of discrete and often individually meaningless data, intense specialization of inquiry and the intellectual commitment to discovery over advocacy or disputation. Ultimately, then, what we have called the age of printing was an era in which the *methods* of learning and communication changed radically. Mill's autobiographical and systematic writings at the end of this period illustrate the profound character of this transformation, and the strength of the forces which created and opposed it. Mill's explicit intellectual intentions[104] and the steps he took to realize them in his *System of Logic* indicate that, still in the nineteenth century, the major intellectual battle was between empirical scientific method and scholastic (intuitive) epistemology. This was a debate, beginning with the Renaissance, over the nature and uses of human knowledge, including the methods whereby man might preserve, expand and declare its certainty, and by the time of John Stuart Mill, rhetoric was largely, if not wholly, irrelevant to such a dispute.

Notes

1. This is not to suggest that classical rhetoric was a discovery technique in any way comparable to experimental science. Rhetoric was concerned more with the ordering and consistency of a relatively narrow sphere of received information and perceptual data; it was not aimed at the enlargement of society's store of knowledge or equipped with a method by which man's

knowledge would advance into the unknown. However, it can be said that rhetoric was capable of handling new kinds of information as compared with the received poetic tradition of Greek culture. Rhetoric, as a critical and logical method, could address itself to questions and adopt forms and tests of validity that could not be countenanced by the Greek poet. This enabled the rhetorician to establish arguments on the basis of information, and logical processes had nothing to do with, or indeed were inimical to, the figures and maxims of Greek mythology. This is discussed at length in Chapter III.

2. James J. Murphy, *Three Medieval Rhetorical Arts* (Berkeley, Calif., 1971), pp. viii *et seq*. For bibliographical reference, see J.J. Murphy, *Medieval Rhetoric: A Select Bibliography* (Toronto, 1971), and "The Medieval Arts of Discourse: An Introductory Bibliography", *Speech Monographs* (XXIX, 1962), pp. 71–78.

3. Murphy, *Three Medieval Rhetorical Arts* (cited hereinafter as *Rhetorical Arts*), pp. viii–ix. For additional treatment, see Friedrich Solmsen, "The Aristotelian Tradition in Ancient Rhetoric", *American Journal of Philology* (DXII, 1941), pp. 35–50, 169–90.

4. Chief among these were Fortunatianus, a Roman of the late fourth century A.D., and Cassiodorus, Martianus Capella and Isidore of Seville.

5. Murphy, *Rhetorical Arts*, p. ix. Two helpful summaries of the Ciceronian tradition are Martin L. Clarke, *Rhetoric at Rome* (London, 1953), and Donald Lemen Clark, *Rhetoric in Greco–Roman Education* (New York, 1957), pp. 67–142.

6. Murphy, *Rhetorical Arts*, pp. x–xii.

7. Ibid., pp. x–xi. Over a thousand manuscript copies of Donatus still exist.

8. The Grammatical tradition is treated briefly in R.H. Robins, *Ancient and Medieval Grammatical Theory in Europe* (London, 1951). The period called the Second Sophistic (50–400 A.D.) which produced the forms of "sophistic rhetoric" is briefly discussed in the first chapter of Charles Sears Baldwin, *Medieval Rhetoric and Poetic* (New York, 1928).

9. Lee A. Sonnino, *A Handbook to Sixteenth-Century Rhetoric* (London, 1968), offers classical definitions for these terms. Quintilian (VIII, vi, 1ff) defines *tropus* as follows: "By a trope is meant the artistic alteration of a word or phrase from its proper meaning to another ... There are two kinds: those involving change of meaning and those which are employed in the oration for ornament and amplification but do not necessarily change the meaning". (p. 187) Quintilian defines *figura* (*schema*) as follows (IX, i, 1ff): "They add force or charm to our matter ... " Fraunce in the *Arcadian Rhetorike* (1588) (26) defines it thus: "A figure is a certain decking of speech, whereby the usual and simple fashion thereof is altered and changed to that which is more elegant and conceited". (p. 99)

10. The classic biography is Charles Waddington, *Ramus (Pierre de la Ramée)sa vie ses écrits et ses opinions* (Paris, 1855). A notable biography in English is F.P. Graves, *Peter Ramus and the Educational Reformation of the Sixteenth Century* (New York, 1912).

11. Wilbur Samuel Howell, *Logic and Rhetoric in England, 1500–1700* (Princeton, 1956), pp. 146–281. For a number of biographical and critical works on the influence of Ramus on logic and rhetoric, see footnote 1, p. 146. The author is deeply indebted to Professor Howell for much of the discussion below concerning the transition of rhetorical conceptions in the sixteenth and seventeenth centuries, and also to his encouragement, criticisms, and personal warmth as this study developed.

12. Ibid., pp. 148–49. This is Howell's translation of the *Institutiones Oratoriae*

from *Petri Rami Professoris Regii, & Audomari Talaei Collectaneae Praefationes, Epistolae, Orationes* (Marburg, 1599), pp. 15–16.

13. Howell, *Logic and Rhetoric* p. 149.
14. Ibid. An excellent treatment of Ramian reform, tracing his influence through primary texts on the Continent and in England, including the writings of Ramus himself, his disciples and other contemporaries. Howell traces the Ramian influence, including its advocates and enemies, through the 17th century, particularly in England. This analysis is carried still further in Howell's more recent book, *Eighteenth Century British Logic and Rhetoric* (Princeton, 1971), and is summarized in a fine introductory essay in *Fénelon's Dialogues on Eloquence* (Princeton, 1951). See also Charles Waddington, *Ramus* (Paris, 1855), F.P. Graves, *Peter Ramus and the Educational Reformation of the Sixteenth Century* (New York, 1912), and P.A. Duhamel, "The Logic and Rhetoric of Peter Ramus", *Modern Philology*, XLVI (February 1949), pp. 163–71.
15. Howell, *Logic and Rhetoric*, pp. 148–51. Ramus set forth his arguments with regard to logic and rhetoric in *Dialecticae Institutiones* (1543) and *Aristotelicae Animadversiones* (1543), books which were expanded and given several editions in the following ten years. It is interesting to note that Ramus himself translated and published the former work in French under the title *Dialectiqve* in 1555 (Paris) and 1556 (Avignon) so that his reform of the liberal arts could receive a broader reading.
16. Ibid., pp. 153–54. Howell's translation of Ramus's dedicatory epistle to Cardinal Charles of Lorraine, who had protected Ramus from Aristotelians who had attempted to suppress his Latin version of the book. *Dialectiqve* (1555), fol. 2V. This preface appears in Waddington, *Ramus*, pp. 401–7.
17. Howell, *Logic and Rhetoric*, p. 153.
18. Ibid. at pp. 154–55, quoting from *Dialectiqve*, pp. 2–4.
19. Ibid., p. 160; *Dialectiqve*, p. 120.
20. Ibid., p. 161; *Dialectiqve*, p. 122.
21. Ibid., p. 164; *Dialectiqve*, p. 134.
22. Ibid., p. 165.
23. This development is carefully documented in Howell, *Logic and Rhetoric*, pp. 173–281, and is the essential task of Howell, *British Logic*.
24. Howell, *Logic and Rhetoric*, pp. 178ff. Also see Neal W. Gilbert, *Renaissance Concepts of Method* (New York, 1963), pp. 197–212.
25. Howell, *Logic and Rhetoric*, p. 150.
26. Ibid., pp. 173–75.
27. Ramus reports in a preface to his *Dialecticae Libri Duo* that he would like to be remembered for his contribution to logic: "as for me, if you wish to inform yourself about my vigils and my studies, I shall want the column of my sepulchre to be taken up with the establishing of the art of logic or dialectic". In the *Dialectiqve*, Ramus expressed the idea that "God is the only perfect logician, that man surpasses the beasts by virtue of his capacity to reason syllogistically, and that one man surpasses another only so far as his address to the problem of method is superior". Howell, *Logic and Rhetoric*, p. 153, notes 15 and 16.
28. Ibid., p. 282. See Ch. 5, pp. 282–341, for a detailed account of the reaction to the spread of Ramist reforms.
29. Ibid., p. 318.
30. René Descartes, *Descartes: Philosophical Writings*, N.K. Smith ed. and trans. (New York, 1958), "Discourse on Method", p. 97.
31. Ibid., p. 94.

32. "*Pour bien conduire la raison, & chercher la verité dans les sciences*".
33. Descartes, *Discourse*, p. 95.
34. Ibid., p. 96.
35. This title is given by Hobbes to an essay written early, but in an unknown year, by Hobbes. The essay was incorporated into *Leviathan* as Part III, Chapter 46. See *Leviathan* (New York, 1958), pp. 3–20; also textual note, p. xvii, H.W. Schneider, ed.
36. Descartes, *Discourse*, pp. 126 and 129.
37. Ibid., p. 129. See also Lucien Levy-Bruhl, *History of Modern Philosophy in France* (Chicago, 1924), p. 1; Leon Roth, *Descartes' Discourse on Method* (Oxford, 1937), pp. 13f.
38. Descartes, *Discourse*, p. 143.
39. Ibid., p. 99.
40. Ibid., p. 103.
41. Ibid., p. 104.
42. Ibid.
43. Ibid., pp. 106–107.
44. Ibid., p. 107.
45. Ibid., p. 106. Emphasis added.
46. Ibid., p. 136.
47. Ibid., p. 137.
48. Ibid., pp. 137–38.
49. Ibid., p. 138.
50. The use of a word whose Latin derivative—*scientia*—means "knowledge" in the sense of a knowing or skilful acquaintance to convey the idea of a "pure" knowledge or "pure" inquiry is probably unfortunate. Below, we shall see that Descartes certainly anticipated practical applications of scientific knowledge to advance man's mastery over nature. See ibid., pp. 130–31. Nevertheless, we can see even in Descartes how scientific inquiry has an intrinsic bias in favor of experimentation, discovery, and the accumulation of knowledge, and consequently less interest in the introduction of this knowledge into public discourse. "In this respect, as also in their distaste for the labors of expository writing", notes N.K. Smith, "Descartes and Newton very closely resemble one another. Like Newton, Descartes was primarily interested in the process of inquiry and discovery; and as Descartes has stated (to Father Vatier, February 22, 1638), the 'ordre pour chercher les choses . . . est assez différent de celui dont j'ai cru devoir user pour les expliquer' ". Ibid., p. 130, note 23.
51. Ibid., p. 126.
52. Ibid., p. 94.
53. Ibid., p. 126.
54. Cf. *supra*, note 50. The expression of this attitude enables us to appreciate the depth of the tradition that has come to be identified as the optimism and progressivism of the *philosophes* of the 18th century French Enlightenment.
55. Ibid., pp. 130–31.
56. *des expériences* in the French text; rendered *experimentorum* by Descartes in the subsequent Latin translation.
57. *expériences*.
58. Descartes, *Discourse*, pp. 131–32.
59. Howell, *Logic and Rhetoric*, pp. 346–49.
60. Several editions of these works are available. Citations from *The Port-Royal Logic* will be from the translation by Thomas Spencer Baynes, 4th ed. (Edinburgh, 1857). A recent translation is available under the title *The Art of Thinking, Port-Royal Logic* and attributed only to Antoine Arnauld, trans.,

and intro. by James Dickoff and Patricia James, in the Bobbs–Merrill Co. Library of Liberal Arts series (Indianapolis and New York, 1964). A facsimile edition of the *Grammaire Générale et Raisonée*, 1660 edition (Menston, England, 1967) presents the modern reader with the original aspect of the work.

61. H.C. Barnard, *The Little Schools of Port-Royal* (Cambridge, 1913) provides an account of the aims and accomplishments of the Port-Royalists. Also, Dickoff and James, *The Art of Thinking*, pp. xxvii–xxxvii.

62. See Dickoff and James, *The Art of Thinking*, pp. lix–lx. Also see Howell, *Logic and Rhetoric*, pp. 352–54 and notes 32, 34 and 42.

63. T.S. Baynes, trans., *The Port-Royal Logic* (4th ed., 1857), pp. xl–xlii. The influence of *The Port-Royal Logic* and its incorporation of Cartesian philosophy has been recognized in recent scholarship by Noam Chomsky, who credits Descartes with being the source of the Port Royal approach to logic and grammar. See Chomsky, *Cartesian Linguistics* (New York and London, 1966).

64. *Grammaire Générale et Raisonée*, p. 3, A ij.

65. Baynes, *Port-Royal Logic*, p. 8. The authors of *The Port-Royal Logic* directly credit Descartes's four steps in his method and cite them in full in their notes to Part IV, Ch. II, pp. 315–16, adding that they "may be useful for preserving us from error, when seeking after the truth in human sciences, although, indeed, they apply generally to all kinds of method, and not specially to analysis alone".

66. Ibid., p. 40. A helpful discussion of the Port-Royalist reform is Howell, *Logic and Rhetoric*, pp. 352–63.

67. Baynes, *Port-Royal Logic*, p. 23. Also see note 9, p. 380.

68. Ibid., p. 25.

69. Ibid., p. 309.

70. Ibid.

71. Ibid., pp. 309–10.

72. Ibid., p. 315.

73. Howell, *Logic and Rhetoric*, pp. 358–59, correctly argues that the *Logic* does not eliminate the presentational function entirely, and is thus not a total break with the traditional conception of scholastic logic. This is recognized in the *Logic*'s treatment of "synthesis" as discussed *supra*. However Howell does not mention the tendency signified by the introductory sentence of the *Grammar*, which claims for that discipline "*l'Art de parler*".

74. Baynes, *Port-Royal Logic*, p. 265.

75. Ibid., pp. 179; 373–74.

76. Ibid. See Parts II and III.

77. Ibid., p. 315.

78. Ibid., pp. 25–26. Also, Howell, *Logic and Rhetoric*, pp. 361–63.

79. Baynes, *Port-Royal Logic*, p. 276.

80. Ibid., p. 16.

81. Ibid., p. 144.

82. Ibid., p. 16.

83. The edition used here is the two-volume eighth edition (London, 1872).

84. This is clear from Mill's *Autobiography* (New York, 1924), pp. 12–16, 40, 85–86, 127. Also, see Howell, *Logic and Rhetoric*, p. 350, and Howell *Eighteenth Century British Logic*, pp. 695–717, for a discussion of Mill's relationship to the tradition of scholastic logic.

85. William Whewell (1794–1866), *History of the Inductive Sciences* (1837). Whewell argued that the methods of the inductive sciences could not be regarded as a procedure assimilable to the formal arguments and proofs of systematic logic. See Mill's *Autobiography*, p. 156, for a further discussion of this point.

86. Mill, *Autobiography*, pp. 145–46.
87. Ibid., p. 157.
88. Ibid.
89. Ibid., pp. 157–59.
90. Howell, *Logic and Rhetoric*, p. 350.
91. Mill, *System of Logic*, I, p. 11.
92. Ibid., p. 4.
93. Ibid., p. 327.
94. Ibid., pp. 437ff, Ch. VII, "Of Observation and Experiment".
95. Ibid., pp. 448–503. Howell, *Logic and Rhetoric*, p. 350, emphasizes the congruence between Descartes and Mill on the requirements of logic and experimental method.
96. Mill, *System of Logic*, p. 4.
97. Ibid.
98. Ibid., pp. 4–5.
99. Mill, *Autobiography*, pp. 157–59; *cf.* p. 167.
100. Ibid., pp. 159–64.
101. Mill, *System of Logic*, p. 10.
102. Ibid., pp. 472ff.
103. This is meant to encompass the discovery, organization, preservation, and transmission of specialized knowledge.
104. Mill, *Autobiography*, pp. 153–59; Mill, *System of Logic*, I, pp. 1–14.

6

Oral Discourse in Linear Culture

> The state of England is lyke to chyldren, sitting rechlesse
> in the market steede. We playe and pipe to them, but they
> relent not: our sermons are like vnto the Musick which *Aristotle*
> speaketh of. Which when once doone, there is no remembrance
> of it. They beleeue Lawiers in lawe matters, and follow them:
> Phisitians, and follow them: Councellors, and follow them: they
> heare Preachers, but they doo not follow them.
>
> *Thomas Drant, Bishop of London (1584)*

It is easier to trace the evolution of rhetorical theory than to
establish a correspondence between changing theories and trends
in actual public oratory. The practical effects of a new rhetorical
method must nevertheless be considered, even if only as a subject
of speculation. Students of language have greatly troubled themselves to arrive at a definition of the "existential" aspect of
communication as a species of meaningful contact between speaker
and listener. This endeavour has been largely unsuccessful. The
temptation has been to focus on speech as a problem of individual
behaviour—the competent or ideal speaker (or listener)—while
conceding without serious examination that this is a phenomenon
characteristically occurring as a social relationship. Consequently,
we may anticipate what difficulties must be faced in attempting
to establish theoretically or empirically the impact of a specific
genre of public oratory.

If it has been difficult to make progress in understanding such
an available social reality as communication, it is all the more
hazardous to speculate about distinct rhetorical settings (as in, for
example, political oratory) or to identify periodic changes in the
relationship between speaker and listener due to new rhetorical
techniques or a technologically altered linguistic environment.
Nevertheless, this is a task which calls for some attention. Long
ago, St. Augustine proposed that public oratory, specifically preach-

ing, was intended "to teach, to delight and to move"—*docere, delectare et movere.* To state the intentions of, or to describe, the communicative act does not suffice to explain it, but at least Augustine's idea reminds us that communication does bind together a speaker and his audience. Speakers do delight and move—as well as offend and bore—their audiences, and we know this has something to do with the speaker's intention, something to do with the rhetorical tools at hand and, finally, something to do with the accidents of personality, charm and the fortuitousness of events. It is with the second of these three factors, the tools of rhetoric, that we are now concerned.

We have already given an account of the important changes which occurred in the function of rhetoric and logic dating from the fifteenth century and continuing into the nineteenth. It is this same period which we have identified as the linear age: the epoch in which printing technology radically transformed the possibilities of language communication. The alteration in the theoretical status of rhetoric, as well as the diminished importance of formal oratory, cannot be solely explained by the rise of printing and expanded literacy. As we have already argued, the immediate intellectual force compelling a revision in the role of rhetoric was the ascendency of science and its attendant methodological developments. Scientific method required a form of discourse, and forms of observation and proof, that simply did not depend upon the classical relationships between rhetorical persuasion, public discourse and the use of sheerly deductive tests of consistency and coherence. These theoretical and methodological evolutions were also crucial social events because they were accompanied by radical changes in educational institutions and curricula, developments which were manifestly aided by the contemporary emergence of printing.

The task of saying anything useful or true about four centuries of public discourse during the epoch we have called the linear age is fraught with many dangers, not the least of them being over-generalization. What is to be included in the category of "public discourse" is especially troublesome for a study emphasizing political language and rhetoric. We have already discovered that rhetoric, being an art or "technique", cannot be separated from its philosophical, methodological and therefore pedagogical spheres of discourse. An examination of oratory in the age of printing cannot fail to draw attention to sermons, another form of public discourse whose social and political significance cannot be denied, even though homilitics would seem, at first glance, to be wide of the mark of strictly political language. Finally, there is a class of speech that can be called "political rhetoric", however varied its members may be.[1] To anticipate a later discussion, it is important to note the comparatively recent emergence of the common forms of strictly "political" rhetoric. Indeed, it is substantially a phenomenon of the eighteenth and nineteenth centuries that parliamentary, electoral, ministerial and presidential oratory have emerged as dominant types of public discourse. For this reason, much of what can be said about public discourse in earlier times must depend upon examples of public oratory that may not strike the modern reader as straightforward political rhetoric.

Changes in Learned Discourse

There can be no doubt that rhetoric, including actual public oratory as well as its theoretical conception, underwent a substantial change in sixteenth and seventeenth-century learned discourse. In the outstanding scientific accomplishments of this period, as embodied in the major works of such figures as Bacon, Descartes, Hobbes and Locke, we detect a pervasive reaction to "disputations in the schools". These writers contributed to a virtual uprising against the dry and pointless rhetoric of school and university pedagogy. We have recorded Descartes's opinions in this regard in the previous chapter, and his attitudes reveal with remarkable precision the discontent of his contemporaries, who were straining away from theology, scholastic philosophy and rhetoric in favour of demonstrative and empirical studies: mathematics, geometry, physics, chemistry and other sciences.[2] From this evidence we may infer that disputation and classical rhetorical composition were increasingly unsuitable forms of pedagogical discourse. This is not to say that the first boring lectures were delivered in this age. Nor should it be overlooked that, especially in the English universities, changes in university governance imposed by religious factions at Court or in Parliament resulted in a discrediting of scholarly disputation. In an age when authority was more than ever before revealed as a question of parties in power; when theology and scholastic philosophy served as alleged justification for every side of a dispute; and when new areas of study, with radically different methods, were becoming more widely understood, it is all the more obvious that disputation and dogmatic scholasticism were subjected to attack and even, as was quite often the case, outright ridicule.

By the late seventeenth century, therefore, methods other than disputation and rhetorical discourse were sought for the advancement and communication of knowledge. Instead of copying the master's oral dissertations on classical authorities, one was to doubt all. Instead of accepting dogma, revealed truths and classical proofs, one had to experiment and learn for oneself. Instead of endlessly picking over old axioms and disputing the adequacy of the necessary conclusions of deductive logic, one had to search out new information and accumulate evidence whose validity rested upon the techniques by which it was ascertained. Those disciplines in the schools which failed to accept this new method were consequently relegated to what C.P. Show eventually called another "culture": scholastic philosophy, theology, aesthetics, politics, morals and other disciplines in the liberal and fine arts. Thenceforth only this old culture would require a rhetorical tradition to keep alive its received values, its formal styles and its public and ceremonial appeals.

Persons interested in the physical sciences were only too happy to retreat to the laboratory and ignore the problem of communication as an issue of secondary or even negligible importance. Public discourse was increasingly impractical due to the highly specialized mathematical character of the information, the esoteric conceptual presuppositions and vocabulary, and the growing assumption that "pure" science did not have an immediate obligation to the general public. These same factors contributed to the formation of the Royal Society[3] and other groups devoted to the advancement of science through the intimate exchange of findings among a select membership. It is true that such societies offered the opportunity for a public forum for the presentation of scientific papers and the debate of contradictory hypotheses. There is good reason to believe, however, that the formal sessions of these groups were little more than a tribute to traditional forms, as well as convenient opportunities to highlight the importance of scientific interests through the ceremonial gatherings of renowned intellectuals. Certainly the meetings themselves were not regarded as the advancement of scientific knowledge through purifying rhetorical disputation, but merely as an opportunity to disseminate new findings and curiosities achieved in the laboratory or in the field. Indeed, there is good reason to believe that the Royal Society of London was poorly attended in formal session, and that its members prized the group most highly as a source of research subventions and a way of making individual contacts.[4] Much more important in the way of communication among the members of scientific societies than their regular meetings were their specially subsidized and periodical publications—the *Philosophical Investigations* of the Royal Society being exemplary of the publications which put into print the latest experimental findings and techniques, the curiosities and enigmas noticed by travelling members and a great variety of reports on work in progress. If the question had occurred to the founding members of scientific societies concerning their obligation to communicate the fruits of their labour to the general public, their answer would surely be to point out the availability of the published books, papers, journals and proceedings produced by these groups. It is unlikely that oral discourse would be regarded as a plausible method of communicating scientific knowledge in an intelligible, much less useful, fashion.

The effect of the seventeenth-century assault upon scholastic tradition was to establish a "method of rightly conducting the reason" that gradually rendered oral discourse dispensable as a means of learned communication. The vestiges of the rhetorical tradition that remained, as they remain in the twentieth century, were perfunctory, ceremonial and a matter of convention—a term that comes down to us in a way that discloses the secondary and reportorial expectations, at best, of learned debate in a public forum. The rhetorical method of learned discourse—where men of special knowledge of a received culture disputed inconsistencies, contradictions and paradoxes born of ancient mysteries and linguistic puzzles—was appropriate for an epoch devoted to retaining and clarifying knowledge. The new, scientific method, which was devoted to expanding the range and scope of man's knowledge of the natural world through direct empirical observation, was simply not in need of a generally useful pattern of public discourse. The former was a method of retention, the latter a method of discovery, and while this tidal change in epistemology did not rise up directly as a reaction to public discourse as disputation, such a reaction was implicit in the transformation. The effect of this change, if not the direct intent, was to render rhetoric in the public forum, as well as the connection between oratory and specialized knowledge, obsolete.

The importance of visual or graphic concepts to a science based upon experiential data is only one example of the extent to which the new methodology required forms of expression distinct from the rhetorical tradition. It is easy to see that mathematics, astronomy and optics, all of which relied upon geometry, and the study of solid bodies and the influence of forces upon them, could not effectively be developed, much less communicated, by oral discourse. The articulation of these sciences required the visual dimension implicit in the notion of observation to illustrate proofs, effects and phenomena, the accomplishment of which would be very difficult, if possible at all, through linguistic expression alone. It is notable that advances in these fields were made in conjunction with printing and the appearance of books. On the printed page could be presented clearly and powerfully the relationships between objects, the spatial arrangement of lines, angles and bodies, and even the tendencies of vectors and bodies in motion. An illustration of this development can be seen in Descartes's three essays—*The Dioptric*, *Meteors* and *Geometry*—for which the *Discourse on Method* served as an introduction. The usefulness of graphic representation in mathematical and geometric conceptualization, particularly in communicating theorems and proofs to others, was a fact known by Euclid and Pythagoras as well as many other civilizations interested in the movements of the stars long before the invention of printing. So it is notable that the interest of early modern science in mathematical proofs and the presentation of hypotheses and data concerning natural phenomena emerged in conjunction with a medium capable of producing uniform graphic reproductions to be bound together with printed texts. The way in which graphs and figures are able to communicate information and ideas without the use of regular language is only an early analogue to the use of symbols, algebraic equations and encoded formulae in modern science. Graphic and symbolic "language" has thus played a major role in the articulation of science, even though it cannot be fully expressed orally (especially without the aid of a printed text), does not conform to common grammatical or semantic rules, and is not comprehensible to the otherwise competent speaker of a natural language.[5]

The emergence of experimental science does not, of course, imply the disappearance of speech as a medium of public communication for the expression of information.[6] Yet it would be unwise to overlook the fact that inherent in the rise of modern science is an ever-expanding separation between oral discourse and the accumulation, ordering, communication and application of human knowledge. In consequence, the methodological and epistemological functions of rhetoric were dealt a severe blow, and formal rhetorical discourse as an oral performance has been reduced to a kind of ceremonial indulgence in all circles having a claim to the accumulation of scientific knowledge. The peculiar character of scientific communication is readily apparent in contemporary society, where specialized knowledge is expressed in increasingly non-grammatical forms, such as equations, mathematical symbols, statistical tables, computing languages and other semi-linguistic orthographies. The distinguishing feature of these expressions is that their usefulness in specialized communication is roughly in proportion to their susceptibility to electronic processing, which is in turn roughly inversely proportionate to their susceptibility to oral articulation. The impact of scientific communication on public discourse in the seventeenth to the nineteenth century may not be so easily grasped as its twentieth-century effects, and yet it is important to understand these earlier relationships.

If rhetoric, as a theory of logic and communication, assumed a new identity and social function as ceremonial convention while surviving as the archaic vehicle of scholasticism so far as the exponents of a new "method" in science and education were concerned, this does not mean that professors, lawyers, politicians and other public figures no longer addressed audiences, nor even that learned societies and universities suddenly excused themselves from public discourse. But the survival of the spoken word was not nearly as important as the growth of the printed word as a medium of communication. Society, by comparison to earlier periods, was becoming massively literate. While schools were gradually accepting and emphasizing the new empirical sciences, the impact of printing was reflected in the growing numbers of books, journals, newspapers and libraries and in an educational system completely dominated by books, from grammar school lesson books for oral recitation to the massive texts compiling mathematical formulae and scientific data.

One may easily understand why public discourse, especially learned discourse, underwent a change of identity, not only in the organization, content and manner of its delivery, but also in the way an oral performance would be received by a literate audience. Consider, by way of illustration, the effect of schooling based upon a curriculum using standard textbooks. In such circumstances, the student is not informed or enlightened by disputation, dialogue and the persuasive powers of an eloquent orator. Rather, the book itself becomes the source of authority—in fact, the authority itself. The school master is—as is richly supported by legend—an anachronism to be scorned and jeered, or simply feared as a physical threat.[7] The erudition of a teacher is replaced by the method of a pedagogue charged with accomplishing a new task: "book learning". Apart from the printing of sacred and liturgical texts, the very earliest printing was devoted to the production of textbooks and epitomes of Latin and Greek texts for use in the classroom.[8] The book, therefore, became not only a godsend to pedagogy on a scale never before possible, but eventually impinged so greatly upon the pedagogue as to make him superfluous as a source of information and a standard of authority.

Religious and Political Rhetoric

In the Roman Catholic Church the impact of printing was initially limited to scholarly and administrative spheres due to the retention of a Latin liturgy and formulaic litanies for the mass of communicants. Protestantism, however, exemplifies the modern focus upon the "written word", that is, the printed scriptures upon which such worship was based. Here the "Holy Word" regained some of its magical and mysterious force at the same time as it became inextricably tied to the physical presence of the Bible, the books of common prayer and hymnals. It is clear that Protestantism was closely linked with the rise of literacy and the broader availability of printed texts,[9] and it is equally important to see this relationship as a fundamental re-definition of public discourse. The pulpit, after all, was the most visible forum for oral communication, and its official function to deliver religious homilies did not disguise the coincidence between doctrinal dispute and moral, that is, political, exhortation. The sermon and the pulpit gained unprecedented significance in the Reformation and, by way of reaction, in the Roman counter-Reformation that followed it.[10] Pulpit oratory can be seen as a by-product of emerging secular literacy, which combined the humanist revival of classical thought and the growth of secular scholarship in biblical philology and law with the demands created by mass literacy for the availability of unsophisticated doctrines.

What appeared in the Reformation as a reaction to ecclesiastical authority and its supporting hierarchy is an analogue to the dissatisfaction with the scholastic curriculum. As Luther exemplified, only the simple word of the scriptures and "evident reasoning", as opposed to learned casuistry, were necessary to enable the Christian to establish the truth sufficiently to stake his life upon it. No amount of canonical tradition, priestly authority, collegial will or doctrinal subtleties could change his mind. "One thing, and only one thing, is necessary for Christian life, righteousness, and freedom. That one thing is the most holy Word of God, the gospel of Christ. . . . Man shall not live by bread alone, but by every word that proceeds from the mouth of God . . . where the Word of God is missing there is no help at all for the soul.[11] The Protestant movement, including the Lutherans, Puritans,

Presbyterians and others, can actually be identified by its emphasis upon the reading of "his Holy Word". This was a profound reorientation, eschewing the visual and oral ceremony of the Roman tradition, which relied upon the theatricality of the mass as its paradigmatic mode of public "discourse". In place of the mass, whose language was fundamentally incomprehensible to the communicants, the Protestants created a service with a simpler ceremony (in some cases dispensing altogether with the mass as the central feature of worship), the reading of scriptural texts, and great, pedantic sermons devoted to expounding "the Word of God". In the Protestant service, eyes moved from "book" to preacher, not because he was dramatically involved in an act of creation and transformation of the "body" of Christ, but because he was reading the "word". The celebration of the mass was essentially a re-creation, a performance depending upon the priestly access to a sanctioned field of discourse to which the communicants were necessarily mere spectators, and generally uncomprehending spectators, at that, so far as the language itself was concerned. By contrast, the Protestant service was less of a "performance" than an encompassing dialogue based upon a "textbook" of unquestioned authority. The preacher in the Reformed pulpit did not shrink back from speaking on behalf of authority, but neither he nor his auditors had any doubt that the "Book" was the source of that authority.

The distinction between secular political discourse and pulpit oratory is far clearer in the twentieth century than it was in the Reformation period.[12] Indeed, the religious sermon was the dominant form of public rhetorical performance at least up to the appearance of nineteenth-century electoral reform, when enfranchisement and the increasing importance of parliamentary assemblies gave rise to the electoral campaign platform. Theological debate and doctrinal controversy were the predominate idioms within which important issues of social policy and political authority had been disputed throughout the Christian period, but it was not until controversy within the Church moved outside the narrow circles of legalistic and scholastic dispute and was taken to the people that the sermon came into its own as a rhetorical medium. The Reformation may be defined, in effect, as the emergence of doctrinal controversy which the Church could not contain within its own sphere of discourse, canonical interpretation and collegial disputation, despite its efforts to do so in reaction to the publications and public sermons of Luther, Zwingli and Calvin. Tied directly to classical models of rhetoric, based upon a clearly defined body of received truth, aimed at resolving conflicts and describing the compass of authority and policy in the secular realm, the religious sermon was undoubtedly a species of political discourse. One has only to think of the issues to which pulpit oratory addressed itself to see that "preaching the Word of God" was anything but a sacred and other-worldly occupation: the several Protestant movements on the Continent concerning princely authority and religious toleration; Puritanism and the relationship between Church and crown during the Civil War; the parliamentary movement, the Protectorate and the restoration in seventeenth-century England; the Puritan church in the American colonies; and even the relationship between social reform and the evangelical, unitarian and Emersonian movements in America in the nineteenth century.

The pulpit was also important as a forum in which clergy and laymen alike could hold forth against established temporal authority. Having a captive audience, the clergy and other churchmen were able to use a form of political language dressed in the garb and assuming the colour of religious sanctity and authority. The frankly political arguments made in the pulpit often served to undermine the credibility of secular political rhetoric and to impinge upon the fidelity of the citizen toward secular political institutions.[13] This effect could even be accomplished by subtle indirection—with the ostensible aim of blessing such authorities—in the perfunctory prayer invoking God's blessings upon the prince and his council, or in the formulaic prayer of forgiveness for the transgressions and ill intentions of "those whom God has placed in positions of authority over us; that they take care to do His holy will". The pulpit as a forum of political dissent should not draw attention away from its use as an organ of established orthodoxy. The Reformation period did not sweep away entirely the coincidence between princely and sacred authority. In Geneva's Calvinistic theocracy, in the early Anglican church and in colonial New England congregations, for example, pulpit oratory was simply a voice of political orthodoxy.

The formal language of public discourse for this period may be expressed, albeit quite generally, according to this distinction: in religious discourse, the foundation was scriptural,[14] and in secular political rhetoric (as it emerged) the foundation was increasingly legalistic as distinct from scholastic.[15] Both these foundations were reliant upon the expansion of literacy and the expanding use of printed materials. The growth of vernacular literacy and broadened exposure to the newly available Bible accompanied the profound structural changes in the Church and its procedures for making authoritative interpretations of religious dogma, the culmination of which was a kind of congregational or presbyterian democracy.

With the entry of vernacular languages into religious liturgy, the Protestant service had a far more intense rhetorical setting for the presentation of a much broader range of topics and information. Consequently, not only did the language of the sacred texts come alive to the general congregation, but the role of the preacher took on a new significance. The congregation was placed in a position of listening to an orator who, however ineffective he might be as a elocutionist, and however much he confined himself to orthodox topics and treatments, used a language that was commonly intelligible and identical, even in idiom, to the newly translated Bible. He was *speaking to* the congregation. Whether he wrote the sermon the day before, or was addressing them *ex tempore*, it was directed to them for that unique occasion, a feature greatly in contrast to the Catholic mass and its variants based upon the religious calendar.

The effect of Protestant rhetoric, however, diminished the aural and visual dimensions of public communication. The sombre service and stark atmosphere of the Protestant church contrasted greatly with the rich visual imagery of the Roman service and sanctuary. Much of the Catholic mass that had great visual appeal was eliminated: the spectacle of the mass in all its enacted ritual and symbolic tokens; the rich use of the plastic arts, including paintings, stained glass, sculpture, priestly robes; the dramatic use of perspective and space in the architecture; the sonorities of the prayers and chants, which were no more than sonorities for those who did not know Latin; and the use of light and music. The effect of these theatrical qualities was, of course, to keep the eyes and emotions of the congregation focused in a very different way from that in the severe Protestant sanctuary, where eyes and minds were to be devoted solely to the Word. Thus the Protestant tendency to enhance and emphasize pulpit oratory also led to a greater emphasis on the printed word. The sermon devoted to "the understanding of the Word" led inevitably to one of two extremes: a new scholasticism of narrow doctrinal and scriptural pedantry; or a rhetoric of inflammatory, demagogic emotionalism. Both these streams are evident in the Protestant tradition.

Secular political rhetoric followed a similar pattern of increasing reliance upon printed texts. As princely government was still the predominant institutional form of secular authority, even in the Reformation States, few occasions existed for the display of political rhetoric in the modern sense before the eighteenth century.[16] Party politics and electoral campaigning, the typical forums for secular politics in which appeals were made directly to the general public, were features largely confined to the latter part of the period in question.[17] Thus political rhetoric still conformed to the classical categories: speeches delivered in the council chambers of the King; speeches made in the early forms of Bench and Bar (often in the "court" of the King, himself, when the latter made himself available as an audience to the grievances of lords and commoners); the early French *parlements*; ceremonial occasions when a public address was made by the prince; and, in the case of the early Renaissance city—state republics in Italy, even electoral and Great Council legislative debates. Here we perceive Aristotle's three general categories of rhetorical performance: legislative (policy) debate, judicial and forensic debate, and ceremonial oratory.

It is difficult to make generalizations as to the form and subject matter of political rhetoric within these categories, as compared with the narrow scriptural and formal constraints upon pulpit oratory. Political rhetoric had no institutional setting to compare with the pulpit, and one cannot readily be identified until parliamentary bodies, political parties and election campaigns began to leave records in print. Political speeches which are available for study, and which would appear to typify the form and subject matter of political rhetoric, were frequently composed in the form of essays or pamphlets.[18] Indeed, this suggests a direct relationship between this rhetorical *genre* and the availability of the resources for printed publication. We cannot possibly reconstruct the oratorical settings for courtly declamations, dedicatory speeches or early parliamentary debate, but at the very least we can be guided by the texts reputed to be examples of political oratory during this period.[19]

English parliamentary oratory from the Elizabethan period to the late eighteenth century cannot fail to be an appropriate scope for considering secular political discourse in the age of printing.[20] We are not surprised to find that, as it appears, every age has had orators who, according to their individual merits, have been fiery and pallid, concise and vague, convincing and specious. Thus it is not our present intention to suggest that certain generations or epochs were peculiarly eloquent, or that the growth of printing and literacy was somehow necessarily accompanied by an increase in the power of political rhetoric, or by its declining impact. What we are concerned to show is any alteration in speeches due to the direct influences of printing technology or the indirect effects deriving from changes in rhetorical theory.

From such a perspective, two points deserve special mention. The first is the tendency of parliamentary rhetoric to take on the form of lengthy essays which were, even for contemporary auditors, far more pleasing to read than to hear.[21] Indeed, the distinction between speech and essay—in the form of a letter, pamphlet or book—was never very clear, a distinction that became virtually imperceptible with the appearance of comprehensive parliamentary journals.[22] The nearly eradicated distinction between the sermon as an oratorical act and a literary effort was admitted quite bluntly by Dean Swift when he said "I never preached but twice in my life, and they were not sermons but pamphlets". Swift's contemporary, Henry Sacheverall, was a more prolific preacher, and his sermons served as the foundation of a political career. One of his sermons, "The Perils of False Brethren in Church and State", delivered at St. Paul's on 5 November 1709, was a blatant attack upon the Whig Government. This sermon was quickly printed as a pamphlet, selling 40,000 copies.[23]

The second point is the appearance in the eighteenth century of what historians of English rhetoric call the "elocutionary movement", which has been concisely defined as "the historical trend in which rhetoric as a formal discipline not only renounced her previous interest in the classical doctrines of invention, arrangement, and style, but undertook also to confine herself to the study of oratorical delivery and its twin aspects of voice and gesture".[24] Although this movement has to do with the tradition of rhetorical theory—a consideration of which was the major task of two earlier chapters—it is a subject bearing upon our present attention to actual public discourse. The elocutionary movement illustrates how as late as the eighteenth century pulpit and political oratory were regarded as inseparable forms of public discourse, and should be guided by common principles. These principles, it should be noted, were entirely divorced from the content of the speech: invention, arrangement and style were now understood to follow the dictates of logic; rhetoric's contribution to this effort had only to do with voice and gesture in the act of delivery. The effect of this development upon oral performance, whether in pulpit or parliament, is clear. Public discourse was caught on the horns of a dilemma. Either it must compete with the power of the printed word by attempting to match the length, detail and compactness of book or pamphlet, thus producing an oration of an exhausting duration; or it must offer itself as elocution, *tout pur*, hoping by sheer excellence of delivery to persuade its audience, as if to admit that its proper task was artifice, precious refinement and dazzling technique, rather than the communication of a body of information. This dilemma has evidently not been solved in any successive period of modern political discourse, and it is for this reason that we have two primary images for the word rhetoric today: the monotonously droning pedant and the sheer stylist of baroque puffery or emotional bombast.

Speech became dependent upon printing for its unprecedented circulation, just as it came to rely upon printed works as the primary source of information. These benefits did not come without a price. In oral or early literate culture, tropes, commonplaces and *adagios* added authority to speech. The effect is quite different in the linear age, where signs of indebtedness betray a lack of originality. Commonplace utterances appear less striking because their presence in books has made them mere quotations, no longer a sign of erudition and a command of the culture but a sign that one's language is derivative, unimaginative and plagiaristic.

The judicial proceeding is an example of the subordination of oral performance to the printed record. Oral argument at the bar is largely devoted to perfunctory and formulaic exchanges, since the all-important legal briefs have already heen printed, distributed and read by all parties to the case. It need hardly be added how important printing is in the preparation of the briefs by reference to precedent cases in the printed reports of court decisions, statutes and codes, law digests and other bodies of literature. Using the law case as a corresponding analogy to parliamentary debate (with its Hansard and revised statutes) and pulpit oratory (with its considerably narrower texts based upon scripture and encyclicals, canons and ecclesiastical writings), it is possible to argue that the trend of oral discourse in the age of printing was "legalistic" in character. The argument of a case was now less of an occasion for the presentation of new or special forms of information than a *pro forma* debate over the case by case application of standardized data and common principles of procedure already set down in authoritative printed sources.

In the political sphere, the power of speech was similarly reduced by the emergence of printed sources of information. Speaking became, especially in official capacities, reportorial in nature. The speech was no longer the final object. Books, official texts, data and other records were always "back there", somehow being referred to. Speech, then, became a sign of something else—a report or reflexive reference to something outside itself. By virtue of this condition, speech tended to the ceremonial, the public display of something understood to be far more complex than what could be presented in the utterance of "mere" speech. The speech was therefore perfunctory, prefatory, a distillate of the "body of information" that could be found elsewhere.

The Audience

The classical rhetorician in the early literate period had an impressive facility, as compared with the poet or fabulist, to hold an audience's attention, to exhibit his knowledge and to sway the opinions of those not favourably disposed to him. The rhetorician's ability to outline, organize and present a syllogistic argument by *writing* a speech constituted a powerful new technology, and it became—as technological developments often do—the standard by which other techniques are judged. One can imagine the effect on a literate audience, for example, of a speaker trying to combat the rhetorician's logic by using a clever fable or a sentimental vignette. But the question arises concerning the advantage of rhetorical technique in the age of mass printing and extensive literacy.

One enters upon dangerous ground when attempting to evaluate or say anything at all intelligible about the "effect" or "impact" of a speech. Generations of rhetoricians have tried to define or explain the communicative relationship between speaker and listener. The result of this effort has largely been to characterize the phenomenon with an alternative nomenclature. Eloquence, illocutionary force, charisma and inter-subjectivity are a few of the terms rhetoricians and philosophers have used to indicate the substance of this relationship or the essence of successful or persuasive communication. These terms, of course, accomplish no more than a re-statement, rather than an explanation, of the object of inquiry. Consequently, the effectiveness of the rhetorical act remains defiant of generalization so far as that act is taken to mean a dynamic relationship in which speaker and listener affect each other in a designed, or at least explicable, fashion. We are left with the somewhat unsatisfying task of accounting for the effect of a speech with explanations limited to hypotheses about the skills and methods of the speaker, or the character and susceptibilities of the listener. Yet we know that such hypotheses can never quite grasp the relationship of speaker and audience, any more than they will contribute to a "psychology" of the phenomenon—a "moving speech"—which often takes place before our very eyes. The difficulties are only compounded when the inquiry looks for effects upon the rhetorical setting due to such related conditions as expanded literacy or alternative communication techniques.

Religious rhetoric during the post-Reformation era illustrates in a perceptible way the effect of printing and literacy on liturgical conventions and audience response. With a service in the vernacular and a congregation possessing minimum literate skills, the people entered into a responsive dialogue with the preacher—although it is characteristic that this dialogue was anchored to printed scriptural and devotional texts. Other forms of participation appeared when deacons, presbyters and other laymen took oratorical roles, primarily as readers of scriptural texts. Congregational participation can be seen as a reflection of the Calvinist idea of the "priesthood of the believers", in which, at least theoretically, there was a de-emphasis of the role of the priest as an hierarchical figure in relationship to the congregation.

Such changes did not necessarily mean that the Protestant minister no longer enjoyed a superiority, or at times even a charismatic dominance, over his congregation. Still the contrast is strong between the minister and the Catholic priest. The latter was relatively isolated from the communicants, especially and symbolically so during the mass. His sacramental superiority to the people, routinely but powerfully expressed by his celebration of the mystical communion, placed the priest beyond the need for rhetorical or charismatic dominion. So just as literacy and the availability of scriptural texts created involvement for the Protestant congregation, it is also possible to discern how these innovations led to pulpit oratory that was unrivaled in its intensity, duration and demagogic character.[25] An Anglican preacher delivered a sermon at St. Mary's, Oxford, in 1660 which attacked such tendencies among Puritan preachers who made use of "strange new postures" such as "shutting the eyes, distorting the face, and speaking through the nose". These Puritans stood accused for their "whimisical cant of *issues, products, tendencies, indwellings, rollings, recumbencies,* and scripture misapplied".[26] In Protestant services from the seventeenth through the nineteenth centuries, it was not uncommon for sermons to last for several hours on end, from mid-morning to the mid-afternoon. One of the duties of church deacons in some early American congregations was to move about during the sermon with a long rod having a feather attached to one end. This device was used to reach down a pew from the aisle to awaken the slumbering faithful.

Another effect of printing upon religious discourse was the tendency toward the standardization of sacred texts and, as a consequence, the spoken word. Textual standardization, including the emergence of orthodox spelling, punctuation and abbreviations in addition to formal grammar and the idea of "definitive" editions, has been widely documented.[27] A convergence toward grammatical and orthographic uniformity was an inevitable result of the capacities and limitations of moveable types, the customary rules of important printers and the publication of translations, reprintings and revised editions. Not the least of these changes was an enhanced regard for the standardization of the sacred texts. Ancient texts became increasingly corrupted through the errors and eccentricities of many generations of copyists. It was not unusual to have several versions of a single text, due to the compounding of translation and orthographic errors during the many centuries of manuscript book production.[28] In the sixteenth century, Erasmus and other humanists were energetically devoted to publishing accurate and, where possible, comprehensive texts of Greek and Roman classics. The publication of the Authorized King James Version of the Bible in the early seventeenth century, after other less intensive efforts had been devoted to the same task, is an important example of the tendency to establish authoritative editions.[29]

The relevance of textual standardization to religious discourse is that the trend in Protestantism—to broader literacy, and the availability and use of vernacular texts in the liturgy—was by comparison with the Latin mass a narrowing of the gulf between the language of authority and the language of everyday use. A sacred text, even in the vernacular, took on a form of authority formerly reserved for the sacred orders of the clergy. This transformation introduced, from the standpoint of scholastic and Church tradition, a quality of public discourse that could not help but be seen as debased, distorted, less elegant and somehow less truly sacred. Thus William Tyndale, who first published an English translation of the Bible, was accused of distorting the scriptures and burned at the stake in 1536. Seen from the point of view of the people, however, this development assumed quite a different aspect. The biblical texts, in their vernacular translations, were most certainly not the language of the streets and shops. Tyndale had two degrees from Oxford; the translators of the King James version were professors at Oxford and Cambridge.

The preachers and lay persons who gained a proficiency in the standardized vernaculars represented by these translations, far from finding in them a debasement, were using a fluency of style and a quality of grammar which were, if anything, more imposing and impressive to the barely literate congregation, especially unschooled women, precisely because they could understand it. This difference of articulation became reflected in customary and reverent forms of speech which constituted a kind of religious dialect appropriate to the discourse of the church service. Although such language had pulpit oratory as its model and a man of some education as its speaker, its broader use among the congregation was accompanied by tacit—and with the Quakers, explicit—assumptions about where, when and with whom this idiom should be used. The Quaker "plain speech" is only one of several contemporary derivations of the vernacularization and standardization of sacred texts and liturgy. Religious language, exemplified by the vocabulary of the pulpit, actually called upon the congregation to assimilate formulaic speech patterns, scriptural texts and epitomes of eloquent and proverbial commonplaces, deriving from a tradition of literacy of which very few of its members had any knowledge at all. For the common person, then, the vernacular service was decidedly not a debased form of communication. Rather, it called forth an effort to rise to the occasion. Indeed, the artifice of religious language made available to the common people the equivalent of a popular rhetorical style. Thus it is possible to claim that the standardization of language brought about by printing, along with the parallel forces of literacy, the availability of books and translations in vernacular languages, left their marks upon religious observance and ultimately the language of the people.[30]

A final point concerning the impact of printing and mass literacy upon public discourse is the tendency for oral address to become a performance and to be received as such by the audience. Such a development would only be a natural outcome of the practice of the new rhetorical theory which emphasized the manner of delivery,[31] although it is unlikely that the elocutionary movement was a response to theory alone, apart from adjustments within the actual content of subject matter, speaker and audience. Of course, we have no way of gauging the degree of appreciation a particular audience may have had that a speech was more impressive as a piece of acting than as a method of informing and persuading. With this difficulty in mind let us examine the proposition that the speech, as perceived by a literate audience, is primarily evaluated according to tacit assumptions discriminating what is being said from how the speaker said it. This is not to suggest that a literate audience has less of an appreciation for words and arguments than an illiterate one. Rather, the perception of what is heard is inevitably influenced by images in the literate mind which translate oral utterances into their literal equivalents. The audience focuses upon the manner of delivery of an oration, not because it has no interest in the literal contents, but precisely because of the tacit assumption that any speech, however well or poorly delivered, can only be reportorial and referential, that is, merely a symbolic schema of the speech's "real" contents. The audience thus assumes that the most important thing about the speech is the very fact that it is a speech, that is, an oral performance. During nineteenth-century electoral campaigns in England, the United States and in Europe, debates and speeches drew audiences that numbered many thousands, and were held under conditions which suggested that they were regarded as valued public entertainment.[32] Only when a speaker's fame has gone before him "in print" can a "personal appearance" have any meaning as a special occasion. Under such circumstances, the audience is far more likely to be impressed with the flair, fluency and "personnage" of a speaker—or at least his voice, if they can not see him from their place in the crowd—than with the substance of what he has to say. The unlettered in such an audience will be unmoved by the force of the speaker's logic, and those who feel a degree of competence in the subject will easily recognize how inadequate the speech is compared to treatments to be found in books, especially books written by the speaker himself.

Like early Puritan pulpit oratory of the seventeenth century, political rhetoric in the nineteenth century seemed to place great importance upon eloquence that stirred the emotions as well as displayed the oratorical skills of the speaker.[33] This was especially true of occasions when great numbers were present. An illustration of the separation between the manner of delivery and the actual content as objects of audience attention is the occasion of Abraham Lincoln's Gettysburg address in 1863. Lincoln's memorable address was counted a failure on that day, and was briefly dismissed as such in the next day's newspapers. Complaints were expressed to the effect that it was a brief, mumbling effort heard by scarcely anyone. Lincoln's appearance at the dedication of the military cemetery was an afterthought, and the major address for the occasion was given by Edward Everett, a Unitarian minister and professor of Greek at Harvard. The latter's effort was a long and rambling piece, delivered with the force that was required to address a throng of thousands. The newspapers noted the success of the speech with generous praise. What is doubly interesting is that although Lincoln's piece became celebrated in print as one of the finest compositions of the English language, and Everett's speech was quickly forgotten, the latter was actually a finely detailed account of the military campaigns at Gettysburg based upon his own careful study of the battlefields and information provided by surviving participants, including General Meade. The speech was, as a narration, one of the finest and most informed accounts of the series of battles.[34] The substance of this speech, which took more than an hour and a half to deliver, was clearly not what the audience roundly applauded, but the conventional stentorian eloquence of delivery. The audience, who after all did not have to be told about the battles, since they had managed to live through them, appreciated the ceremony of the occasion and the way in which Everett's performance observed it with the appropriate rhetorical *tour de force*. Lincoln had simply stood up, read his few lines in a half-audible voice, and then sat down again before five minutes had elapsed. As a performance, the speech was a failure.

Oral discourse as a rhetorical display does not, of course, rule out the possibility that the composition of the speech may include important information and arguments of a logically persuasive quality. Both the speeches just referred to illustrate, in different ways, that the content of a speech can be important and accredited according to standards outside the rhetorical setting, for example, literary merit and historical scholarship. What is important for the present argument, however, is the fact that the rhetorical display fails or succeeds quite independently of the content of the speech; and, because of the medium of print, the content of the speech has a life of its own quite independently of the rhetorical display. The point to be emphasized here, although it must be largely speculative, is that the audience, as well as the speaker, seemed to understand and acknowledge this division.

Elocutionary theory in the eighteenth and nineteenth century, which was devoted primarily to the style and gestures of delivery, implied that the orator's impact owed more to skilful performance than to the intrinsic logical or factual merits of the speech. At the same time, there was a developing relationship between public oratory, especially religious discourse, and the book trade. The popularity of collected sermons in the book shops of the seventeenth and eighteenth centuries portended the expanding influence of, and in effect a subservience to, a technique of communication that simply could not be ignored by the orator. Milton noted the trend toward publishing and selling sermons as early as 1644. "But as for the multitude of Sermons ready printed and pil'd up, on every text that is not difficult, our London trading St. *Thomas* in his vestry, and adde to boot St. *Martin*, and St. *Hugh*, have not within their hallow'd limits more vendible ware of all sorts ready made: so that penury he need never fear of Pulpit provision, having where so plenteously to refresh his magazin."[35] A bookseller in Henry Fielding's novel *Joseph Andrews* (1742) is made to say:

> The trade is so vastly stocked with [sermons], that really, unless they come out with the name of Whitefield or Wesley, or some other such great man, as a bishop, or those sort of people, I don't care to touch; unless now it was a sermon preached on the 30th of January; or we

could say in the title-page, published at the earnest request of the congregation, or the inhabitants; but truly, for a dry piece of sermons, I had rather be excused; especially as my hands are so full at present.[36]

If the availability of the printing press gained the preacher a much larger readership than his own congregation, printing also enabled the preacher to use the sermons to different purposes. Published sermons, singly and in collection, could serve as an elaboration of doctrine, especially for theologians and seminary students. The printed text of a sermon, in other cases, might serve as a defence against heresy or an attacking manifesto against established doctrine.[37]

The influence of printing upon the content of sermons, and the function they served both for preachers and disciples of the faith, are suggested by the frequency of their publication from the earliest days of printing. While noting this influence, it is important to remember that preaching itself was guided by principles seeming to ignore the growing literacy of the congregation and the important literary role of published sermons. The task remained one of performance. As late as the Victorian period in England, the orator "held forth with an air of authority and indulged in verbal pyrotechnics with an élan his modern counterpart may well envy. Not that he was personally more flamboyant, but the oratorical tradition as he inherited it allowed him—almost forced him—to be aggressive and authoritative."[38] It may well be that the hortative style assured the attention of the auditors, as well as their entertainment, in a setting that was less and less dependent upon the pulpit as a source of informed discourse. The change in the function of the preacher is recognized in broad scope by G.R. Owst, whose two books on the medieval English pulpit argue for the existence of a flourishing tradition of pulpit oratory in the middle ages. Contrasting the situation of the modern preacher with that of the medieval one, Owst suggests the change in communicative function of the sermon. We may infer from what he says why "pyrotechnics" may be resorted to by a preacher struggling to retain what Thomas Wilson had called in the sixteenth century "the fickle ears of our fleeting audience":[39]

In a world devoid alike of the newspaper and the printed book, of the means of rapid communication by land or sea, the itinerant [medieval] orator had surely an opportunity which any man of ambition might envy . . . Modern preachers, eyeing the spoilt children of our modern pew, may well envy the prospect that lay before our medieval friar. Traveller, friend of the outcast, master alike of the ecclesiastical and the popular tongue, with intimate knowledge of the world as well as of books, he could mingle in his discourse the latest "narration" with the mysteries of nature . . . for ever bringing forth out of his treasure things new and old.[40]

Given the "spoilt children of our modern pew" as his congregation, the modern preacher's performance before a literate audience had to be a kind of entertainment. If in some cases the congregation, in its influential parts, was more widely travelled, more educated and more fully in possession of an "intimate knowledge of the world", this was all the more reason for the sermon to be a kind of ceremonial performance that would, substance aside, win congregational feelings and reaffirm the uniqueness of the preacher's task. The latter interest was not an idle concern, since the great quantity of, and heavy demand for, printed sermons led on the one hand to plagiarism in both preaching and publishing sermons written by another, and the production of "sermons" for the book market by lay writers. Dr. Johnson, who claimed to have written forty sermons, is quoted by Boswell: "I have begun a sermon after dinner, and sent it off by the post that night".[41] This remark, as well as any, illustrates how printing severed the tie between composition and oral performance, the latter becoming incidental to the primary interest in offering a written piece to the reading public.

Notes

1. This class of speech would include, *inter alia*, judicial opinions and decrees, edicts, official addresses, parliamentary debate, party convention and political campaign speeches.
2. Both Hobbes and Locke made frequent references to their distaste for the scholastic curriculum and their desire to study mathematics and science. Francis Bacon's *Advancement of Learning* (1605) is another seventeenth-century example of the tendency for re-classifying knowledge with a view to more efficient production and use of scientific knowledge. Bacon's *Novum organum* (1620) was a proposal for an entire new system of reason, amenable to empirical investigations, which was intended to replace Aristotle's system upon which the scholastic tradition had been built.
3. Thomas Birch, *History of the Royal Society* (London, 1756), I, pp. 3–6.
4. This is an unmistakable impression received from Locke's private views about the formation, meetings and activities of the Society of which he was a founding member. H.R.F. Bourne, *Life of Locke* (London, 1876), I, pp. 245–48.
5. It is noteworthy that symbolic languages have nevertheless developed according to a certain uniformity. Scientists or mathematicians of varying language competences can easily convey, test and reformulate information expressed in symbolic formulae.
6. Perhaps a severe medievalist or Renaissance historian would note the rise of science as the beginning of the decline of articulate speech and the jealous

veneration of classical languages. This would seem to be a case of the seeds of destruction being sown within. The very technology—mass printing—that made mass literacy possible has also led to a vulgarization that must culminate in what amounts to "illiteracy" and the misuse or disuse of language. Many university professors of English might be tempted by this thesis, although they would probably be more prone to blaming television for their students' grammatical shortcomings rather than the ill effect of reading too many books.

7. One is tempted to make the comparison between such teaching and the oral tradition, in which elementary education was also based upon oral recitation, but with the teacher, rather than the book, as the source of knowledge. In the oral tradition, one learned about wars, great men and gods; in the literate tradition, one learns "history".

8. See Chapter IV.

9. The relationship between Protestantism and literacy is two-fold. The reformed church was associated with expanding literacy for the purpose of enabling the faithful to read the Bible, especially in the vernacular. On the other hand, there is a prior connection between Protestantism and printing in the sense that the movement itself was an outgrowth of increasingly secularized higher education (both Luther and Calvin had studied law), a new tradition of textual criticism (emerging from the search for textual purity and uniformity) and the debate over doctrinal interpretations (a matter closely related to questions arising from efforts in translating scripture into the vernacular).

10. A number of general studies are available on the subject of Reformation and post-Reformation preaching. The most voluminous one is useful as a reference work: Edwin Charles Dargan, *A History of Preaching*, 2 vols. (New York, 1968, reprint of 1905 ed.). A good study of the early English pulpit is J.W. Blench, *Preaching in England in the Late 15th and 16th Centuries* (Oxford, 1964). Two studies which show the political significance of pulpit oratory are Michael Walzer, *The Revolution of the Saints* (Harvard, 1965) and Paul S. Seever, *The Puritan Lectureships: The Politics of Religious Dissent 1560–1662* (Stanford, 1970).

11. Martin Luther, *Christian Liberty* (Philadelphia, 1957), p. 8.

12. Actually, the distinction even today is not so clear as might be expected. The role of the church and pulpit oratory in the Negro civil rights movements in the United States in the 1960s and the position of the Church on such social issues as divorce and abortion in Europe are cases in point.

13. Luther's letter to the German princes "On the Peasant Revolt" and his sermons on the same question are illustrative documents.

14. Strictly biblical in the Protestant movement and the canonical tradition in the Roman Church, which included the scriptures, canon law, writings of the Church fathers and papal bulls and encyclicals.

15. We suggest a distinction here between "legalistic" and "scholastic" in the sense that discourse became centred less on philosophical and deductive argumentation confined to religious and classical authorities, and more on legislation and basic documents of a juridicial and constitutional nature.

16. There are important exceptions. E.g., parliamentary debates in England, and political discourse in the American colonies, both legislative and electoral in form. The difficulty of distinguishing between "political" and "religious" discourse is apparent, for example, when examining the political rhetoric of the Genevan republican city-state, or the assemblies of New England town meetings.

17. Again, there are important exceptions, e.g., the much earlier Italian city–states, especially in Venice, which produced institutionalized political rhetoric in

legislative councils and periodic, often very elaborate, electoral campaigns.

18. Illustrative examples would form a list of England's notable men of letters: Hobbes, Locke, James Harrington, Thomas Paine, Edmund Burke are only a few.

19. Chauncey A. Goodrich, *Select British Eloquence* (New York, 1852); Loren D. Reid, "Speaking in the 18th Century House of Commons", *Speech Monographs*, XVI (1949), pp. 137–40; R.F. Howes, ed., *Historical Studies of Rhetoric and Rhetoricians* (Ithaca, 1961), esp. pp. 225–52; 271–93. For a discussion of the earlier, Elizabethan, parliaments see R.H. Tawney, *A Discourse upon Usury by Thomas Wilson, 1572* (New York, 1925) and J.E. Neale, *The Elizabethan House of Commons* (London, 1949).

20. Howes, *Rhetoric and Rhetoricians*, pp. 225–52; Neale, *House of Commons*.

21. D.C. Bryant, "The Contemporary Reception of Edmund Burke's Speaking", in Howes, *Rhetoric and Rhetoricians*, pp. 271–93.

22. The first official compiler of English parliamentary proceedings, Luke Hansard (1752–1828), began his work in the late eighteenth century.

23. James Downey, *The Eighteenth Century Pulpit* (Oxford, 1969), p. 18.

24. Wilbur Samuel Howell, "Sources of the Elocutionary Movement in England: 1700–1748", in Howes, *Rhetoric and Rhetoricians*, p. 139: also biblio., pp. 397–401.

25. James Downey, *Eighteenth Century Pulpit*, pp. 22–23.

26. Robert South's sermon, "The Scribe Instructed", quote from Downey, *Eighteenth Century Pulpit*.

27. See references in Chapter IV, *supra*.

28. J. Carter and P.H. Muir, eds., *Printing and the Mind of Man* (London, 1967), introductory essay by Denys Hay, pp. xviii–xx.

29. *The Oxford Annotated Bible* contains a brief summary of the establishment of the English translations and earlier editions of the Bible, pp. ix *et seq.* (Oxford, 1962).

30. This impact is especially important, perhaps, in the cultures dependent upon modern English, where there are no pronominal and verbal provisions for an intimate form of address. This deficiency must be patched over by the retention of certain archaicisms—*Thee, Thou*, etc.—which make religious language all the more a distinct dialect appropriate to religious ceremony, but little else.

31. W.S. Howell in Howes, *Rhetoric and Rhetoricians*, pp. 139–44.

32. One of the most famous examples of this phenomenon was the series of debates by Abraham Lincoln and Stephen A. Douglas during the Illinois senatorial campaign of 1858, which Douglas won. See R.A. Heckman, *Lincoln* v. *Douglas: The Great Debates Campaign* (Washington, 1967).

33. A distinction between Puritan oratorical bombast and Anglican "fine" preaching was so apparent as to become an object of satire and ridicule from both pulpits. See Downey, *Eighteenth Century Pulpit*, Ch. 1.

34. W.S. Howell, *Poetics, Rhetoric and Logic* (Ithaca, 1975), p. 251. Also, see William E. Barton, *Lincoln at Gettysburg* (Indianapolis, 1939).

35. Downey, *Eighteenth Century Pulpit*, p. 4, quoting Milton from *Areopagitica*.

36. Ibid., p. 5, quoting from Bk. I, ch. xvii. Downey's study of the 18th-century pulpit nevertheless credits the 17th-century pulpit as unequalled in pre-eminence, naming such great preachers as Lancelot Andrews, John Donne, Jeremy Taylor, Richard Baxter, Isaac Barrow, Robert South and John Tillotson. W.F. Mitchell, in *English Pulpit Oratory from Andrews to Tillotson* (London, 1962), suggests how these preachers, by printing their sermons in periodic collections, virtually served a journalistic function (pp. 3–4).

37. Downey, *Eighteenth Century Pulpit*, p. 3.

38. Ibid., p. 1.
39. W.S. Howell, *Logic and Rhetoric in England 1500–1700* (Princeton, 1956), p. 107, quoting Thomas Wilson's *Rhetorique*.
40. Downey, *Eighteenth Century Pulpit*, pp. 81–82, quoting from G. Owst, *Preaching in Medieval England* (London, 1926).
41. Downey, *Eighteenth Century Pulpit*, p. 8, quoting from Boswell's *Life of Johnson*. Downey has an interesting discussion of the excesses of sermon publishing which shows how this genre was affected by the book trade, and in turn, as Johnson himself claimed, became an important part of England's national literature.

7

The Universal Medium

> Broadcasting cannot compete with other amusements. Broad-
> casting does not encourage association or herding, and can,
> therefore, never compete with the theater, the concert, the
> church, or the motion picture. Radio's greatest benefit is to
> isolate persons. It will, however, serve most effectively the
> sightless, the bed-ridden, the farmer, and the deaf.
> *Amercian Journal of Sociology*, 1927

The third of the major propositions outlined at the beginning of
this study argued that political rhetoric in the twentieth century
is a technologically superseded form of communication, and that
its cultural aspect as a language performance bears no resemblance
to the social and political functions of classical rhetoric, that is,
to inform and persuade. This proposition compels us to survey the
techniques of communication which have evolved, largely in this
century, in such a way as to suggest to many the formation of a
new cultural era, an "electronic age" of mass communication. Of
particular concern is the relationship between political discourse and
the most powerful of the electronic media—radio and television—
so that we may determine how political discourse, and especially
oral address, have been altered by the new technology both in form
and social effect.[1]

The development of the electric telegraph by Samuel F.B. Morse
in the first half of the nineteenth century marks the origin of
electronic communication. With this device men were able for the
first time to overcome time and distance in communicating with
one another.[2] While it can be argued that the telegraph was not
a totally revolutionary mode of communication,[3] its invention was
an initial step in the development of electronic techniques of
transmitting, recording and reproducing aural and visual information.

The "electronic age"[4] will be used here as a convenient term for the era in which this technology has developed into elaborate systems of communication—an era that is considerably briefer and better defined than the age of printing, even if it has produced effects upon language and oral communication that are far more complex than those attending the previous era. McLuhan and others have used the term "non-linear" to distinguish electronic means of communication from those based upon chirography and printing. The essential distinction centres not so much on the production as on the perception of sense data. Thus a non-linear medium is one that creates images that can be perceived by eye and ear without requiring the (literate) skills necessary to observe the rigid rules of attention, sequence and context.[5] Electronic techniques of communication are able to carry words and sounds to the auditor's senses as intelligible items of graphic and phonetic information as well as visual images of the speech act itself. Have these techniques changed the character of public discourse, and by implication, altered the role of political rhetoric within modern society? This is the central question before us in this chapter.

In our analysis of political rhetoric in an age of printing and expanding literacy, we noted that rhetorical acts were performed in the shadow of the printing press and the printed record. Rhetoric in that age came to be divested of any special obligation, in theory, to the coherency and discovery of knowledge, and thus survived as a body of elocutionary precepts. In practice, rhetorical performance allied itself with printed communication in such representative forms as the sermon and pamphlet. In this way, rhetoric[6] acknowledged superior methods of acquiring and disposing of specialized information and a superior technique of communication. In much the same way, an "orator" in the electronic age is aware of the subordinate, increasingly dependent, status of words, voice and gesture as communicative tools. The speaker sitting before the videotape camera must always be conscious that his words are not sounds breaking the silence that, by their very ephemeral utterance, become transitory fragments of meaning projected to willing ears —as assumed in classical rhetoric. His words, gestures and intonations are preserved on tape; they are simply raw material for editing, rather than the elements of a communicative act; and there is no audience, except for the crew of technicians whom the speaker must, so far as he is able, pretend do not exist.

In such circumstances, communication with an audience becomes quite a different rhetorical problem, with an array of technological strategies far more complex than those possessed by the orator. The speaker must regard his utterances as a relatively primitive and preliminary behaviour offered up to the production studio, where his efforts will be subjected to the superior techniques of the electronic medium, where what has not already been accomplished by lighting, amplication and make-up may be supplied with cutting, re-sequencing, interspersions of charts, graphs, supplementary film, music and better footage from previous takes. Compared with audio-visual technology, the speaker becomes a minor character in the rhetorical settings—not an orator but an actor. In place of the orator addressing the attentive masses, the image emerges of a speaker sitting in a bare cubicle, addressing not a throng, but merely a microphone and camera lens. Outside the cubicle the sound of his voice cannot be heard, but that is where the volume and tone of his voice are determined, the liveliness or serenity of his gestures created by camera angle, focus and proximity. The dimension of time is lost altogether, along with the quality of what must now be conceived as a "live" performance. The transmission may communicate the speaker's voice at the speed of light to a widely dispersed audience or, alternatively, abstract the utterance out of the sweep of time and cut it up, collate it, experiment with different tracks, and eventually put it in a can or throw it away.

One need not be misled by these not at all imaginary vignettes to think that they imply a powerless, tyrannized orator wholly at the mercy of the production studio. The power of electronics is awesome in the face of the "unaided" voice, but power may run in the other direction, with the production studio at the service of the speaker. If there is truth to the statement that the speaker is at the mercy of electronic technology, it is also true that the technology—along with the audience—is at the mercy of the speaker should he appropriate these media for his rhetorical aims. We have more than enough evidence to show that the electronic media are at the service of powerful men and powerful aims.[7]

Re-defining Rhetoric

It is significant that we cannot meaningfully discuss political rhetoric in the electronic era in isolation from the technology available. Indeed, as the previous paragraphs suggest, rhetoric and technology are virtually indistinguishable. Thus we are forced to reconsider the very substance and form of political rhetoric as oral discourse. If we insist upon a narrow conception of rhetoric—a formal speech before an audience to inform and persuade on behalf of an acknowledged subject—we would almost certainly be ruling out the most significant portion of the matter under investigation. To focus upon live, personally delivered public speeches before a live (even if broadcast) audience is to emphasize the directly oral, unmediated rhetorical setting of classical oratory at the expense of missing far more significant aspects of public discourse.

If a new conception of rhetoric were designed to include mediated oratory, thereby admitting the dispersed listeners into the rhetorical setting—as in a televised "fireside chat" or a major policy speech —our attention would still be restricted to occasions retaining the traditional characteristics of an actual person speaking in "real time" to an audience, with a coincidence of oral and visual experience bound together into a single moment of time. Such a definition of political rhetoric ignores the kind of communications to which modern political parties devote up to ninety per cent of their budgets: pre-taped and highly edited speeches, candidate "biographies" on film, brief advertising spots replete with fast cuts, sound track overlays, and even cartoon figures. The variety of public relations media techniques used by public officials and bureaucracies to communicate to the general public would also be ignored. Clearly, political campaign communications, press conferences, slogans, and the sophisticated selling techniques used by governments to win and retain support for policy administration[8] make up a significant part of modern political language which must be accomodated by any study of the relationship between language, communication technology and society.

We are faced therefore with the obsolescence of the term rhetoric, in so far as the term refers to principles of persuasive speech. Whether we attach to this term the Greek and Roman meaning which encompassed logical organization and delivery, or use the eighteenth-century elocutionist's view that rhetoric is concerned with the principles governing effective delivery alone, it remains equally true that the term referred to persuasive oratorical performance. There are many precedents for using the term rhetoric very loosely for language forms other than classical oratory,[9] and it is common for the term to be applied to any use of language that does, or intends, to move and persuade: poetry, political slogans, or even literature as a whole. We are now drawn, however, to consider that some of the most powerful techniques of communication dispense with words and language in the ordinary sense altogether, and that is why we must question—if not answer exactly —whether rhetoric remains a legitimate category in an analysis of modern political communications.

If the broader term "political communication" be supplied in place of rhetoric in recognition of the non-oratorical and non-verbal characteristics of electronic communication, there remains one important respect in which rhetorical theory may be re-applied to the most sophisticated electronic presentations. The possibility of seeing radio and television as intrinsically rhetorical media requires a distinction between their potential to convey and extend (by broadcasting) an ordinary speech act and their potential to *create* audio-visual information. It is suggested that in the latter case, the electronic media reach their most significant potential for rhetorical communication.

The fundamental distinction that must be emphasized in the various uses of the electronic media in political communication is that between broadcasting and production. In broadcasting, the speaker uses the transmitting potential of electronic technology to extend his utterances to greater numbers and to more remote locations than could otherwise be accomplished by the unassisted voice—or even with the assistance of printing, where broadcasting's superiority is illustrated by its speed as well as its scope of access to an audience. The use of electronic devices to produce a rhetorical setting that did not or even could not actually be presented directly to an audience is significantly different from simple broadcasting. The special function played by the mediating devices in this case is creative, rather than merely extensive.[10] It is the use of electronic technology not only to extend and expand the transmission of a speech act, but actually to produce a rhetorical performance that literally never occurred and could not have occurred as a speech act. Thus any broadcast of a produced performance—such as the advertisement clip, edited speech, or other examples mentioned above—is precisely a technique of reproduction because it involves a separation in time between broadcast and performance. What is conveyed is a replica or an artifice of a rhetorical act, and like any form of reproduction, the technique can be repeated indefinitely in reproducing identical facsimiles. The "power" of this technique, therefore, depends not only upon the broadcast media's advantages (and disadvantages) in projecting images instantaneously and to a potentially universal audience, but also upon the opportunity of reproducing a message in a standard image indefinitely.

The production and reproduction of what we must call, for want of a better term, rhetorical performances by electronic techniques, amounts to a revolutionary method of political communication. It is as if the classical divisions of rhetoric—invention, arrangement, delivery, among others—were appropriated by the electronic studio and fashioned into a new "art of rhetoric".

We may be justified in including such artificial audio-visual creations under the heading of rhetoric, precisely because in both the classical and elocutionist definition, rhetoric's task is to present a coherent, well-organized statement in a manner that disposes the audience to be pleased and persuaded by the effectiveness of the speaker's delivery. The ability of audio-visual technology to create a pseudo-oratorical record out of several "takes" and supplementary sound and visual images (background overlays of voice or music, documentary graphic illustrations, rapid combinations of images for psychological impact) in an endeavour to produce a concise, impressive and persuasive statement would seem to be the epitome of electronic technology's power as a rhetorical medium. The denomination is all the more appropriate because the audio-visual production aims at moving and persuading its aduience by techniques that correspond to the elements of classical rhetoric: invention (the resources and materials used, i.e., the "script"); disposition (sequence, arrangement and "mix"); style (the audio-visual techniques of composition and expression); delivery (utterance and gesture, achieved by cutting, editing and staging); and memory (the mastery of material, which is fully replaced by the reproduction facilities of the technology).

The effectiveness of the rhetorical image may be subjected to "pre-testing" on an audience or panel and corrected to assure that the device produces the desired emotional and attitudinal effect.[11] The actual broadcast of the piece requires the exercise of additional features of the new rhetorical method. The composition of the audience and the intensity of contact with it can to a large extent be controlled by "placing" the device for broadcast in terms of the choices available in the various "media markets". The size and composition of the audience can be controlled by "time-slotting" so that one can, alternatively, reach or avoid housewives, commuters, teen-agers, popular or classical music listeners, radio or television audiences, people who tune into news programmes, or tune away from them. By manipulating these variables, as commercial advertisers (for whom these marketing techniques were developed) typically do, radio and television operators can virtually "guarantee" an audience of known size and demographic composition. Audience selectivity enables the communicator to produce different material designed to appeal to each region and composition. Varying the frequency of reproduction, as one's aims and budget allow, enables the broadcaster to achieve extensive or intensive saturation of the audience. Even this brief review of broadcast advertising illustrates the great flexibility and adaptability of electronic techniques as tools of communication.

The implication of the distinction between broadcast and produced rhetorical events is quite clear. We have drawn a line between rhetorical performances that are actual and those that are not, between those which actually happen and those which could not have. This amounts to a distinction between the actual and the artificial, in terms of linguistic performance. If rhetoric as compared with casual conversation is art, the electronically produced programme is still more artificial because of its divorce from any conceivable linguistic performance apart from the technology. In making this distinction we do not intend to condemn or to establish a metaphysical standard against which electronic communication is found morally deficient. Normative considerations are certainly possible and available to the reader as he chooses, but that is really beyond the present endeavour. The immediate interest is in the analysis of the form, function and effects of the use of language within contemporary discourse. Thus it is important to note how electronic technology presents a distinction between rhetorical performances that fall into relatively clear categories of the real and the apparent when actual human behaviour is used as the standard of measure. An 'old' rhetoric of oratory contrasts with a powerful "new" rhetoric which has at its disposal an array of communication techniques and an unlimited range of audio-visual materials to use in affecting an audience. This "extra-linguistic" rhetorical communication is especially significant as it gradually becomes the standard for rhetorical performance in contemporary electoral politics.

Electronic Extension and Political Rhetoric

It is often remarked that radio and television have offered the possessors of political or economic power an unprecedented access to public attention. George Orwell's vision of this in *1984* is probably as good an expression of this idea as any appearing since he wrote the novel in 1948. For whatever reasons of policy and commerce, entire societies have developed embracing networks of radio and television, and the fact is that a broadcast medium now exists which enables speakers to address either a small, well-defined audience or an entire population. A potential audience, in other words, is available and can be selected according to time, place, scale and composition in a way that makes the electronic media truly revolutionary in comparison to any other technique of communication. The mere existence of this technology and its near-universal distribution in industrialized societies does not however guarantee universal and unrestricted access to these channels, nor the desired audience for those who do have access. The potential of electronic mediation is limited precisely by its expense, sophistication and public character,[12] but in another sense, the very potential of radio and television as a powerful means of communication generates political restrictions and limitations upon its use quite apart from questions of expense or expertise. One should not overlook the parallel here with much earlier technological innovations such as a standardized alphabet or the printing press which, in turn, also gave rise to legal sanctions and political regulation.

The electronic media, both in theory and in practical comparison with any previous medium of communication, have set an absolute standard—the instantaneous and universal audience—and have established outer magnitudes of speed and scale for language performance. That these criteria are relatively, rather than absolutely, achieved in everyday experience does not detract from the fact that radio and television have access to listeners on a scale that no other means of communication can even come close to approximating. The singular feature of the electronic era is the achievement for the first time in history of a virtually inclusive communications medium. No fewer than ninety seven per cent of households in the United States have at least one television set, a proportion that exceeds that for homes with a telephone. The universal accessibility of these truly "mass" media is not restricted even by the standard of literacy, since the listener has only to bring the minimal skill of attention to image and sound. The theoretical capacities and practical developments of the electronic media need not, however, lead us to ignore a fact of equal importance, that is, how seldom the potential is exploited, particularly toward the outer magnitudes of speed and scale, for purposes which we could plausibly identify as within the province of political rhetoric.[13]

So far as the broadcast audience is concerned, radio and television are uniquely sophisticated but easily operated techniques of communication. The listener neither needs nor acquires any skill whatsoever. In this sense, electronic technology is greatly different from printing, whose effect was to demand the skill of literacy which in itself implied great changes in the methods and availability of education. Radio and television were technological advances which, unlike every preceding advance in language technology, required no accompanying language skill in order to universalize the technique as a medium of mass communication. This ease of access to the electronic audience is not without certain drawbacks, especially for the audience. The word may have always been, in a certain sense, more powerful than the sword. The rhetorician's ability to sway the crowd, the priest or lawyer's undermining of institutional authority with a pamphlet, and the novelist's power to create outrage and define the public opinion are examples of this. But the power of the spoken or printed word is hardly a match for the modern politician's use of electronic communications to gain and wield power.[14] A speaker's assembly can never be large or easily gathered, and a readership will always be limited by literacy levels and literary tastes. But no such limitations exist for radio and television, which are frequently left switched on in homes for more than half the waking hours each day.

The ease with which the electronic media obtain access to an audience is matched by the minimal demand placed upon individual listeners, but despite this convenience a very difficult question of access is involved. The efficiency of electronic media—measured, say, as cost per listener and elapsed contact time—contrasts sharply with the problem a speaker may have in gaining access to radio and television. This is due not only to the direct control of electronic media by governments and commercial enterprise, but also by the more complex barriers of technological sophistication, the high cost of facilities, the relatively small number of clear channels and, finally, the level of attention of listeners, especially where alternative programmes are available. Thus the potential abuses implied by the electronic media's monopoly of access to mass audiences is compounded by additional opportunities for abuse flowing from the inevitable restrictions of access imposed by limitations of time, resources and expertise.[15] The potential of the broadcast media for extending and intensifying political discourse is, therefore, qualified by constraints of policy, technological resources and popular interest.

If we consider only such formal rhetorical acts as the political orator's speech, one might conclude that the broadcasting potential of radio and television is barely tapped. This observation may seem to contradict the general impression that political figures are seen and heard with great frequency. Indeed, populations are probably more familar with the facial expressions and voices of public officials than ever before in history. Yet it can hardly be denied that their appearances are only rarely the occasion of a formal address. The power to reach an audience of millions, even if available, does not mean that the power will be used, or used effectively. This is especially true in the case of formal oratory, although notable exceptions come to mind. Radio and television have been used for a number of memorable political addresses, and these media are now an integral part of party convention rhetoric, inaugural ceremonies, formal press conferences and other official speeches.[16] On the whole, however, radio and television present political figures and their utterances in a manner that either fragments the rhetorical setting or serves as an alternative to it. We have in mind here not only the daily news programming, in which political figures are shown in short clips (often without sound), in interviews, or performing ceremonial duties (signing Bills, disembarking from an airplane and such) where the action itself, rather than an oration, is the item of interest. Even more characteristic of broadcast appearances of political figures are the advertisements, "documentaries", and excerpted "statements" popular in political campaigns. The importance of newscasting, public relations efforts and advertising campaigns is not to be underestimated for its impact upon public opinion, but the point to be emphasized here is that formal oratory plays only a minor and occasional part in this process. In the United States, where many hundreds of commercial radio and television stations provide a greater access to local populations than in any other society, the broadcasting of formal rhetoric is almost solely a national phenomenon. There are many contributing factors to this situation—prestige of national office, high cost of broadcast time, competition with commercial "entertainment"—but the fact remains that the viewer seldom finds himself confronted with a speech.[17]

The viewer does, however, find himself confronted with studio-produced events. News broadcasting, which rarely does more than present a newspaper format of headlines and brief lead-in paragraphs, does its best to encapsulate actual speeches by showing brief excerpts aiming to represent the speaker's topic stripped bare of context and secondary (or complex) material in the speech. Political figures often find these efforts to be distorted because the news editor fails to emphasize the topics or sentences which the speaker wished to be emphasized—a disagreement in itself pointing up how different the television newsroom product is from the rhetorical event it treats.

The politician has his day when he controls the studio. It is becoming a routine condition of political life, especially at the national level, that public officials rely upon staging techniques, videotape editing and special effects to present themselves to the public. The election campaign is no longer the only period during which politicians use the electronic media for their special powers of communication,[18] but it is still at this time that the airwaves are saturated with political salesmanship. During the campaign the viewer is presented with slick audio and video excerpts of the candidate at his best. Slogans, songs, photomontage, sound overlays, animated graphics, professional narrators and other sophisticated media devices have made electoral campaign advertising a new business enterprise in the United States and in a growing number of European countries. The 1972 federal parliamentary election in Australia, especially the campaign of the Australian Labor Party, introduced the entire range of marketing and electronic media techniques.[19]

Apart from political campaigns, rhetorical performances are usually limited to a few national political figures whose broadcast appearances are typically the occasion of major policy announcements, State ceremony or national emergencies.[20] Public affairs programming on regional radio and television stations is, in fact, so unpopular (with producers as well as with the audience) that regulatory and licencing commissions typically require a minimum of public service programmes and "local content" for the granting of broadcasting rights.

The content of commercial broadcasting is remarkably similar in substance and presentation, and is generally apolitical. In countries such as Australia and Great Britain, where major public broadcasting systems compete with licenced commercial networks, a degree of diversity in programming is assured, but the competition has had the effect of forcing public stations to adopt the style and emphases of commercial broadcasting. In any case, only a small portion of each day's broadcasting could be called political programming, even if that be loosely defined. Publicly financed broadcasting, despite its potential as an outlet for government propaganda, is to the contrary often bound by its regulatory apparatus to avoid controversial or partisan materials. This seems especially to be the case in Australia. The uniformity of programmes—music and news on radio, serials on television—and programming contracts between local stations and national broadcasting corporations hardly amount to an actual "network" or "system" of broadcasting. The mere existence of vast arrays of broadcasting stations with a capacity for periodic relays and integrated "network" transmissions does not imply—nor do we find empirically—that the electronic media operate as an intensively-used mass medium for political discourse. The use of broadcasting for its powers of audience extension is a rare exception, taking place primarily during periodic election campaigns or in times of national or regional emergency. In this sense, the term "network" as applied to radio and television is, from the perspective of political discourse, somewhat misleading. Only for the few ceremonial occasions when political speeches are broadcast to a national audience do radio and television function as a "mass medium" for the broadcast of rhetorical performances. The reasons why this is so vary from place to place, and do not necessarily have to do with forms of State ownership and intervention. The present argument need not go beyond the mere recognition of the status quo,[21] namely, that the outstanding feature of the potential of the broadcasting media is how greatly they remain unexploited for purposes of political rhetoric.

Every technique of communication involves limitations. This takes the form of discrimination in the selection of "information" content, as well as in the form of inevitable and planned restrictions relating to competence and access in the use of the technology. The development of handwriting was accompanied by the emergence of scribes whose competence became a valued and scarce commodity. The advantages of literacy led to questions of access to writing skills, which in turn implied economic, religious and sexual discriminations in the dissemination of the technique. In the same manner, broadcast technology has given rise to several levels of competency: research scientists and engineers, technicians, marketing experts, production engineers, camera-men, editors, script-writers, actors and professional broadcasters. The technological complexity of the electronic media is therefore reflected in the complexity of the groups possessing this competence.

Access to the actual use of electronic media, apart from the technical skills involved, is an equally complicated issue. Hopes about the "mass" and democratic character of radio and television were expressed when the technology was first developed, and many hopes (or ideological illusions) still remain, but access to broadcast technology remains highly restricted. This restrictiveness is not simply due to the sophisticated technology required for broadcasting, nor to the small number of clear frequency channels, a limitation now practically overcome through the development of cable transmission, the technological feasibility of higher frequencies, and alternative techniques of signal transmission. Indeed in certain respects the equipment available and on the market today —video-recorders, sound recording and reproduction units, simple portable cameras, to name a few—makes it easier in terms of sheer technical knowledge and skill to broadcast radio or television programmes than to set and operate a printing press.

Access to electronic technology is a complex subject, and a full inquiry would have to touch upon such far-ranging matters as the regulation, licencing and ownership of stations, the legal status of broadcasting, compatible and non-compatible technology, signal strength and direction related to national boundaries, "public" and "private" broadcasting, and broadcasting as it is related to other industries, including journalism and publication enterprises. Here we will focus upon broadcasting access from the point of view of political discourse. The generalizations required in such an approach would in any case be necessary if we are to arrive at any conclusions about political broadcasting which are common across cultural and national boundaries.

Although legal restrictions vary from country to country, administrative regulation of political communications generally operates with regard to sponsorship (where stipulated persons or groups are denied access), content (if even minimally, e.g. libel laws), scheduling (e.g., broadcast advertising prior to election dates), accountability (as to sponsoring organization), and sums spent for the purchase of time, or time allocated for parties by State-operated stations. Non-partisanship in selling advertising time, the right of reply and equal time are issues receiving close scrutiny by regulatory bodies as electoral campaigns have increasingly used radio and television to reach potential voters.

The general conservatism of agencies (public or private) which control broadcasting is certainly an important factor bearing upon the question of media access. In so far as broadcast organizations enjoy success in reaching an audience with a kind of programming that has produced this success, their tendency to discriminate against potential "clients" who wish to broadcast radically new, or potentially unpopular material is understandable. This restriction operates at the managerial level, where buyers of broadcast time are refused for reasons of station policy or (as is much the same case) are informed of the illegality of such material, and also appears in the form of self-censorship by persons or organizations who remove established broadcasting from their range of possible communication techniques. Thus legal restrictions, cost of broadcast time and institutional conservatism combine to diminish access to the broadcast media. Moreover, the side of the technology in contact with the public, the "industry", has established a cultural image of élitism, prestige and social distance. This image is nurtured for purposes of institutional morale in both commercial and State-owned networks by promoting broadcasting as show business, an art, or a profession.

Notes

1. No attempt will be made here to present a continuous history of communications technology from the age of print to the contemporary era of electronic communications. Such an attempt would lead away from the present focus upon the relationship between political discourse and electronic technology.

2. This general proposition is useful even though relatively efficient forms of "instantaneous" communication existed even in pre-historic times: drums, smoke signalling, horns, lanterns and fire seen from hill-top to hill-top. The difference that must not be overlooked, however, is that these earlier forms of communication were limited in extensiveness by the capacities of the human senses (sight, earshot) and could not be retained or stored without being translated into another medium.

3. The telegraph was in a technical sense only an improvement upon earlier methods, such as semaphore, light and smoke signals, drums, etc. Although the telegraph obviously had powerful practical applications in newsreporting and battlefield communications very soon after its invention, the telegraph transfers information in a way that is dependent upon earlier techniques, namely chirography. The actual data conveyed by the telegraph are totally abstract "sounds" which have meaning only as they are symbolically related to an alphabet or other code base. This process of encoding is totally reliant upon chirography and linear communication. Compared, therefore, to telephone, radio, or television, which we might refer to as "immediate " media in that they convey information (albeit linguistically and visually) *directly*, we can see that the telegraph partakes of the enormous speed of electricity, but little else that has made electronic communication so powerful.

4. The most comprehensive study of the history of American broadcasting is Erik Barnouw, *A History of Broadcasting in the United States*, 3 vols. (New York, 1972). Another study is Herbert I. Schiller, *Mass Communications and American Empire* (New York, 1970). For the history and social context of Australian television see Australian Senate Standing Committee on Education, Science and the Arts, *Broadcasting and Television*, 2 vols. (Canberra, 1972–74); John Western, *Australian Mass Media: Controllers, Consumers, Producers*, Australian Institute of Political Science Monograph No. 9 (Sydney, 1975); Department of telecommunications, *Broadcasting, A Report on the Structure of the Australian Broadcasting System* (Canberra, n.d.); S. Hall, *Supertoy: Twenty Years of Australian Television* (Melbourne, 1976). For reference to the literature see Ross Curnow ed., *Australian Broadcasting Index, 1900–42*, Univ. of Sydney Dept. of Government Media Monographs (Sydney, 1977), and *Media Information Australia* (Sydney, triennial), from 1977. Marshall McLuhan's two major works on the electronic media are only too anxious to place communications technology in historical and technological perspective: *The Gutenberg Galaxy* (Toronto, 1963) and *Understanding Media* (New York, 1964). A survey of the state of research in mass communications is W. Phillips Davison and F.T.C. Yu, *Mass Communications Research: Major Issues and Future Research* (New York, 1974).

5. The difference between linear and non-linear media is perhaps best seen as a difference of degree, rather than kind, and one that is not an exact or exclusive distinction between technologies. E.g., a political cartoon, display advertisement and banner headline may all be regarded as "non-linear" fields of perception, while the same edition of the newspaper will contain traditional "linear" printed format. The electronic media, of course, constitute the largest and most important class of non-linear techniques of communication. The technological

features distinguishing these techniques are the use of transmission signals
operating at the speed of light, the broadcasting and storing of information
by decodable electronic impulses and the capacity to transmit and reproduce
audio-visual content. The number of instruments for electronic transmission
and reproduction—from telephone and radio to computers and laser beams
—increases every year, and they are familiar enough to require no classification
here. What is notable, however, is that so many of these instruments can be
used in complementarity, e.g., audio-visual recording on tape or disc for
television broadcasting; computers, telephone links (using both cable and
wireless) and photocopying terminals; computerized typesetting and high speed
photolithography. A further complementarity is that the technology required
for "live" transmission is adaptable to and in part indistinguishable from the
technology for recording, storing and reproducing. The "network" of communications based upon telephone lines and electric "wireless" devices is thus
greatly complicated and intensified: communications satellites, cable-connected
television and computer centres and micro-wave relays. These, combined with
more traditional telephone links, radio signals and various recording devices,
make possible a remarkable combination of multi-use and multi-media communications. E.g., a television programme conducting telephone interviews will
use ultra-high frequency signals for the visual, FM radio waves for the audio,
telephone lines for the caller, a tape recorder for a time-lag screening of the
calls; and the programme will perhaps be recorded on video tape for re-
broadcasting at a later time.
6. The term *rhetoric* is intended here in the broad sense of formal public discourse,
i.e., a speech or public address.
7. In most nations, the electronic media are wholly or largely controlled by the
State. Where this is not the case, the media remain at the service of powerful
interests. The State control of the media in developing nations has recently
become an international political issue, and debated at length in UNESCO
conferences in Nairobi (1976) and Manila (1977). Charges against UNESCO
proposals on media policy were made by the International Press Institute, *New
York Times* (7 June 1977), p. 8, and the World Press Freedom Development
Committee, *ibid.*, (13 July 1977). p. 8. Debates in the earlier conference are
reported in *ibid.*, (5 November 1976), p. 23 and (19 December 1976), p. 17.
For a survey of mass communications around the world see Brenda Maddox,
Beyond Babel: New Directions in Communications (Boston, 1974), pp. 15–62;
H.I. Schiller, *Mass Communications*, Chs. 1, 2, 7 and 8. On the regulation
of Australian broadcasting see Kenneth Wiltshire and Charles H. Stokes,
Government Regulation and the Electronic Media, C.E.D.A. Monograph 43
(Sydney and Melbourne, 1977); Nicholas Johnson and Mark Armstrong, *Two
Reflections on Australian Broadcasting*, LaTrobe Univ., Media Centre Papers
No. 6 (Bundoora, Vic., 1977); Australian Broadcasting Control Board,
Television Programme Standards, 2nd ed., "Determined by the Board in
pursuance of the Broadcasting and Television Act 1942–69 together with
certain other information for commercial television stations" (Canberra, 1975).
For discussions of the political uses of mass communications in the U.S. see
E. Barnouw, *History of Broadcasting*, Vol. 3, The Image Empire; H.I. Schiller,
The Mind Managers (Boston, 1974); Daniel Boorstin, *The Image* (New York,
1961); and Frank Mankiewicz and Joel Swerdlow, *Remote Control: Television
and the Manipulation of American Life* (New York, 1978). The skilful media
campaign used by Richard Nixon in the 1968 presidential election is traced
by Joe McGinniss, *The Selling of the President 1968* (New York, 1969).
Similar communications techniques in Australian political campaigns are

analyzed in Henry Mayer, ed., *Labor to Power, Australia's 1972 Election* (Sydney, 1973), pp. 6–16, 18–28 and 198–223; Laurie Oakes and David Soloman, *The Making of an Australian Prime Minister* (Melbourne, 1973), Ch. 7, "The Media and the Elections", pp. 171–210; Andrew Clark, "The Men Behind the Election Campaign", *National Times* (Sydney, 14 Nov. 1977), p. 5; Les Carlyon, "Images Built on Dull Scripts", the *Age* (Melbourne, 23 Nov. 1977).

8. Dan Nimmo, *The Political Persuaders* (New York, 1970), is a good summary of communications practices in modern American electoral campaigning, as is Joseph Napolitan, *The Election Game* (New York, 1972). A pioneering survey in this field was Stanley Kelley, Jr., *Professional Public Relations and Political Power* (Baltimore, 1956). The Australian government is estimated to spend about $16 million per year on advertising, promotions and public relations. The *Age* (8 February 1978). Australian political parties have retained professional advertising agencies since at least 1949, and now use them for continuous "image development" in addition to mapping out and undertaking the advertising responsibilities for electoral campaigns. An example of such work is an unpublished and confidential report by Spectrum International Marketing Services, *Political Parties, Leaders and Issues—A Pilot Study of Voters' Attitudes* (Sydney, August 1971). This report is quoted in some detail by Neal Blewett, "Labor 1968–72: Planning for Victory", pp. 6–16, and Vicky Braund, "Timely Vibrations: Labor's Marketing Campaign", pp. 18–29, in Mayer, *Labor to Power*. The Australian Labor Party's advertising agency, Hansen–Rubensohn–McCann–Erikson (Sydney) commissioned the Spectrum study and presented its "book" for the 1972 New South Wales election campaign, titled *It's Time*, based on its findings. The Hansen–Rubensohn agency developed the 1948–49 Liberal Party campaign, the first one to use radio extensively.

9. For example, Thomas de Quincey insisted upon a distinction between the literature of knowledge and the literature of power, and offers a conception of rhetoric that amounts to *any* use of language that is poetical and emotive. In effect, rhetoric is equated with all non-scientific communications. For an elaboration and critique of this view, see W.S. Howell, *Poetics, Rhetoric, and Logic* (Ithaca, 1975), Ch. 6. *Rhetoric* has also traditionally referred to written texts not necessarily intended for oral delivery; also to the principles of grammar and style.

10. Produced transmissions would include speeches which have been edited, dubbed, excerpted, or otherwise assembled in a non-sequential pattern (such as repetitions, flashbacks, etc.); speeches interrupted with music, narration, or any kind of animation or simulation; and any form of technical effect that is projected as an informative or persuasive "statement" or "gesture" resulting from studio production, including the use of sound and light enhancement, professional voices and actors and simulated audience response.

11. This technique is a direct application of sampling and survey techniques originally developed as marketing research for manufacturing interests. Vance Packard, *The Hidden Persuaders* (London, 1962), discusses market research in Chs. 1 and 2, and illustrates in Ch. 17 how these techniques are used in political campaigns and in the shaping of public opinion. Also see works cited in notes 7 and 8, *supra*.

12. By "public" we mean the necessary technical regulation to ensure equipment standardization and compatibility, and clear-channel frequency assignments; but also the necessarily public and political character of the problem posed by the restriction of access (in terms of control, ownership and opportunity

to be heard), the very necessity of which creates political forces seeking to govern access and programming content.

13. For present purposes, we shall exclude from consideration the effects upon attitudes, opinions and culture deriving from the viewing of consumer-oriented advertisements and entertainments (i.e., the implicitly ideological character of "non-political" programme content), although these effects are clearly of sociological importance. For a general guide to the literature on the sociological significance of television see George A. Comstock and Marilyn Fisher, *Television and Human Behaviour: A Guide to the Pertinent Scientific Literature* (Santa Monica, Calif., 1975); also E.A. Rubinstein, G.A. Comstock and J.P. Murray eds., *Television in Day-to-Day Live*, Vol. 4, *Television and Social Behaviour* (Washington, 1972). A specialized Australian study is R.J. Powell, *Television Viewing by Young Secondary School Students* (Canberra, 1974) for the Australian Broadcasting Control Board; Australian Senate Standing Committee on Education and the Arts, *Impact of Television on Children*, Official Hansard (Canberra, 1977); and a general introduction to the subject, Trevor Barr, *Reflections of Reality* (Adelaide, 1977). See literature cited in notes 7 and 11, *supra*, for material related to the impact of television on public opinion.

14. Hitler's use of radio and a comprehensive telephone network were essential in his rise to power and his ability to maintain personal control over both domestic and military policy. Instantaneous telephone communications were crucial in fending off a plot to assassinate him. Albert Speer, *Inside the Third Reich* (New York, 1971), pp. 486–93. It is also illustrative of this point that *coups d'état* in countries around the world frequently begin with the seizing of the government broadcasting facilities even before an attempt is made to capture the chief of State.

15. Whether restriction is politically partisan in character or there is an "independent" commission to administer legal and technological aspects of broadcasting, policy questions are inevitably involved. The regulation flowing from the latter case, however *laisser faire* in terms of programme content, would itself be a matter of political policy. For an analysis of this issue in Britain, see Tom Burns, *The BBC: Public Institution and Private World* (London, 1977), esp. Ch. 6, "The Servant of Two Masters".

16. Franklin D. Roosevelt's depression-years "fireside chats", Winston Churchill's wartime radio addresses and Richard Nixon's "Checkers speech" (made in 1952, before the days of videotaping and the relatively rapid forms of editing) have become rhetorical classics. Party convention keynote, nominating and acceptance speeches, "state of the nation" speeches and presidential inaugural addresses are now primarily "media events" in American politics. In Australia, ceremonial rhetoric, especially in electoral campaigns, is increasingly staged as a broadcasting opportunity. This is particularly true of the important party policy speeches delivered by the leaders of each party as a formal opening to the election campaign. This trend originated with Sir Robert Menzies's policy speech in 1963, when it was televised for the first time—a party decision recognized at the time to be of major strategic importance. Colin A. Hughes and John S. Western, *The Prime Minister's Policy Speech: A Case Study of Televised Politics* (Canberra, 1966). Sir Robert, and Gough Whitlam (prime minister from 1973–75), are both credited with being gifted orators; Evelyn Heath, "Representative Speeches of Gough Whitlam", *Australian Scan* 3 (December 1977), pp. 23–24. Specific "issue" speeches in electoral campaigns are staged in various capital cities as media "teasers" to maximize free air time. See N. Blewett, "Labor 1968–72", p. 9

17. Even on ceremonial occasions an entire speech may not be televised. In the U.S., television addresses by the President seldom last for thirty minutes, often less than fifteen. During the Nixon administration, the President gave periodic addresses on radio only. These were often broadcast at noon on a weekday, and devoted to specific and complex legislative issues. The apparent aim was to place an official position "on the record"—although there was probably no intent of actually informing or persuading a massive national audience by this means. Televised speeches by Prime Minister Whitlam often lasted for only five or ten minutes, and they were generally devoted to stating broad generalities and policy aims, with little attention to complex information. Studies of the 1972, 1975 and 1977 federal elections in Australia suggest that campaign use of the mass media fell primarily into these categories: television —thirty to sixty second advertising spots; radio—party leaders appearing on live "talk back" programmes (at no cost for time) and paid spots for sound track duplicates of the television ads; and newspapers—"logical information" advertisements to support policy issue slogans. See Braund, "Timely Vibrations", pp. 23–26; Blewett, "Labor 1968–72", p. 14–15; Also, P.D. Jack, "It's Time, the Tombstone Series, Mr. Nice Bloke and Graphics Plus", in Mayer, *Labor to Power*, pp. 212–15.

18. Public officials now commonly employ a "media staff" to foster their "image". This personal staff is usually supplemented by consultants on retainer from professional advertising firms who make market studies of the public image of the politician (the "profile") and offer recommendations as to alterations and improvements. There is frequently a free exchange of staff between the advertising firm and the politician's personal staff. See David Wise, "Are You Worried About Your Image, Mr. President?", *Esquire* (May 1973), pp. 119ff; Kevin P. Phillips, *Mediacracy: American Parties and Politics in the Communications Age* (New York, 1975); and Mayer, *Labor to Power*, pp. 6–28 and 198–232.

19. Two informative articles on the 1972 Australian election are Blewett, "Labor 1968–72" and Braund, "Timely Vibrations"; see notes 4, 7, 13 and 24 of Chapter VIII, *infra*, for other references to these studies. For the use of mass communications in elections prior to 1972 see Hughes and Western, *The Prime Minister's Policy Speech*, and Murray Goot and R.W. Connell, "Presidential Politics in Australia", *Australian Quarterly* 44, 2 (June 1972), pp. 28–33. For more recent elections see Howard Penniman ed., *Australia at the Polls: The National Elections of 1975* (Canberra, 1977), Ch. 7, "The Media and the Elections", pp. 171–210; and Andrew Clark, "Behind the Election Campaign", p. 5.

20. Of course political figures are regularly scheduled by their public relations staff to appear on local radio and television programmes in a variety of informal settings: for example, press conferences, interviews and telephone "talk back" shows. These appearances are coordinated with frequent ceremonial "photo opportunities"—dedicating buildings, visiting hospitals, etc.—in the day-to-day "image development" of the electorate's perception of the politician's personality and issue profile. These are typically selective and local uses of the media, and distinguished here from more formal and extensively broadcasted rhetorical performances.

21. Enid Campbell and Harry Whitmore, *Freedom in Australia* (Sydney, 1967), pp. 120 and 126–29. It is often claimed that radio and television are of critical significance in winning and retaining political office, shaping public opinion and gaining acceptance for public policy. However, recent research in Australia, Great Britain, Israel and the United States suggests that "user selectivity"

in television viewing leads most frequently to such non-political functions as diversion and "killing time", as well as for the partly escapist, partly socializing functions of dramatizing personal relationships and identity. See Susan Kippax and John Murray, "Using Television: Programme Content and Need Gratification", *Politics* XII, 1 (May 1977), pp. 59–69. This research was originally published in E.A. Rubinstein *et al.*, *Television in Day-to-Day Life,* esp. J.P. Robinson, "Towards Defining the Functions of Television", pp. 568–603.

8

Political Rhetoric and Electronic Technology

> Language, if it do not uphold, and feed, and leave in quiet,
> like the power of gravitation or the air we breathe, is a counter-
> spirit, unremittingly and noiselessly at work, to subvert, to lay
> waste, to vitiate, and to dissolve.
>
> Wordsworth, *Essay on Epitaphs*

We have so far suggested that the broadcast media extend the range
and scope of communication, as well as actually create material
for transmission that is analogous to the rhetorical act in construction and aim, even though its production is essentially independent
of oratorical or verbal elements. In addition to these effects, we
must inquire into the possibility of direct changes that have taken
place in the substance of traditional political rhetoric due to the
electronic media.

The "rhetorical device", typified in the short political advertisement, is transparently a product of electronic studio techniques and
bears a functional, if not formal, relationship to the rhetorical
tradition, in so far as it aims to produce an emotional reaction.
Yet it does so with little if any linguistic content. Turning our
attention to oral performance, that is, actual cases of oratorical
discourse, two questions arise concerning the relationship between
political rhetoric (in the sense of oral performance) and electronic
technology: does the technology affect the verbal content of ordinary
rhetorical performance and in what sense has the "linguistic
setting" itself been transformed by the formation of mass media
audiences? In brief, we shall attempt to continue our inquiry from
the same perspectives used in examining the effects of printing and
the development of mass literacy.

The role of the broadcast orator is problemmatical in a far more
radical way than for the orator facing an audience, whose very
physical presence implies some degree of competence or interest.

There at least the existential condition of speech—the speaker and his audience—was intact. The predisposition of the audience to the speaker, and he to them, may be affected by such "technical" intrusions as literacy and printing, but the speech remains a public occasion with an indeterminateness which must always accompany a public act, no matter that the orator reads from a text, or that the audience has read in the newspaper that it is identical to the speech delivered the night before. Something might happen. The speaker might throw aside his text, or the audience might force him to do so.

On the other hand, broadcast rhetoric, even a "live telecast", cannot avoid impersonality and isolation—a type of total privacy —for both speaker and listener. The speaker faces an unresponsive microphone, the listener hears a disembodied voice, or a voice appearing to accompany a telescreen image, in a variety of contexts. But the listeners collectively, as an "audience", combine only in an abstract way, and remain atomized by the nature of the medium. There are, undeniably, elements of immediacy and emotional confrontation between the speaker and his television audience. He may cause them to laugh, or cry, or be bored. Some have argued that an audience reacts to a person's television image in the same way as they would to a personal appearance,[1] but this does not alter the fact of physical separation. Reactions from a broadcast audience simply cannot be registered, and thus the speaker cannot react to responses associated with changes in his pacing, intonation and manner of delivery. The audience, atomized as it is, cannot and individually knows that it cannot, affect the speaker as he goes about his delivery. The rhetorical setting itself is transformed from a public occasion to the speaker's isolation and the audience's dispersion into so many thousands or millions of units at leisure in living room and bedroom, driving a car or working in the office.

Techniques may be used to "personalize" the rhetorical setting through staging, sound-track "audiences" and other attempts at intimacy (often mistaking the formal character of oratory by placing the speaker in a casual setting—before a fireplace, in an easy chair—in an attempt to establish contact with the speaker). Alternatively, it may be decided to capitalize on the remoteness of television rhetoric and actually emphasize the distance in order to highlight the lofty inaccessibility of public office, thus making the speech a kind of oracular utterance. Finally, one may simply concede the absence of a rhetorical setting. In this case, a formal "speech" is taken as an imposition upon the time and attention of busy individuals, for whom radio and television are primarily

means of diversion and entertainment. Thus the formal address—
which characteristically relies upon minimal standards of grammatical precision, logical sequence and the presentation of subject
matter to form a persuasive argument—is abandoned due to its
technological inappropriateness. By this path, which follows the
apparently natural strengths of electronic media, the speech is
shortened to the point of elimination. The emphasis is placed upon
a rapid succession of images, action, and sound which contribute
to the visual sense of motion. In short, the electronic rhetorical
"device" offers itself as the heir to "just rhetoric".

Political Campaign Broadcasting

What we have called broadcast "devices"—the audio-visual record
of a speech event produced in whole or in part by studio techniques
—have achieved a remarkable degree of sophistication (although
this is nothing to the credit of politicians, whose use of them is
largely derivative of commercial advertising expertise) and they are
now the primary method by which political parties and candidates
for office articulate their campaigns, as well as the most expensively
supported means by which ideas, issues and "images" are communicated to the public.[2] Professional politicians commonly refer
to their own and their opponents' broadcast media campaign in
terms of how successfully or unsuccessfully it produced a "candidate
image", gave an identifiable style to the endeavour, and whether
or not it had "audience appeal". For all intents and purposes, the
media campaign *is* the campaign, and actual public appearances
are referred to in terms of their being "good media". Public
appearances by the candidate take place early in the morning as
a general rule, so that television coverage will produce free "news
spots" on both afternoon and evening television news shows.
Campaign organizers refer to these appearances as "media events";
they are, as it were, not real, but merely convenient items
contributing to "candidate visibility". Campaigns stay close to
urban centres, not because rural areas produce few votes, but
because carefully selected cities are effective "media markets"
which cover the rural areas as well as adjacent smaller cities with
regional television. This is the language of the modern political
campaign.

   Political parties spend a lot of time and a good deal of money
to have their candidates make brief, highly staged public appearances. This is done not only to obtain local "free" news

coverage of the candidate set amidst a favourable backdrop, but also to give the campaign's *own* "media team" (sound, video and still photographic technicians) "reality opportunities". This footage is quickly edited, spliced and juxtaposed into credible "action" clips on thirty and sixty-second television spots in order to update the campaign from week to week. A study of language might well consider the jargon of modern media campaigning, but that is a matter of secondary importance to the present interest in the "devices" appearing as rhetorical events on radio and television.

Campaign "ads" tend to be thirty or sixty second spots; sometimes they are only twelve or fifteen seconds in length. In fact, these spots rarely present the candidate actually speaking—except as a voice-over while the video shows the candidate "in action". A popular technique is to show the candidate in a series of still photographs, with a professional "voice-over". Some of the most forceful spots have been drama in microcosm. Here the candidate does not appear at all, except perhaps for his name in bold letters in the fade-out frame.[3] The advertisement may actually be difficult to detect as a campaign spot. Children happily playing in the surf, an elderly woman walking down a derelict city street at night, street scenes of riots and demonstrations juxtaposed with photos of a smiling opposition candidate have all been the subject of thirty or sixty-second "image equations" calculated to produce a desired emotion in the viewer. These productions, complete with musical sound-track and cinematic polish, mesh with the larger strategy of the campaign, and the viewer may not even need the candidate's name or slogan to cross the screen as a signature line, since the message of the "ad" has already been conveyed by the image that has been established in weeks of running "ads" similar in technique and style. A media campaign is successful when the "message"— the candidate image and issue orientation—"takes" in the viewer's mind as the solution to a puzzle.[4] The rhetorical objective is achieved precisely when it is superfluous to name the candidate or to project distracting "information".

Longer television spots—of about five minutes' duration—frequently show the candidate in a relatively formal setting behind a desk talking straight into the camera. Careful viewing shows that the speech is highly staged and edited, or alternatively it may be a carefully edited condensation of a speech delivered to a live audience. Finally, recent presidential campaigns in the United States suggest a trend toward longer television spots—between thirty and sixty minutes—in which the candidate delivers a fairly extended "policy" or "position" speech in which several topics are discussed in some detail. These may be straightforward speeches delivered from a text; sometimes they are broken up with documentary material and graphics so that the impression of a formal speech is avoided. These speeches are, of course, carefully staged and carefully edited, having been filmed in the studio. The viewer has the impression that the candidate and his staff have made every effort to broadcast the candidate at his rhetorical best, and the candidate's objective in the set speech is to appear "presidential". The Australian Prime Minister's and opposition leaders' campaign policy speeches opening the formal campaign period play much the same role. They are integrated with the party's larger media strategy and are prepared with great concern for technical detail, although the speeches are delivered before a pre-selected "live" audience.[5]

The final day of the media campaign is either reserved for an extended formal speech by the candidate as a last appeal to the voters, or there is a virtual blitz of spot advertisements for a saturation effect, or both. In any event, professional campaign managers in America commonly assume that the only wise course is for seventy-five per cent of the entire campaign budget to be invested in radio and television advertising during the last week or several days before the election. The one-month Australian campaign period naturally leads to a concentration of advertising in a brief period. The prohibition of broadcasting political messages in the final three days further affects the party's advertising policy. Television costs appear to be greater than the combined costs of radio and newspaper advertising, the latter being, in the view of some advertising agencies, a waste of money on "linear logic" that does not fit into the "image mosaic of the television campaign".[6]

What, if anything, is to be concluded from the evolution of "ad spot" political campaigning? The first, and most obvious, conclusion is that the electronic media have been used for their powers of production and creation rather than simply for broadcast extension. The second conclusion is an apparent trend toward very brief rhetorical events—one is tempted to call them rhetorical gestures instead of speech performances. In the five-minute speech a concession is made to tradition, although the art of the studio technician is called upon to show the candidate at his elocutionary best, evoking slogans and weighty admonitions. The intent is not to persuade or inform, but to present a "presidential" image. A third point concerns the high cost of radio and television advertising. Effective "ad" spots and five-minute speeches may be very expensive to produce, but at least they can be used repeatedly for a higher return on the investment, and there is no risk incurred over the content or the candidate's performance. By the same token, a brief "ad" spot represents a much smaller outlay for air time than would be necessary for a speech, and there is much less danger of losing an audience. Even a five-minute spot, tagged onto the end of prime time programming, can be assured of a large audience of known composition, thanks to market research and programme ratings. A thirty-minute speech enters into direct competition with other programming, and risks alienating an audience deprived of its regular programme, as well as perhaps boring and so losing it. When political campaign organizations *do* sponsor a thirty-minute or longer speech by the candidate—thus investing in costly air time and running the risk of alienating rather than impressing the audience—a barrage of fifteen-second "ads" are broadcast the day or two before; they advertise an advertisement, in effect, and as with any other commodity for sale, make a large investment in it to assure an audience for it. Viewed in this way, it is easy to understand why a thirty-minute speech would not be left to the luck of having the candidate in fine form for a live appearance and delivery of the speech. Such a large investment—not only the air time but the lead-up campaign of "ad" spots to build the audience for the speech—must obviously be one that is as safe as the medium will allow, which in this case means a well-rehearsed, well-produced and well-edited performance. If the candidate himself is not a good speaker, or there are other reasons to keep him from appearing before the public, an adept surrogate may well be a sounder investment.[7] This exception to the rule that formal addresses are avoided in broadcast campaigning is made, apparently, when it is deemed necessary to invest in public exposure, image development, or in correcting the candidate's "public profile" as measured by market research opinion polls.

Otherwise, recent experience in political campaigning seems to demonstrate a preference for communications designed to convey images and symbols rather than argument, scenes rather than speech, actions rather than words, emotions rather than thoughts. "Ad" spots have the capacity to achieve these objectives by catching the attention of ear and eye with fast cuts, sound overlays, striking visual techniques and virtually complete control of the content. Their advantage lies in appealing to the elusive and fugitive listener, impressing him for a few seconds with evocative imagery, while taking care not to risk losing his attention by confronting him with demands upon his powers of concentration, or requiring him to assimilate new or difficult information.

The formal epitome of this kind of political communication in political campaigns would seem to be the extremely brief, cinematically sophisticated audio-visual "drama". While it differs radically from anything traditionally regarded as formal oratory, there is some justification for calling the studio-produced political advertisement a rhetorical device. Even if it is only tenuously related to a speaker–language–audience paradigm, there can be no doubting the fact that it is a species of rhetorical communication: it attempts to move in a symbolic or emotional way, if not to persuade. The techniques applied to its production and broadcast are specifically aimed at predisposing the audience, in opinion and perhaps in action, in a way desired by the creator.

Status in Broadcasting

An assessment of the relationship between political discourse and the electronic media must also take account of incidental communications touching upon public office and public policy. Here we have in mind such things as the broadcasting of press conferences, interview formats, official hearings and other examples of oral performance which are not direct forums in the sense that a paid political advertisement or official oration is. As we look to this broader field of discourse, the status of the speaker and the associated phenomenon of distance between speaker and audience are elements which enable us to place diverse forms of communication within the rhetorical tradition.

In classical rhetorical theory, there was an assumption of a social and intellectual distance between the rhetorician as the possessor of specialized knowledge and the listener who, by his attention, submits to the guidance and authority of the prepared mind. In the classical model, there was a direct link between the superior status of the speaker and the specialized character of what he was saying. Moreover, the very fact that the orator sought a public forum implied that his information and arguments constituted a public concern. Social and political dimensions were intrinsic to the rhetorical performance, even if this required, as in a case of law, the presentation of specialized or esoteric information about whose importance the public (in this case, the jury) had to be convinced. The status of the speaker in the classical setting, therefore, was inevitably tied to the presentation of specialized information.

In the practical experience of modern broadcasting, by contrast, it can be argued that the links between status, expertise and access to the forum have substantially changed. The very terms "announcer" and "news-reader" express the medium's use of professional "orators" who specifically eschew the status of authority and expertise. As a kind of journalist, the broadcaster's performance is credible to the extent that he has "informed sources" or is able to quote or interview an expert or official connected with the item in question. This is not, of course, to suggest that the popularity of a broadcaster depends necessarily upon the neutrality with which he selects the public issues and their respective authorities, but it does point up the specialization of the forum as regards the subjects and substance of public discourse. In effect, broadcasters are professional elocutionists: they are specialists, primarily, in delivery alone, and their status depends very much upon that speciality.

The sources and authorities used by professional broadcasters are assumed to have expert information at their disposal, and these are perhaps more closely the rhetorical participants analogous to the classical orator. It can be argued, nevertheless, that the relationship between status, expertise and access is fundamentally different in broadcasting. In effect, the selection of the expert reverses the flow of authority established in classical oratory as deriving from the substance of what is actually said. It is as if access to the medium (in a news interview, for example, or in testimony before a televised legislative hearing) confers or at least certifies status.[8] This, of course, raises questions about the openness of the media for the dissemination of new or controversial information, but our present concern has to do with the way in which the audience receives information, and what authority it carries, when those who articulate it have a status based, in effect, upon appearance or access alone. Thus it is not difficult to imagine such a case as the following. When a person who is not widely regarded as an "authority" delivers information or an opinion on issues ranging from predicting an election outcome to selling toothpaste, the characteristic retort from the viewer is "What right does *he* have to be saying that on television?" Such a question is obviously answered in terms of *who* the speaker is, and not what he is saying, and it may not matter whether he is a recognized authority or simply "famous". Indeed, if there is no title, office or standard authority reference associated with the face to tell the viewer who he is, the assumption is immediately available that what he is saying is not to be believed. Authority flows from the speaker to the information, in contrast to the classical model, in which authority flowed from the information to the person who possessed and could articulate it.

Although modern broadcasting has been described as the "public forum of the airways", this figure of speech is somewhat misleading, as it suggests a medium devoted to topics of general public interest. In fact, the programming content of broadcasting is largely made up of light entertainment designed for specific sub-groups of the population. The statutory principle governing American broadcasting—that the Federal Communications Commission ensure that broadcasting be devoted to "the public interest, convenience and necessity"—obviously offers much flexibility in defining what the public interest is. The "best interests of the Australian community" are also identified as the primary objective of the Australian Broadcasting Act, which calls for moral and social issues to be aired according to standards of common sense and good taste, and with respect for the law and social institutions.[9] The special category of "public interest" programming—news, emergency broadcasts, coverage of elections and special events, documentaries—satisfies, at least in part, the metaphor of the broadcast media as a forum for the airing and debating of public issues. However, not unlike market-oriented commercial programming, public interest broadcasts are typically devoted to subjects of interest to limited segments of the public, and this limitation is narrowed in proportion to the degree of specialized treatment given the issue. Consequently, the broadcast audience as "the public" is an abstract fiction. In fact, members of broadcast audiences routinely assume that, far from a public forum, radio and television constitute an entertainment medium which rarely disturbs the listener with programmes of a persuasive or overtly political character.[10] Programme ratings verify that, with an implicit vote of confidence in market research and network programming, viewing habits are based upon avoidance of programmes which "haven't got anything to do with me". As news broadcasts, documentaries, stock market reports, sports telecasts, children's programmes and "soap operas" clearly illustrate, the broadcasting industry has developed special, selective audiences.

An elusive and fragmented audience confronts any speaker who does wish to address an issue and convey information of a general public concern. This is a major problem faced by the media consultants of governments and campaign organizations. The technological structure of the "forum" is available but it is often difficult to find the "public". Indeed, there is no evidence to suggest that individuals perceive radio and television, much less themselves, as constituting a public forum or political assembly. Turning on the television, far from being a public or civil act in which one undertakes a personal responsibility to make a critical evaluation of informed argument, is generally just the opposite: an opportunity to escape, to suspend reality and to avoid complex judgments in favour of simple diversion and entertainment. Ignoring for the moment the cumulative effect upon the viewer, we must appreciate how radio and television, at a given moment for a given broadcast, are instruments over which the individual has considerable control. Persons responsible for programming, political or otherwise, must always bear this in mind. The listener-viewer has a continuous option to change stations or turn the receiver off at any moment. These elements of choice simply do not exist in an immediate rhetorical setting. The fact that each listener has these options and is isolated in an auditory setting—home, work, car, or a variety of other locations—means that any broadcast must either capitalize on a given opportunity of audience selectivity and be projected to a specially defined group, or must anticipate the isolated, ill-attentive audience and devise a rhetorical approach which is sufficiently powerful to create a general level of attention.

If recent developments in political advertising are any guide, the aural and visual impression made upon the immediate attention of the audience is far more important than presenting, say, a summary exposition of information that might over-extend the listener's level of attention and remind him that such "facts" exist in more suitable media—books, magazines, computers—which he would consult if he were interested in them to that degree. To such an audience, factual data and logical argument recede in importance. Radio and television do not effectively place facts, figures and logical relationships before the listener; the data are lost from moment to moment and image to image. What the electronic media do effectively is convey, perhaps even create, a perceptual world that is constantly changing, in which both information and impressions are fragmented. The images themselves are spatially and chronologically indeterminate—"live" or "on tape"—and "objective facts" about such a world are useless in forming an accurate impression of it.

A speaker on radio or television can be assured that when his voice and image flicker away, his words will have vanished with him. Whatever impression may have been created at the moment, no evidence remains unless the listener has taken care to use a sound or video tape recorder. The impression may linger for a time, but it cannot be re-created for others in any satisfactory way, and will eventually disappear completely—except perhaps as an emotive memory. The comfortable viewer who did not have to take the trouble to leave his living room to be a part of the audience is not likely to take himself to last week's newspaper or to the community library to verify or discredit information presented in a campaign advertisement. Far from this being a licence to broadcast facts and figures at will, it suggests that such information is irrelevant and ineffective as a means of establishing an impression. In the case of a political speech or "ad spot", all that will remain (if anything) in the viewer's mind is a heightened or diminished interest in the subject at hand (elections, candidates, issues, a local flood), a more or less intensified awareness and a mental impression of the total performance. What is in question is the viewer's mental disposition, and not his conscious command of a body of information. Indeed, after the political broadcast is over, it is altogether likely that the audience, individually and in various collective segments, will go right on being an audience for a continuous stream of other performances: opponent candidates, a Ford automobile, a bank robbery, or a favourite comedy series. Taken as a whole, this sort of experience only reinforces the fragmentation of time and space, the discontinuity of events, and the irrelevance and impossibility of locating facts and sources that would "validate" an argument and place it into a coherent and meaningful sequence.

Rhetorical Techniques

In spite of the tendencies favouring non-verbal, technologically sophisticated rhetorical devices, oratorical skills remain an important resource for political communication. Electronic instruments actually enhance certain rhetorical skills, and of course audio-visual records of "talking heads" are an important content (if only as the raw material of unedited footage) of most political broadcasting. The survival of vestiges of oratory therefore enables us to trace the remnants of classical rhetoric in such communications. As an example, we may notice how the very possibility of artificial continuity, editing, retakes and audio-visual synchronization establishes the ideal of the perfect, error-free broadcast.[11] There is no technical reason why the broadcast should include grammatical errors, mispronunciations, awkward pauses and the like. This is reminiscent of classical rhetoric's *copia*, the fluency of speech which never lacks for a well-turned phrase and at least the appearance of continuity of thought. If, as is normally the case, the broadcast orator is reading from a speech text, the "free flow" of copious oratory may be simulated—by TelePrompter or other hidden techniques. On "live" broadcasts, the loss of continuity remains a possibility; on studio-produced broadcasts, it is simply unnecessary because the desired effect can be created in the studio.

Those ancient devices of rhetoric—tropes, figures and commonplaces—also survive. Particularly when a speech has as its primary aim the creation of an impression, rather than informing or persuading, the use of impressive language is essential. The phrases resorted to have little if any resonance with a literary or poetic tradition, but they achieve the effect of copious speech by filling in what might otherwise be silences and by lending the performance a certain cadence and formal style. The following are familiar examples:

I come before you today . . .
No effort will be spared . . .
Let every nation know . . .
. . . nothing could be further from the truth . . .
We are in the midst of the greatest . . .
The time is at hand . . .

Obviously these phrases are far less rich in metaphor and poetic allusion than the tropes, figures and *apothegmata* of Greek and Latin rhetoric.[12] They cannot be said to strike the listener with a pleasing or familiar image, nor do they reproduce in common speech valued cultural information. The only oratorical contribution they offer is, perhaps, a platitudinous tone while sustaining the flow of speech. But their use is a signal that the speaker intends to offer something that is worthy, useful and in the public interest—a means of appeal and an invocation of authority reminiscent of the classical use of the commonplace.

Under the heading of commonplace speech we should also take note of two other rhetorical devices, the cliché and the slogan, which have significance on a wider plane of discourse than broadcasting. The cliché and the slogan not only appear in formal oratory, but seem to have become fully realised "rhetorical events" in political language. Campaign rhetoric in modern electoral politics illustrates how a slogan or catch-phrase will be seized upon to give a kind of thematic continuity to the campaign. This strategy is pursued in newspaper advertisements, billboards, radio and television spots, automobile bumper stickers, buttons and even in a candidate's five-minute "speeches" during a whirlwind tour of the constituency. "It's time" set the tone of the entire 1972 Australian election, while "Turn on the Lights" was the Liberal Party's response in the 1975 campaign. These up-beat, mostly nonsense phrases carry a subliminal message that makes them memorable and susceptible to a range of interpretations. "I like Ike" and "All the way with L.B.J". were captivating American electoral slogans, although any meanings they had were probably not as important as their qualities of rhyme and rhythm.

The use of slogans in campaign oratory, as well as the reliance upon social science and computer-language jargon by bureaucrats, seem to indicate—along with the use of the commonplace—the survival of formulaic speech in an age that is supposed by many to take pride in originality and new forms of expression. Although a slogan is capable of conveying information in either very specific or very ambiguous ways,[13] its condensed and repetitive character reinforces the evolution of a rhetorical style which aims at stimulating emotions and forming images rather than conveying information and persuading with logic. How far contemporary political language has travelled toward a rhetoric of formulaic catch-phrases can be seen by even a cursory analysis of contemporary political language.[14] Here one finds the virtual abandonment of sustained argument or logical sequence, and in their place are one-sentence paragraphs, bald and emotional assertions, clichés, an over-all epigrammatic tone and the absence of connection between one paragraph and another.

The use of legal phraseology and scientific neologisms is another factor in the formulaic character of modern political language. Although these styles are more characteristic of bureaucratic and administrative press releases or other public statements which are carefully phrased, such as press conference oratory, legislative debate and (especially) formal testimony, they are certainly important elements of contemporary political language. Characteristic of this vocabulary are grammatical forms which are resistant to the presentation of factual information or logical development: conditional and passive verb structure, impersonal pronouns and finely drawn categorical exceptions. Although the primary objective of this language is to obscure or render meaningless a particular field of reference, rather than evoke images or emotions with the efficiency of a slogan, the grammatical process by which this is accomplished can be reduced to only a few formulae which produce language approximating the cliché style.

One notable effect of broadcasting that departs from classical rhetoric is that persuasion is finally abdicated as its primary aim. The classical conception of rhetoric held that persuasion was the effect of sound argument (logic) and effective delivery (*pronuntiatio*). Rhetoric responded to the age of printing by emphasizing delivery and assuming a role of summary exposition and reference, but persuasion was nevertheless invited in terms of the printed sources external to the speech act. The use of the electronic media for campaign oratory and political advertising would seem to suggest that persuasion is not a primary objective of such broadcasts. Neither inductive nor deductive argumentation appears to be compatible with electronic communication simply because both logical methods require the kind of performance which is ill-suited to broadcasting: the presentation and manipulation of discrete data according to fairly clear guidelines of evidence, proposition, inference and conclusion. A feature of broadcast oratory that is less clear, but worthy of note, is that *elocutio* and *pronuntiatio*—those elocutionary tools of style and delivery by which an orator might reduce his audience to tears or spellbound conviction—are also relinquished.

Replacing persuasion as a rhetorical aim is the process of identification. Here the speaker invokes symbolic commonplaces, by which he endeavours to associate himself (especially) and his proposals (if any) with images, ideas and values which are far from new or specialized in character—uncontroversial within the dominant culture. These conventional items,[15] as might be expected, are little more than platitudes such as order, brotherhood, peaceableness, the new and the good (progress) the old and the familiar (tradition), and synonyms for the common will of "the people".

It will be readily observed that speeches based upon conventional identification have little need of persuasion or the livelier devices of gesture to win a point or the acceptance of a new body of information. Nor will such speeches require a logical method to convince the audience of the truth of conventional values. Of course, identification is a form of persuasion aimed at gaining a desired response from an audience, even if its use does not require the resolution of controversial propositions or the mastery of new subject matter. The objective is the acceptance in the listener's mind of the coincidence between conventional values and the speaker, or, conversely, the lack of coincidence between these values and the speaker's opponent.

The *status* of a speaker becomes a matter of special importance when his function is no longer associated with expertise or valued information, and when he identifies himself with merely conventional ideas. Consequently the status, or more broadly, the "image" of the speaker must become the centre of focus of any rhetorical performance. A president or prime minister will not ordinarily have to be concerned with this problem, further than taking care that the desired "profile" is maintained. But a candidate for public office must either demonstrate that candidacy alone confers status or that he has, for other reasons, an equivalent status.[16] Even if he tries to demonstrate his competence in specific policy areas in private conversations with small groups or influential individuals, so far as the broadcasting media are concerned he will be advised that his public image depends on appearance rather than expertise or eloquence. The aim is not to persuade the public that he has, say, special information or compelling new theories about economic inflation, but rather that he is the kind of "character" entitled to have an opinion about the subject. The public profile, paradoxically, amounts to cultivating subjective impressions about inherent traits of character and personality: trust, competence, compassion, strength, courage and the like.[17]

It is apparent in this process that logic, argumentation and special information are either secondary or irrelevant. The rhetorical object is the speaker himself, rather than a substantive policy dispute or the persuasion of an audience. In fact, the orator may rest assured that his audience neither possesses nor is interested in the substantive information required for comprehending and following an argument to the point of persuasion. Thus any attempt on the speaker's part to introduce information tends to elicit suspicion in his audience because their assumption is secure that the "facts" of the matter are "beyond" them and cannot, in any case, be effectively presented in a brief television format.

A typical example from American political campaigning will serve to illustrate a communications technique which has general application across a range of electorates and candidate images. Suppose there is a candidate running for office who seeks to impress upon his television audience that he has an image as a "liberal, compassionate man" who, in contrast to his "tough cop" opponent (whose campaign may well rest upon *his* status), values human lives over the protection of property. This "liberal" candidate will not quote statistics suggesting that "crime in the streets" and "crimes of violence" are bogus issues. He will not produce official statistics showing that the large majority of homicides are the result of fights between family members or long-time acquaintances who resort to a privately owned gun. Rather, the candidate will present thirty- and sixty-second television spots showing the candidate in shirt sleeves and open collar walking through city slums patting small children on the head and talking "sincerely" with passers-by. Further, he may show film clips of himself presiding over a dramatic investigative hearing, or driving home forceful points before an attentive, friendly audience. In short, the advertisements will project an "image" rather than impinging upon the audience's cognitive faculties with the invitation to digest information and re-evaluate popular preconceptions.

Self-aggrandizement and the attempt to depict one's high popular esteem have not developed as selling points for public figures only with the development of the electronic media. Nevertheless, broadcasting presents a "logic" for the "media image" style of campaigning which is difficult to refute on its own terms, and difficult to defeat if one's opponent uses it. The argument follows this path: it is a waste of time speaking in person to small and scattered audiences when so many more people can be reached by radio and television; the "message" one wants to convey can be driven home again and again with media "ad spots"; why risk an awkward moment or a disastrous slip of the tongue in live appearances when these elements can be eliminated in the studio?; political audiences tend to be already committed loyalists and activists, and the media enable one to reach the undecided, uncommitted and potential non-voter; the broadcast campaign is less expensive if pro-rated on the basis of the size of audience and other cost-effective measures are applied; and in the implicit understanding of the audience the broadcast orator has satisfied a kind of "threshold" status requirement merely by gaining access to the established media. A political candidate may well become a "serious" contender simply by mounting a media campaign. Thus the very availability of broadcasting technology operates as a force which shapes and changes the nature of campaign communications. Not only is the rhetorical dimension—speeches, debates, policy discussion—largely changed or replaced by media image-making, but the candidate himself is subordinated to a media-packaged "candidate image" which is deemed far more advantageous to be projected to the public than the actual person.[18] This strategy has been found to be so effective that major public officials, after election, retain their public relations firms to cultivate the image, or alter it when convenient, throughout their term of office.[19]

The "logic" of political image-making does not necessarily require a vast gullibility on the part of the audience, who may reasonably hold the assumption that status or image is actually a function of ideological interests and group membership. The speaker is thus assumed to be partisan—even if he did offer facts and figures one would not necessarily believe them—and the only question of importance is whether or not the speaker is a recognizable exponent of the group under consideration, that is, are his identification and status secure? Therefore, speakers who pass the media "threshold" by their selection as recognized authorities or as candidates for office are virtually transformed into spokesmen. If such an identity is not already established, broadcast appearances begin to create it. The rhetorical performance—whether in the form of an interview, an advertisement, or even a broadcast speech—becomes spokesmanship, and the speaker has only to represent an image of a broadly recognizable stereotype. Instead of presenting information or a coherent argument, one need only act out an image. When a news programme presents, say, a story on the women's movement, an attempt will be made to present "spokeswomen" for "both" or "all sides". Thus brief interviews and film clips will attempt to offer a "well-rounded" picture—meaning a set of images and identities which successfully reinforce common stereotypes of relevant opinion positions. The practiced listener assumes—even demands—this kind of treatment as the norm. Should the programme present an "unknown" who does offer new information or arguments—new, at any rate, to the audience—the audience may well assume that the contribution was biased, irrelevant, or that this speaker's inclusion is evidence that the programme was "slanted".

By this process political campaigns, official oratory and news broadcasting[20] are virtually forced into truism, simplicity and trivialization. The broadcast threshold effect and the audience's perception of it reinforce the importance of status—the spokesman must be easily identified, a "known leader" in his field. This produces rhetoric by those whose views are already widely known. As spokesmen, they are rightly assumed to be partisans whose views are, by definition, biased, and are therefore not to be taken seriously as a source of information or credible argument. This is as true of the audience's perception of political speeches, "ad spots" and candidate-sponsored programmes as it is of "sources" in network news documentaries. For the listener, the spokesman's argument, say, on abortion, does not need to be taken seriously (because he is a Catholic bishop) since he would not be interviewed in the first place unless he were a well-known advocate of one position, and therefore biased (with nothing new to offer on a clearly defined position). For the speaker, the substance of what is uttered is important only to the extent that it clearly and simply conforms to the standard identity of the position represented. The "good statement" for the spokesman is precisely the one that assures that it will be received favourably only by those who already identify with that position, and will be rejected out of hand by those who do not because the spokesman was the epitome of an "obviously biased source". Persuasion, logic and the evaluation of information are beyond the powers of "spokesmanship", precisely because spokesmanship entails just the opposite: the presentation of commonplace images, identities and stereotypes.

Generally aware of this problem, politicians exercise considerable caution in expounding anything that might be interpreted as a persuasive argument, preferring to rely on the much more useful strategy of reinforcing and enhancing their images whenever the occasion for a rhetorical gesture arises. Both of these objectives— avoiding issues and promoting images—can usually be served by addressing such uncontroversial points as the goodness of patriotism and those who possess it, and the badness of those (such as one's opposition) who do not. This interpretation, indeed, may be taken as an explanation of why politicians, especially candidates for office, scrupulously avoid public debates with their opponents, unless they are confident that their image is secure and that their opponent will decline the challenge. When debates are held between rival candidates it is usually a tactic of local politics with a small likelihood of the debate being broadcast. But in such cases, or in the few examples where radio and television have provided a forum for national candidates, the candidates themselves, their aides, and the audience seem to agree that the one who "had the edge" had it because he succeeded in projecting a superior image and not because he provided more information and sounder logic.[21]

Public discourse in contemporary society manifests a strange eccentricity about "facts" and their relationship to public policy. In a culture which values "hard data" and rewards those who produce and work with them—a culture which claims to accept only objective, empirical and scientific data in conformity with its dominant epistemology—it is peculiar that there is a pervasive assumption that such knowledge can have no bearing upon public discourse in general and the substance of political rhetoric in particular. Perhaps it is the very mystification of "facts" as the only form of knowledge that has led modern populations to conceive of the realm of public discourse as an inferior kingdom grounded solely in opinion, dogma and self-serving human motivations to corrupting power.

Without passing final judgement on this view, it is clear that this perspective—some have called it the "age of positivism"—leads to an intense pessimism regarding contemporary politics. This would seem to be particularly true for the lone individual's confidence in himself and his fellows to make any sort of reasoned decisions or to propose alternative ideas concerning public policy. The emergence of "image politics" is simply the electoral and institutional concomitant of this trend. But what is even more important is that the popular pessimism about the possibility of reasoned public discourse is not without a rival. This pessimism or skepticism lives, paradoxically, with the additional popular assumption that authority is indistinguishable from official status—or that, even if they are not the same, there are no resources at hand by which they can be reliably distinguished. The public, having no capacity in public discourse except as an audience-accomplice in the building of image recognition, does not want to be persuaded or provided with information. Thus a surprising degree of skepticism concerning the content of mass communications is coupled with a remarkable passivity in accepting the images projected.

The American public at large throughout their government's involvement in the Vietnam war repeatedly held to the view that U.S. involvement must be justified on the basis of information available, necessarily, only to a few men in Washington.[22] "They" must have the "facts", and the war was being pursued by them, so the war must be justified. The circular reasoning was complete since individuals chose to think "as I obviously do not have the facts, how can I oppose what I do not really understand?" In just such a manner partisans against the war were rejected out of hand as "biased" and "uninformed". For years the American public relied upon a presumed wedlock between status and "facts", and credited a governmental bureaucracy with the possession of the facts ("If they don't know, who does?") that endowed them with the authority to pursue the war while ignoring the partisans whose rhetoric protested against it. In this case it is clear that the public's loyalty to a governmental élite—or a supposed élite—was the determining factor in the vacuity of public discourse in this period, although the emptiness and sheer falsehood of such discourse was considerably influenced by lies, secrets and public relations smokescreens indulged in by government officials.[23] Rhetorical protestations against the war, even when they became vociferous mass demonstrations, were clearly unpersuasive to the public at large, who broadly accepted, not the government's own rhetoric (which was blithely assumed to be riddled with "credibility gaps"), but the offices and identities of those in power. The irony of this entire process is that this remarkable demonstration of fidelity, appearing as a passive approval, was conceived in the minds of so many as a preference for governmental policy based upon "facts".

The unavoidable conclusion to this survey of political language in an age of electronic communication is that by technique and design, political rhetoric has virtually become a barrier to communication—if we still take communication to be "the conveyance and exchange of information".[24] This does not mean that political language and rhetoric have ceased to exist as instruments of power. Yet the conclusion is clearly available that they have ceased to be tools in the service of the aims of classical rhetoric, that is, to inform and persuade. This development amounts to the removal from public discourse of the function of communication referred to throughout this study—the disposition of information necessary for the maintenance and elaboration of culture, a result that was foreshadowed prior to the emergence of electronic technology, but finally achieved by it. Now the appearance of political rhetoric, especially as shaped and refined by the broadcast media, serves as a kind of anti-communication, simply because it is so useful in serving two ancient functions of language—the assignment of status and the selective suppression of knowledge—while being so useless in offering itself as a technique of collective expression and deliberation.

It is difficult, therefore, to avoid the conclusion that the broadcasting media have contributed to a kind of inversion of rhetorical discourse. Reminded that classical rhetoric aimed to inform, persuade and move, we see the remarkable way in which radio and television—widely supposed to be so potent toward those ends— have rendered these classical aims more difficult. This effect, in fact, most clearly obtains when audio-visual techniques are marshalled in their most sophisticated forms, and the attention of tens of millions of people is rewarded with the latest sixty-second episode of a politician's media package. Here the intention is not to stimulate thought but to prevent it; not to communicate information, but to conceal or trivialize it; not to persuade but to placate and entertain; not to move but to enlarge quiescence; ultimately, not to use language at all if cinematic artifice and a musical soundtrack can be used to conjure the desired image and elicit the favourable emotion.

The forms in which political rhetoric now appears, and the vocabulary (both linguistic and visual) which it uses, seem uncannily appropriate to this new task of establishing an embargo on public discourse. Thus in an age of remarkable advances in "communications technology", contemporary political rhetoric evolves steadily beyond the slogan to jingles, cartoons and the artifice of professional actors and studio cosmetics. Even in the rhetoric of bureaucratic administration the same steady trend appears. Complex issues (or even very simple ones) are reduced to acronyms, impersonal forces and silly slogans, so that the public's only path is to look for helpful images—which of course is precisely the aim of bureaucracy's increasingly sophisticated public relations managers. Gradually, then, the substance of discourse is drained away, and rhetoric succeeds in its task of offering images in place of information, identifying these images with the resources and expertise required to dispose of information and policy. As the world of public policy becomes darker and more remote from everyday life, the public is only too willing to believe in these images which are, after all, consoling and sometimes even entertaining.

Notes

1. The chairman of Dwight Eisenhower's 1956 presidential campaign made a survey to see if the candidate's closed-circuit television speeches to 53 fundraising dinners were sufficiently effective: "We found the full impact was there —the same emotion, the same tears—just as if the President had been there in person". Quoted in Vance Packard, *The Hidden Persuaders* (London, 1962), p. 158.
2. Television advertising has become the single largest expense in U.S. presidential campaigns. The bulk of the campaign budget is expended in the final one to three weeks on "saturation" broadcasting of short ad spots. Joseph Napolitan, *The Election Game* (New York, 1972), pp. 143–44. Radio and television spots in Australian elections are also the most costly campaign items. Steve McLean and Paul Brennan, "Press Advertising Strategies and Democracy", in Henry Mayer, ed., *Labor to Power, Australia's 1972 Election* (Sydney, 1973), p. 205.
3. There is reason to believe, based on recent trends in U.S. elections, that local and regional candidates whose faces are not well known to the public concentrate on the "image" of their surname in radio and television spots, on the theory that this is essential for recognition at the moment of balloting.
4. The advertising agency for the Australian Labor Party secretly recorded and attempted to release a "soft rock" tune—"It's Time"—months before the formal election campaign in 1972. Its political origins became known before it received much commercial radio play or popular sales. Nevertheless, the record continued to sell, and the theme song was used in intensive radio and television "ad" spots performed by leading entertainment figures. The objective was to create an "emotional bridge" early in the pre-campaign period as a basis for the "image mosaic" to be developed in later weeks. A survey on election day found that "It's Time" was spontaneously chosen by more voters as a reason for voting ALP than any other reason offered. See Vicky Braund, "Timely Vibrations: Labor's Marketing Campagin", in Mayer, *Labor to Power,* pp. 20–28.
5. Neal Blewett, "Labor 1968–72: Planning for Victory", in Mayer, *Labor to Power*, p. 15. The cultivation of party leader images is discussed in Murray Goot and R.W. Connell, "Presidential Politics in Australia?", *Australian Quarterly* 44, 2 (June 1972), pp. 28–33. An overview of the media techniques of the 1977 Australian federal election is Les Carlyon, "Images Built on Dull Scripts", the *Age* (Melbourne, 23 November 1977).
6. Braund, "Timely Vibrations", pp. 25–26. Costs for 1977 Australian campaign

advertising are discussed in Andrew Clark, "The Men Behind the Election Campaign", *National Times* (Sydney, 14 November 1977), p. 5. Also see Howard Penniman, ed., *Australia at the Polls: The National Elections of 1975* (Canberra, 1977), Ch. 7.

7. An example is the thirty-minute speech by John B. Connally, a former governor of Texas and widely regarded as an effective speaker, as a "Democrat for Nixon" in the 1972 presidential election campaign. His television address was a prime example of a slick, carefully rehearsed, staged (even choreographed, as Connally moved gracefully around a sumptuously appointed study), and professionally edited product. After its first national showing, even the opposition referred to the speech as "dynamite", and the videotape was shown again several times on network television. Shown at prime evening time, the speech was obviously felt to be worth the hundreds of thousands of dollars spent by the Nixon organizers to air it. See C. Keever, *John B. Connally: Portrait in Power* (Austin, Texas, 1973), pp. 364–66. A similar campaign technique, although developed as a series of newspaper display advertisements by "Business Executives for a Change of Government" in the 1972 Australian election campaign was very effective in satirizing Prime Minister William McMahon's personality and popularizing his malapropisms. The photos, copy and layout were so thoroughly humourous that they set the tone for the final weeks of election coverage in the press. See P.D. Jack, "It's Time, The Tombstone Series, Mr. Nice Bloke and Graphics Plus", in Mayer *Labor to Power*, pp. 214–15. Pre-testing and mid-campaign surveys encouraged the Labor Party to spend half of its media budget airing the successful "It's Time" "ad" spots. *Ibid.*, p. 212. Aiming purposely at a "blurred" image of the ALP, since surveys showed that party leaders were perceived largely in negative terms, the ALP advertising agency wanted to avoid issues and personalities in order to "plug into a mood". The goal was to build a purposely ambiguous image of the party: "the way we want people to believe it is . . . as they themselves perhaps would wish some party would be". Braund, "Timely Vibrations", pp. 25–26. Also Blewett, "Labor 1968–72", pp. 12–13. Such a media strategy prohibited lengthy rhetorical performances by party leaders, especially by Gough Whitlam and Bob Hawke, respectively the parliamentary party leader and the ALP National Party chairman.

8. This is taken to its logical conclusion when a person becomes famous for simply appearing on television: a "TV personality". A similar, but not identical, case is the use of famous entertainers and sports figures to endorse commercial products.

9. In the United States, the Federal Communications Commission is charged with overseeing commercial broadcasting with a view to serving "the public interest, convenience and necessity", as set forth in the Federal Communications Act, Title 47, *U.S. Code*, Section 307(a). See S.W. Head, *Broadcasting in America* (New York, 1972), pp. 361–68. In Australia, both public and commercial broadcasting comes under the administration of the Australian Broadcasting Control Board, empowered by the *Broadcasting and Television Act, 1942–1975* (Canberra, 1975). Also, see A.B.C.B., *Television Programme Standards*, 2nd ed. 1970 (Canberra, 1970 and 1975); Kenneth W. Wiltshire and Charles H. Stokes, *Government Regulation and the Electronic Media*, C.E.D.A. Monograph 43 (Sydney and Melbourne, 1977); and Henry Mayer and Sara Pantzer, eds., *Media Policies of Australian Political Parties*, Univ. of Sydney, Dept. of Government Media Monographs (Sydney, 1977). The importance of broadcasting was recognized, not surprisingly, by the Whitlam government elected in1972 by establishing a new cabinet post, the Minister for the Media.

10. Some sociologists and political scientists insist that all broadcasting is political and persuasive—commercial advertising, situation comedies, sex role projection, etc.—as a socializing environment. Indeed, research has shown that television programming builds stereotypes, affects attitudes, reinforces valued symbols and stimulates one's social and economic behaviour. See Chapter VII, note 13. While accepting these findings, however, the present argument asserts the importance and the conceptual possibility of distinguishing broadcasting content that is manifestly political and rhetorical in character from entertainment and consumer advertising. It is granted that political candidates and toothpaste are frequently "sold" by the broadcasting of "ad" spots that are virtually indistinguishable in form and treatment, but this does not imply that both "ads" effect the same kind of behaviour or have the same relationship to the obtaining and exercising of political power.

11. The parallel between studio production and the printer's editorial task of producing uniform, "proofed" copy should not be overlooked.

12. It is not argued here that the stock of commonplaces at the command of the modern orator has been accumulated through the retention of a cultural tradition (analogous, say, to the retention of Homer or the Roman historians) or through the cultivation of rhetorical skills in a form of education which explicitly transmits such material. Indeed, when modern orators (and their speechwriters) make use of *Bartlett's Familiar Quotations* to quote from a classic, they more often than not illustrate by contrast the poverty and inelegance of their own prose.

13. Such slogans as "In the name of God, go" and "End the war" very economically and powerfully convey specific information within their appropriate political contexts. Presidential candidate George McGovern's 1972 campaign slogan, "Come home America", was thought to be effective, however, because it was ambiguous. Anti-war voters saw in the slogan a direct proposal to stop the war in Vietnam, while voters further to the right on the political spectrum were attracted to its agrarian and isolationist overtones. The Australian Labor Party's 1972 slogan, "It's Time", also had an appealing ambiguity, enabling the voter to project his own aspirations into the inspirational mood set by the "ads". The Liberal Party unwisely "replied" with their own slogan, "Not yet", which offered only a closed and negative outlook to the voter. Learning from this experience, the Liberals offered to "Turn on the lights" in 1975. The "It's Time" slogan was derived from theories of the attitudinal impact of television, and was evaluated after the election as "the perfect statement—open-ended to keep communication open and to avoid alienating undecided voters. There was nothing to disagree with in the statement and it conveyed its correct meaning [that is, time for a change of government] to most respondents surveyed, without stating its objective once". Braund, "Timely Vibrations", p. 25.

14. Richard Nixon's two presidential inaugural addresses are emblematic of this trend. A reading of either text quickly demonstrates that each brief, one-sentence or one-line paragraph is nothing more than a simple, undeveloped maxim, and that they follow one another with no apparent order or logical sequence. A more general example of this trend is the use of catchy, concise and stylized frankness in campaign advertisements in newspapers. A contrast is provided between Labor's use of glossy pictorial brochures and catchy newspaper "ads" in 1972 and the Liberal Party's printing of lengthy booklets on specific issues and labeled the "Tombstone Series" by the Liberals' own media staff. See Jack, "It's Time", in Mayer, *Labor to Power*, pp. 212–15.

15. The following examples are illustrative of the genre:
    My fellow (Australians, etc.) . . .
    On behalf of the (whole community, the Trade Union movement, etc.) . . .
    I say to you in all (candor, humility, etc.) . . .
    Never before . . .
    We must never forsake (truth, our allies, peace, etc.) . . .
16. A candidate for the United States presidency customarily takes several tours abroad prior to his formal campaign, especially to areas of current economic and political importance, in order to acquire a status for speaking out on foreign policy. Gough Whitlam's trip to China in July 1971, resulted in much publicity, and was thought to be helpful in building an image of experience and statesmanship. See Goot and Connell, "Presidential Politics", pp. 28–33; and Laurie Oakes and David Soloman, *The Making of an Australian Prime Minister* (Melbourne, 1973). The Labor Party's marketing research firm, Spectrum International Marketing Services, found the China trip to have had only limited impact on the electorate, according to their confidential report of August 1971. Braund, "Timely Vibrations", p. 19.
17. Nixon's 1972 presidential campaign seemed to be based upon two endlessly repeated slogans: his "competence" (In what? Answer: "government".) and the fact that he was "the President". So at pains was his organization—The Committee to Re-Elect the President—to promote this image that the name, Richard Nixon, appeared on no campaign materials and was virtually eradicated as an identity. It was felt that the name, as shown in marketing surveys, could only introduce negative associations concerning the candidate's personality, and thus detract from the effort to develop the desired image.
18. It may well be true that these same forces have established new criteria for determining the kind of persons required as suitable candidates for media marketing.
19. The Liberal Party in Australia prior to 1973 used the marketing surveys and "social barometer" of PROBE, a Sydney marketing research firm, and retained the services of Masius–Wynne–Williams advertising agency. The Labor Party used Spectrum International Marketing Services in 1971–72 and have retained the Hansen–Rubensohn–McCann–Erikson agency periodically since 1934, although this agency was also retained by the Liberals in 1948–49. Jack, "It's Time", pp. 212–13. Also see Clark, "Men Behind the Election" for more recent use of professional public relations personnel. Dan Nimmo, *The Political Persuaders* (New York, 1970) and David Wise, "Are You Worried About Your Image, Mr. President?", *Esquire* (May 1973), pp. 119ff, illustrate the extent to which political parties in the U.S. rely upon marketing surveys and sophisticated communications techniques on a permanent basis. After Labor's total commitment to marketing and communications strategies prior to the 1972 election, students of Australian politics confirmed the arrival of "the continuous campaign" in which elections are merely periodic climaxes in a series of strategic phases. Blewett, "Labour 1968–72", pp. 8–11 and 13.
20. Special interest programming and topical documentaries occasionally rise above the standards implied by this judgement.
21. The 1960 and 1976 United States presidential campaign debates are notable exceptions, although the format of the broadcasts (two or three-minute answers to journalists' questions) actually required the candidates to give bland and predictable answers to predictable questions. The broadcasts were perhaps more notable for the preliminary emphasis placed on them as a kind of political drama in which each candidate's image was to be put to the test on live television, and how the candidates underwent grueling cramming sessions so

that their answers might be calculated to sound good, please everyone and offend no one. Polls after the first 1976 debate indicated that Jimmy Carter's reception by the viewers was hurt by his tendency to recite economic and budgetary figures in surprising detail. He was careful in subsequent debates to avoid factual information and couch his responses in a more platitudinous style. There was an apparent consensus among candidates and commentators that the real meaning of the debates lay in presenting the candidates' "character" to the people, and that in this regard the debates were a great success. Commentators in the press and polling experts agreed that the candidates avoided controversy, "waffled" on issues, and were fastidious in their caution to say nothing definite in the way of policy or legislation.

22. It was not until early in 1970 that the public opinion polls began to show a majority of Americans holding opinions opposed to the war. See periodic survey results published by the American Institute of Public Opinion, *The Gallup Opinion Index* (Princeton) for the years 1965–70; also John E. Mueller, *War, Presidents and Public Opinion* (New York, 1973), esp. pp. 81–98.

23. Neil Sheehan *et al.*, eds. *The Pentagon Papers*, (New York, 1971), in this or other editions is by no means a definitive record of official suppression of public dialogue on the war. Congressional investigations since the appearance of these papers concerning the pursuit of the war have documented many other instances of policies which were developed, carried out in secrecy and denied later in knowing contravention to fact, e.g., support of mercenary guerilla armies, "secret" bombings, and the financing of opposition parties, *coups d'état* and political assassinations. Also see Daniel Ellsberg, *Papers on the War* (New York, 1972), esp. pp. 42–135, and David Wise, *The Politics of Lying* (New York, 1973).

24. See Paul E. Corcoran, "The Obsolescence of Political Language", *Australian Scan* 3 (December 1977), pp. 47–57. Marketing and media specialists involved in the 1972 Australian election campaign, in reflecting upon their success, considered printed materials and hard information a "waste of time" and that "the near-perfect product launch" was due to their "creation of the party's image mosaic". "The theory of influencing emotional response was . . . the cornerstone on which success turned (*sic*). Had the party gone all-out for a rational response . . . loss would have been a foregone conclusion." Speaking of the ALP's "It's Time" campaign, a member of the campaign staff wrote "The image of the whole commercial was intended to be one of energy, enthusiasm and youth. The concept . . . was aimed at presenting a favourable psychological image—the "good vibrations" the party wanted and needed to effect the change in their perceived image . . . The fragments of the mosaic were favourable pieces of media information or messages which together helped build that "perceived" image which the voter carried around. It was control over the building of this image that was the communicator's dearest goal . . . The "linear-logic" people were given the components of a rational decision in their medium—the press . . . TV and radio commercials were never intended to include information communication as one of their functions. Rather, their function . . . was seen as evoking an emotional response . . . The 1972 media campaign . . . was based on a simple theory: that people make emotional, not rational decisions and that these decisions can be influenced to varying degrees by the judicious use of media . . . " Quoted from Braund, "Timely Vibrations", *passim*, pp. 21–28.

9

The Post-literate Culture

> Today the globe has shrunk in the wash with speeded-up
> information movement from all directions. We have come, as
> it were, to live in a global village. Our information comes at
> high speed, electronic speed from all corners. We would seem
> to be living, almost under ear conditions, of a small village
> world.
>
> Marshall McLuhan

A decline in literacy has been a recurrent object of despair for many
centuries. And surely before Voltaire penned this verse, men were
aware of the connections felt to exist between language, culture
and morals, and that a decline in one implied a decline in the others.

Plus que les moeurs
  sont dépravés

Plus que les expressions
  deviennent mesurés.

On croit regagner
  en langage

Ce qu'on a perdu
  en vertu.[1]

It has been argued in the previous chapters that language, in
so far as it is a technique of communication, has undergone a
number of transformations, and that with each technical innovation
in communication there has been a change in the social function
of language. This is an idea which in one sense is very simple and
very obvious—one is intuitively aware that the function of language
in a pre-literate tribal chant is very different from that in a Roman
law court or a parliamentary speech—and yet it is an idea which
posits a distinction between communication as a natural function
of society, and language techniques which in a given culture may

not be able to perform this function. Our argument has tried to establish that language in many of the traditional forms in which we recognize it has ceased to serve as an instrument of communication. The rhetoric of formal oratory, more than any other form, has been transformed into a culturally anachronistic and obsolete language technique, although it is not difficult to argue that prose (both in composition and reading), formal pedagogy, and even the skill of reading are forms of language which seem to be gradually receding as important techniques for the exchange of information necessary for the maintenance and elaboration of culture. It may well be said that this definition is itself obsolete—as many would surely contend—probably because it is so closely tied to language acquisition and performance. The quaintness of this whole inquiry is adequately suggested by the impression we have of the proposition, and the kind of person who advances it, that the art of conversation and the art of letter-writing are not only declining, but moribund.

It happens to be the case that "literacy" is a political issue. In the sense in which we commonly understand this term—the ability to read and write at some minimal level—it has always been a political issue, simply because the scarcity of leisure and expensive resources (and the customs and classes devoted to protecting them) have made it difficult, impossible or even illegal for most members of society to become literate. In the Greek, *schōle* was the word for leisure. In the twentieth century, when some nations finally committed themselves to the virtually unprecedented goal of universalizing literacy, the problem became directly politicized. Hardly disabused of the Enlightenment ideal that education was the panacea of all private and social ills, people of all classes looked to education for their different aims. People with much to lose saw public education as one way to forestall revolution, to provide a lettered work force, and to protect and even reinforce the élite character of the "higher" education due their sons—and daughters. These people now see a political issue in a "decline" in the standards of education and a loss in the literacy of a new generation, and they are not sure if the debasement has come from popular education or the "liberal" educational philosophy emanating from the most élite institutions.

People who had everything to gain for their sons and daughters saw public education as a great opportunity and an equalizing force in society; it was one way to bring the revolution. These people see a political issue in the failure of public education to achieve what it was never in fact intended to do, namely, to provide for them the skills, graces and social contacts available to the middle and upper classes.

The question of declining educational standards and illiteracy is not simply a matter of class or wealth, because there are issues which cannot be sorted out so easily. Rich and poor, black and white alike, find dissatisfactions with their children's schools, and there are a myriad of criticisms: poor and ill-trained (illiterate) teachers; lack of classroom discipline; age and aptitude class streaming which aims at competition to the detriment of those with socio–economic deficiencies; ungraded or un-streamed classrooms which retard the more able pupil; classroom techniques geared to let the child set his own pace, leading to imaginative but un-assessable behaviour and deficient language and mathematical skills; over-structured classrooms which inculcate or attempt to inculcate irrelevant and obsolete skills, but actually injure the child's motivation and learning; socio-economically and racially segregated classrooms which (for the rich) "protect standards" and (for the poor) reproduce inequalities; socio-economically and racially integrated classroom which (for the rich) destroy discipline and lower academic standards and (for the poor) confront the child with a suffocating and alien culture in which he competes at a disadvantage, loses cultural identity and fails; a lack of adequate funds for proper teaching facilities; too much money for trendy studies, non-skill oriented teaching devices and "educational technology".

Our present interest is not to attempt to solve this conundrum, but merely to point out that illiteracy and declining, or changed, educational standards are political issues.[2] From many quarters, there is the clear conviction that standards have fallen, or that promises have not been kept. Some have said that television is at fault, while others claim television has (even inadvertently) started children to count, expand their vocabulary and learn to read years earlier than pre-television generations. Others still claim that the "average" university student cannot be made to read assignments, while surveys indicate that more books are being sold, although the length of books is greatly reduced, along with the size and sophisticiation of their vocabulary.

It is pervasive in all of these widely varying viewpoints that literacy—so long as it is not used as a code word for discrimination —is a good thing, and that the loss of literacy and the lowering of standards of acceptable achievement are bad things.[3] The same kind of moral assumption is inherent in social and literary criticism, which deplores the untraditional and apparently careless prose and poetry of contemporary literature; the vulgarity and obscenity on stage, screen, sidewalk and classroom; and the inchoate stream-of-conscious inarticulateness of natural conversation. In short, the "decline of language" amounts to a loss of moral character.

The viewpoint from which we approach this question is informed by our analysis of the obsolescence of traditional literacy. This is a perspective upon contemporary society as a post-literate, not an illiterate, culture. The debate over declining literacy in education, or the failure of education to live up to the promise of universal literacy, is essentially misdirected. The real question is not whether schools are adequately performing the task of developing language skills, but whether literacy (reading, writing, articulate conversation —that is, what some "advanced" schools call "communications skills") is a communication skill at all. Here, it seems, is the real political issue. There is, of course, no question but that very real skills are required to compose a concise sentence or a thoughtful paragraph, to translate a passage from Cicero or read Shakespeare with comprehension. Very different, but no less real, skills were required for the Mycaean youth to master the origins of his people and the mysteries of the universe in folk song and poetry. But can we expect a society to foster skills which have lost their functional utility, which have ceased to be in any crucial sense culturally necessary? It is a commonplace and a critical lament that schools now offer far better resources for science education, and that by contrast, the "humanities" are impoverished. It is, however, less well noted that few if any critics have raised a voice to suggest that the reverse investment should be made. Whatever the intensity of one's lament for declining standards of literacy, no one seriously suggests that society's commitment to scientific skills is optional, much less dispensable. Consequently, the depth of the political issue of literacy and illiteracy in education is measured precisely by the kind of political force (and the wielders of that force) that would be required to reverse the focus and investment of public education. In fact, very few people would want this to happen, and the small number who would elect such a course would be remarkable in their reactionary conservatism. Indeed, their numbers would be so small that they would be regarded, tellingly, as irrelevant.

It bears repeating that our present intention is not to advocate ideological positions, or lament the passing of the old, any more than the coming of the new. Neither do we intend to paint a landscape in black and white depicting an illiterate, if highly "enumerate",[4] society. There are shades of grey everywhere; and this is why the subject is so difficult to apprehend with satisfaction. Perhaps more people *do* read today than ever before, both in number and proportion of the population. Perhaps what they read is less complex, badly written and poorly understood. What we want to emphasize is the tendency away from a literate culture and the obvious cultural reliance upon both specialized and popular techniques of communication which have only anachronistic integrations of literate language forms. Several examples will illustrate this tendency: computer "languages"; scientific and mathematical notation; "free association" poetry and prose; visual and graphic symbols and phonic stimulation as preferred forms of popular entertainment; alpha-numeric "read-outs" from the computer (telescreen displays have rendered "print-outs" obsolete) for the convenience of human beings who must use computer languages to "communicate" with the computer's far more efficient binary and octal electronic processing capacities.

What appears to many as a "decline in literacy" is viewed here as the emergence of post-literate culture. It would be surprising if this phenomenon were not a cause for moral uncertainty for many people, especially those whose identity, professional endeavours and material interests are grounded in literate culture, as well as those who look to "education" (conceived as literacy) as a fiscal anodyne for ignorance, poverty and social division. Rather than commiserate with this sentiment, it is our concern simply to understand post-literacy as the cultural context within which political language survives as a linguistic performance. In passing to this subject, it may be of interest to point out to the many critics of the "new illiteracy" that their attentions and theories may well be misguided. Indeed, the many "causes" of "declining standards" in contemporary education are much more profitably seen as the effects of post-literate culture, and not causes at all. In the fifteenth and sixteenth centuries, early printers did not produce books in the vernacular because of a declining standard of penmanship or poor Latin instruction in schools. Sixth and fifth century B.C. Greeks did not prepare their sons for public life by procuring their tuition in reading and writing and eventually rhetoric simply because of a declining standard of poetic bards and inferior instruction in Hesiod and Homer. A case for the decline of literacy would have to argue that companies have been compelled to switch to typewriters because of inferior schooling in penmanship and that department stores have begun to use cash register adding machines only because their clerks can no longer add and subtract. Obviously, new language and communication techniques lead to the disuse of older ones, and this technical transformation is accompanied by changes in the content of communication.[5] If lyric poetry was an efficient technique for conveying the historical genealogies and the dramatic relationships of anthropomorphic gods, it was not an appropriate medium for the conveyance of abstract speculation about laws and the first principles of the constitution of the universe, which found dialectic logic (and rhetoric as its oral performance) far more suitable. If formal rhetoric was appropriate as a technique to convey news of an army's victories and defeats to the Roman Senate, and to celebrate the return of triumphant generals, such a technique may not be suitable for an examination of optics, trigonometry or the strategies of modern warfare.

How can we describe the post-literate society and post-literate culture without lapsing into moral indignation and intellectual condescension? Perhaps it is an impossible task to do so. This is, after all, a book, it was intended for readers, and it endeavours to inform and persuade. George Steiner touches upon the difficulty of writing about the decline of literate communication in an essay on Marshall McLuhan, in which the latter's work is found to be an analysis in the form of the problem.

> Many of the irritants, many of the crudities of presentment which exasperate or bewilder, are strategic. The *Gutenberg Galaxy* is an anti-book. It seeks to enforce, physically, the core of its own meaning. Its bearing on traditional modes of philosophic-historical argument is deliberately subversive. It is precisely part of McLuhan's achievement that we should be irked and affronted by the strangeness or inadequacy of his resources. He is saying to us, in a verbal mime which often descends to jugglery but also exhibits an intellectual leap of great power and wit, that books—a linear progression of phonetic units reproduced by moveable type—are no longer to be trusted. He is retreating rapidly from the word.[6]

If McLuhan's work "seeks to enforce, physically, the core of its own meaning", he has at least made his position clear. The reader is never in doubt of McLuhan's conviction that Western culture has been dominated by a narrowed and sterilized sensibility in the reading of linear print, and thus has lost a kind of primal, sensual unity which we can look to have restored by a "sensorium" of a totalized and instantaneous electronic communications network. If McLuhan's approach is morally indignant, but relieved, at the appearance of post-literate culture,[7] it may be that any book on the subject is, even if less overtly committed, a kind of polemical refusal of the trend it reports. Let it suffice to say that our present discussion of a post-literate culture is not intended as a critique or apologia for "the electronic age" on the one hand or the culture of literacy on the other. Indeed, it is assumed that this analytical distance is not abridged by noting the contradictory and reverse logic of those who find causes of illiteracy in what are actually the effects, nor by pointing out that the appearance of language in post-literate cultural manifestations is characteristically emotive, empty of reason and information and more conducive to the prevention than the stimulation of informed thought. To say these things is not to engage in moral or political polemic, nor is it an expression of resignation and despair. It is simply to identify a pervasive social phenomenon. If accomplishing this identification suggests the illogic or futility of certain policies, and if it illuminates certain questions related to politics, culture and the use of language for political ends, so much the better. With this statement of intention on the record, we shall now turn to several questions concerning language performance in post-literate society. In particular, we shall look briefly at language in institutional settings, specifically "political" language, and the prospects for public discourse (that is, language communication in its social dimension) in a post-literate culture.

Pre-Literacy and Post-Literacy

For an understanding of language with respect to institutions, politics and public discourse in post-literate society, we may profitably review the role of language in pre-literate society. This method can, of course, be no more than the pursuit of an analogy, but the effort may be sufficiently heuristic to be worthwhile.

In pre-literate, oral culture we found[8] that language was embedded within society as a cluster of customs and institutions. As *parole*, language was necessarily a performance that not only facilitated casual activities relating to the daily routine of nurture and conviviality, but was formalized into three basic social functions: ceremonial chants and recreational songs which communicated and maintained the cultural history of the group; special linguistic rites which assigned and ordered status; and a language of power, the possession of which enabled certain individuals to claim authority or (in the larger group) to appeal to authority in the form of invocations and curses. In this oral setting, language was pre-eminently *sound*, and therefore was indistinct from the natural environment in a way that is difficult for a literate person to understand. If natural and supernatural forces could manifest themselves in the cries of animals and the sounds of rain and storm, there was every reason to suppose that human sounds could be shaped and used in ways that might please, appease, invoke or ward off supernatural powers. By extension, calls, names or spoken formulae were convenient ways to order the family and tribal setting into roles, power relationships and behaviour patterns. Of course, the most effective way to preserve and transmit this information, without a system of written symbols, was to compose the information into chants, formulaic expressions and other oral devices, which in turn could be placed in the keeping of certain groups or individuals,[9] or associated with totemic rituals which were physical reminders of the information, and therefore contained, or could be used to summon, the powers of the information in question.

Summarizing the special features of language performance in oral culture, in considerably abbreviated form, may well suggest to what extent analogies exist in what we have characterized as post-literate society.

(a) Language is *sound*, an oral performance as opposed to a literate activity linked to reading or writing.
(b) Oral expression is *formulaic*. The range of expression is facilitated by aids to memory and performance: rhyme, meter, epigrams, onomatopaeia, mnemonics and other small-scale systems.
(c) Oral utterance possesses or calls forth a form of supra-sensible power. The spoken word assumes an incantory or invocatory power, e.g., when a curse or oath (even in common vulgarity) endows the speaker with a certain status *vis-à-vis* his subject of address.
(d) Language serves as a medium of retention, in which its content is limited to commonplace or received information, thus making oral performance essentially incompatible with articulations of inquiry or discovery.
(e) "Speakers" are identified with authorities or roles whose object is the maintenance, manipulation and sanctioned use of specialized information.
(f) Public group performance is "choral" in its repetitive, ceremonial and formulaic expression.
(g) Speech is facilitated by totems as an alternative and supplemental mnemonic device—a kind of physical "image" to represent and support formulaic retention.

What is surprising about these descriptive criteria of language use in oral culture is the extent to which they are suggestive of contemporary language. Indeed, if one reviews each of these points, examples spring to mind which would seem to support an analogy between the oral and the contemporary cases. Of course this does not logically "prove" that contemporary "post-literacy" is the necessary conclusion to the proposition that there are similarities between oral culture and current language use. This proposition being true, there may also be similarities between oral culture and, say, the sixteenth century. But our present purpose is only to illustrate the analogy in question—that is, the presence in contemporary society of features reminiscent of language in oral society —and not to attempt a logical demonstration that post-literacy is *in fact* a kind of historical reflex and return to oral society.[10]

Orality and Post-Literacy in the "Youth Culture"

If oral culture emphasizes the phonic and aural in formulaic expression, and assumes that ritual utterance is accompanied by a form of supernatural power, this very nearly resembles a popular description of the contemporary "youth culture". Although this criticism is often based on a concept of "orality" derived from Freudian psychology (which in any case is not entirely beside the point of primitive language use and the cries and oral gestures of infants), the argument proceeds on familiar ground. Thus youth culture is characterized as being suffused and hypnotised by sound —primarily music from omni-present electronic sources. "Sound" is the appropriate term, at its most sympathetic, since it is produced with such complexity and volume that the "words" often cannot be understood and seem to be irrelevant to the aural experience. Indeed, the lyrics of these songs are often so simple and repetitive, and are accompanied by so many nonsense "scat" sounds, that the words as semantic units are irrelevant. In the cases in which words are intelligible, it is clear that they are remarkably formulaic and simplistic, but this does not prevent their extensive repetition by musician, listener or dancer. As for the magical or invocatory power of this experience, one is free to speculate (but that is all, really) that a number of powers are at work, and such speculations range from the sexual to the charismatic, the latter potent enough to remind some people of manipulative mob psychology, mass hypnosis and the stimulation of aggression.[11] In any case, it would not be difficult to find a broad consensus among afficionados and detesters of popular music alike that it is capable of conjuring up supra-rational powers. If we continue the application of oral criteria, we could identify the retentive function of language with the extension of the aforementioned formulaic language in music to the youth culture's behaviour in public discourse. If an individual's speech (not to mention his skill in writing or reading) is said to be rambling, ungrammatical, illogical and filled with clichés, it is not difficult to draw the conclusion that such ideas, opinions and feelings as he has can only be articulated by stock phrases and idioms that reflect his primary participation in aural activity. It would be surprising if this language would facilitate logical tests of validity or consistency, or lead to inquiry and the amassing of new information.

The next criterion—authority roles based on the privileged possession and use of special (sacred) verbal data—is difficult to apply to the "youth culture" without resorting, perhaps, to pseudo-sociology and conspiracy theories. Still, it is probably plausible to say that the entrepreneurs of "sound"—those who write the songs, perform them and promote them to commercial success—have the status, authority and power which graduate them to the privileged positions of celebrity, wealth and control of the "music industry".[12] The final two criteria may be mentioned briefly, as well. Certainly we have an example of "choral" and ceremonial oral performance —including both rhyme and mime—in the rock concert, and also, by extension, in the electronic audience. The musical totems of the youth culture are remarkable analogies to those of oral culture, since the revered objects and symbols—audio equipment, radios, records—are precisely devices which "conjure" up the powerful contents of the aural experience. And there can be no doubt that these totems are valued and revered objects the possession of which confers status within the appropriate peer group.

It is easy to find this "youth culture" application as a cliché in itself, but it must be remembered that this very youth generation is also the reference group for critics of "illiteracy". The discovery of post-literacy, in any case, would appear to be most obvious and certain in reference to educational institutions (presumably charged with reproducing literate culture) and the young people filling their classrooms. Consequently, the fact that the youth culture is, at best, a fleeting and impressionistic reference group, and cannot be taken as any more than that, does not mean that the characteristics of the group may be dismissed out of hand. If we find analogies of pre-literate, oral culture manifested in school and university-aged young people, we can also trace them to other groups. One group that comes to mind immediately is the contemporary housewife. Although some have argued that women have always been on the fringes of literate culture,[13] there is a close parallel between young people and housewives with regard to each group's pervasive contact with radio and television. In fact, commercial broadcasting throughout Western society is aimed at two distinct audiences, teenagers and housewives. The former are offered an environment of music and the latter an environment of melodrama and consumer (quiz show) phantasies. Although a number of parallels can be drawn between the aural setting of the modern home and our model of oral culture, we shall note only in passing that "leisure" time and attention (of the ear if not always the eye) for the housewife (whether affluent or poor, busy or consigned to listless torpor) are devoted to non-literate stimulation.

Other Forms of Post-Literacy

There are other groups and institutions which offer parallels to non-literate culture. Perhaps surprisingly, one of these is modern bureaucracy—both government and business. Although bureaucracies stand as a major monument to the order, routine and rationality of linear culture, and have become the object of satire because of their obsessive dependence upon record-keeping and repetitive procedure, there seems to be some evidence that bureaucratic communication increases in "efficiency" to the extent that it decreases in literacy. Thus information is at its most valuable and reliable when it is quantified and, better still, statistical; and this is also the form in which it may be accepted, stored, manipulated and retrieved by electronic devices. Information that must be written in a "memorandum" is a necessary evil, and this evil is ameliorated by the development of a mechanical style of writing filled with the mimicked jargon of quantitative expression and computerized data processing. The latest innovation in the writing of a memorandum appears to be the "flow chart". Although this could easily be regarded as a reformed type of linear communication, we mention bureaucratic language as evidence of post-literacy simply because it is a clear manifestation of a class of communication which relies as much as possible upon non-literate resources (electronic data processing and communication, and quantitative expression), and eschews (or at least is no longer able or interested in using) traditional techniques of grammatical and literary fluency. It should be added here that education, to the remarkable extent that it is a bureaucracy extending into the classroom itself and into textbooks and teaching methods (as in "programmed learning"), serves as an institution relying increasingly upon post-literate communications and skill development.

A final institution that reflects post-literate tendencies is art, although this is another category at least as difficult to pin down as a youth culture. Of course the plastic or representational arts constitute a direct link to pre-literate and oral society, and in this sense their very existence in literate culture beside the literary arts —*belles lettres*—testifies to a cultural survival of a profound nature. The point of present interest in contemporary art, however, is the refusal on the part of many artists to give a literal interpretation of their work—either as to "meaning" in a moral or aesthetic sense, or even as to the simple objective "identity" of the subject. Clearly this is a kind of return to the "immediacy" of the object to the senses, and the autonomy of the object apart from any reference to or dependence upon external (allegorical, mythical, symbolic, religious) information which is accessible in a literal articulation. In one important respect this is a revival of the magic or inherent power of an object that reminds us of oral culture. On the other hand, such a work does not necessarily stand for or "contain" anything else, even an oral utterance. Rather, it is a visual or tactile medium alone. Having said all this one can point to, say, paintings and sculptures which do have a representational content or "meaning", but one that is not so much literal as physical and quantitative. From Seurat to Mondrian to Vasarely we find a tradition of artists which presents an object to our senses whose primary significance is in reference to the colour spectrum and the way in which particular intensities and juxtapositions affect the retina. Thus our experience of the painting is equivalent to a bio–chemical experiment—a photo–optic–physiological reaction—in which the colour stands only for itself as paint with specific light-reflecting properties, and not as patches of colour that "stand for" a literal content to which it is an allusion. In this sense, then, modern post-representational painting is both a revival of sensual aspects of pre-literate society and an extension of a pre-literate medium of communication into the empirical interests of post-literate culture.

The proposition that contemporary Western culture has entered into a stage of post-literacy is not the kind of hypothesis that a careful historian will try to prove or disprove. This reluctance is not so much due to the contemporary nature of the problem as it is to the simple historiographical difficulty one has in making objective and purely descriptive accounts of a "stage", "trend", or "evolution" in history. The historian who claims to have discovered such a phenomenon is invariably reproached because of the way in which his alleged historical development is either tautological (resulting from the criteria of his discovery being embedded in the methods by which his data is gathered) or subjective and value-laden (resulting from "hidden" assumptions about what constitutes change, development or progress). That is why the present account of post-literacy is offered by way of analogy and definitional criteria. We want to avoid blind alleys. We cannot "prove" that post-literacy exists today, or that it will "intensify" tomorrow. Indeed, we cannot prove that there was ever such a period as "literacy", unless we establish working definitions and arbitrary criteria—for example, a certain percentage of grammar school graduates, or so many books printed per thousand of population per year, or a newspaper circulation equal to fifty-one per cent of the adult population—which would lead directly to the historiographer's charge of circular reasoning.

There are distinctions and discriminations, not only with respect to such amorphous objects as society and culture, which simply cannot be validated by logic or demonstrated by empirical tests. Most things in life are uncertain, and it would appear that just such things turn up as the objects of moral concern and political policy. Aside from this speculation, however, it is easy to grasp that the existence of social processes and transformations is often difficult or impossible to subject to rational or scientific proof. One cannot dispute the reduction (yes, "reduction", a frankly evaluative term) in status of folk-song as a technique of cultural communication or transmission when an illiterate society merges with a literate one, or itself becomes literate. Yet we cannot really prove this. We cannot prove that the social function of the accomplished balladeer changes from something like educator in illiterate society to entertainer in literate society without establishing *a priori* premises and thus predicting our conclusions. In fact, we probably cannot even specify what is meant by the word "changes" in the previous sentence, because this points to a phenomenon not fully commensurable with two elements or functions—the balladeer-educator and balladeer-entertainer—which are supposed, respectively, to undergo and result from the "change".[14] Nevertheless, it strikes us as true in a partly specifiable way[15] that the social function of folk-song is transformed as part of the process of expanding literacy and subsequent achievements in communications technology.

Are we, then, in a blind alley? It would appear that the answer to this question is, unhappily, partly "yes" and partly "no". We cannot, it is true, specify and postulate post-literate culture as an objectively existing state of affairs satisfying certain descriptive criteria. Culture is not an objectively existing state of affairs, unless one reduces it (as indeed many have) to a purely material and mechanistic interplay of supposedly economic forces, or reifies it to a metaphysical, transcendent force. What is possible, however, is to see literacy and communication as separate technical phenomena, with separate functions and cultural inter-connections. The advantage of this distinction is that it makes possible an analysis that neither relies upon normative evaluation nor requires a progressive or regressive view of history. Post-literacy, therefore, is simply a typifying category which points out the relative disjunction between literary skills, on the one hand, and the techniques of communication which have emerged and come into use, in part, independently of those literary skills, on the other. Furthermore, we can now see that what have been called institutional causes of illiteracy—e.g., poor schooling, or advanced pedagogical techniques—are in fact no more than infrastructural responses to the emerging technologies. Literary skills have not been "lost" through moral incorrigibility or historical inevitability; rather, these skills have simply lost their support to new skills, particularly those skills which are associated with scientific and technological activities.[16]

There is no reason for supposing that literate skills will vanish in post-literate society. Oral speech, reading and writing—that is, the literate skills dependent upon language-specific grammars—will surely remain in post-literate culture, just as certain forms of formal rhetorical performance have survived into and beyond the age of printing. Oral argumentation in cases at law is an example of such a survival. Due to our present interest in political language and oral performance, it would be inappropriate to venture too far into speculations about current and future directions of literature. Any number of books and articles have appeared in the past several decades proclaiming that poetry, the novel, serialized fiction and virtually every other literary genre are "dead". The fact that these proclamations appear in the form that is alleged to be deceased suggests that literate culture has a way of persisting.

The survival of literacy in post-literate culture does not necessarily pose a paradox. We have frequently noted that literacy is always a relative characterization of any society, and the general use of the term admits often surprising degrees of illiteracy among the young, or the very old, or within ethnic sub-populations. In the same way, "post-literacy" is a relative term used to draw attention to salient characteristics of a society, in this case, for example, the existence of specialized communication based upon non-grammatical languages and symbol systems in science and engineering;

electronic systems for storing, processing and retrieving information based upon non-linguistic techniques; and the predominance of radio and television in domestic entertainment as replacements for serialized and other forms of popular reading.[17]

The idea of post-literacy entails an interesting form of social élitism. Individuals, families and other elements comprising traditional ruling élites have rarely been, and need not have been, members of literary élites.[18] Ruling élites, however, have made use of persons whose literary talents fitted them to be scribes, lawyers, historians and teachers, positions in which writing was essential. Indeed, in classical Greece and Rome, and throughout the Middle Ages, the literati comprised an official class near to the centre of political power. Nevertheless, they were a serving class, and the need for their skills enabled persons to enter official circles whose social station—for example, monks of ignoble birth—would otherwise not permit it. In modern times, since the invention of printing and the expansion of education, a literate class has continued at the service of power in both commerce and government. As late as the nineteenth century, Marx and Engels pointed to a division in society between those who worked with their hands and those —whom they characterized rather over-broadly as "intellectuals" —who worked with their heads. Without troubling to give too careful a definition of the degree of skills attained by the "educated classes", there can be no doubt that official society depended upon and saw to the cultivation of an educated élite—not necessarily or fully corresponding with the ruling élite. This situation is not appreciably different in contemporary society. In the West, higher education (which was once satisfied by the *quadrivium* of arithmetic, music, geometry and astronomy—precisely those fields of learning turned to after a mastery of literate skills in the *trivium:* grammar, rhetoric and poetry, including Greek, Latin and perhaps elements of one's vernacular) now is conducted at great expense and for a greater number of years than ever before. That this investment of time and money during the recent two or three centuries has not given rise to a literary tradition demonstrably superior in scope or genius to its predecessors—in *belles lettres,* philosophy and history, for example—should not really be surprising.[19] Nor should it be surprising that today, when more resources than ever before are expended on higher education, even in the "liberal arts", there are outcries over the poor literary standards of people who have spent twenty years and more in school. For some impression of these standards, one need only turn to any number of "scholarly journals", which need editors to impose some consistency on behalf of simple rules of grammar, even though they are powerless to guarantee clarity and economy of statement.

It is evident that higher education has really followed tradition in its emphasis upon scientific and technical subjects. Here are the disciplines which, from the time of Peter Ramus and the Port-Royalists and Descartes, freed themselves from the constrictions of a communications theory grounded in classical rhetoric, which was, after all, an "elementary" subject, and in any case always one that was wed uncertainly to logic. In the twentieth century, this liberation is very nearly accomplished in universities, as well as in high schools, where the pursuit of specialized learning is largely independent—both in experimental method and in increasingly mathematical acquisition and formulation of content—of literate skills. In sum, higher education itself is essentially post-literate.

Returning to the question of an educated élite, it is clear that the graduates of post-literate education have inherited the mantle of office formerly worn by the literati. They remain, in a new fashion, the "learned", but they are no longer men of letters. Their function, however, is substantially the same: they—the name "technocracy" is accurate enough—are there to record, process, retrieve and make sense of highly specialized information. Francis Bacon said, in these words, *Scientia est potestas*. Thus the new literati remain the privileged servants of power, and one can even see that, in the broadest sense, they are charged with responsibility for the social function of communication. It remains, as before, an exchange between a relatively small group conversant with special skills and privileged information. Even those who have the responsibility of "communicating" with the general public, no matter what technological medium is used, place oral performance at the disposal of "media advisers" and studio technicians. The composition of speech as a literary feat, and its performance as a rhetorical act, are both literate skills offered up to the devices of specialists whose skills as electronics engineers, cinematographers and marketing specialists have nothing whatsoever to do with the actual content of the speech.

Post-Literacy and Political Language

Political discourse in post-literate culture assumes a stylization which conforms to its extra-communicative function. The effect of radio and television upon political rhetoric has already been surveyed, but it is noteworthy that the surviving rhetorical performances appear as a genre activity. Despite the lip service paid to the "power" of the mass media to "disseminate information", there is a popular assumption—amounting to a world-weary cynicism—that political rhetoric is a display of style with no meaningful content. Thus an actual oratorical performance, such as a campaign speech, offers the broadcast audience perfunctory, congratulatory clichés which are little more than a survival of the formulaic tropes and schema of classical rhetoric. Rhetorical devices such as slogans, rhymes or audio-visual reproductions are less clearly related to oratorical performance, but they strongly reinforce the formulaic, ritual-like stylization of political language. Hence speeches become embarrassingly trite, and the more "innovative" uses of the media for political communication produce a language reduced to slogans and unpredicated incantations.[20] Finally, the genre character of political rhetoric is heightened by the broadcast media's capacity for exact repetition and the constraints of format: an oration becomes a "television appearance", a political endorsement becomes an "ad spot".

Political rhetoric in post-literate culture takes on a two-fold character. At the same time as oral discourse becomes transformed into an archaic ritual and increasingly drained of its linguistic content by electronic media, oratory revives pre-literate modes of expression to articulate a rigidly defined and narrow ground of discourse. While this transformed rhetorical display appears to some as irrelevant, trite, and cliché-ridden grandiloquence, it is also clear that it is a form of oral communication which survives precisely because of its reliance upon simplicity, a familiar stock of received "wisdom", and the invocation of accepted commonplaces. Formal political discourse, therefore, solidifies into a formulaic "residue" of language with a thinness of grammatical, informational, and idiomatic content that is surprising only because of its inevitably stark contrast with other (non-oral, non-rhetorical) techniques of communication.[21] Indeed, if our earlier observation concerning the progressive obsolescence of language techniques is followed,[22] we may draw a rough analogy between folk music and political rhetoric. We noted that folk music becomes a "genre" precisely when an innovation in communication replaces its previous function, and that the survival of that genre depends upon a self-conscious perpetuation of what now (but only now) appears as an original or "authentic" style. Thus the preservation of this genre depends entirely upon easily recognizable idioms; "innovations" are impure and would threaten the authenticity of the genre. In the same fashion, rhetorical commonplace and stylization are the strengths rather than the flaws of political oratory. The power of such a performance derives from a faithful execution of ritual expressions in the manner of a tribal ceremony, with severe sanctions against any departure from the limited stock of expressions,[23] especially if these departures offer new ideas, present factual information, or challenge pervasive values. Persuasion, conflict, or the disposition of specialized information play virtually no part in such oratory.

It need scarcely be mentioned that these conclusions conflict with the entire tradition of enlightenment and liberal optimism concerning an educated public. Thinkers ranging from John Milton to Thomas Jefferson to John Stuart Mill have anticipated a gradual expansion of rationality, and even political liberty, flowing from an enlightened public discourse, an idea which takes for granted that literacy, available lines of communication and freely available (i.e., uncensored) information would perforce lead to the exercise of rational choice and wise public policy. Instead, we find that "public discourse"—at least as it is imagined in Jeffersonian democratic theory: an educated public, served by a free press, engaging in self-interested debate—is an increasingly remote concept. Apart from the survival of political oratory as a ceremonial archaicism, the post-literate needs and techniques of contemporary society imply that "liberal democracy" and its corollaries of public discourse, rational man and progressive intellectual elevation no longer serve even as a plausible ideological description of "advanced" societies. In the place of the "rational man" who steps into the voting booth from the "market-place of ideas" to exercise his choice on behalf of "enlightened self-interest", post-literate society offers the image of a man inured to the idea that the "mass media" manipulate him more than they inform him, that rhetorical displays are estimable only for their surface appearance (dull, slick), and that his apathy to make a choice is reinforced by the feeling that in any case he can never know "all the facts". Here one's interest is served not by active dialogue or participation, but by withdrawal and self-consignment to a group identity (consumers, farmers, unions, etc.) which is primarily attractive because such groups typically have a leadership possessing "all the facts". Few people actually believe this, of course, but subscribing to group opinion is a complement to the intellectual passivity characteristic of post-literate man, and is a kind of rational self-interest, given the reality of technological specialization and the difficulty of communicating or comprehending information related to such specialization.

The residue of political language which persists in post-literate society, and which pre-dates it in the sub-literate strata of all cultures, is largely formulaic in character. Slogans, the rhymed phrase and "mass lines", are representative of this language. Although it is conceivable that a slogan or catch-cry can actually convey an idea—"No taxation without representation"—or serve as a mnemonic for an ideological pattern—"Better dead than red" —it would seem that the associative power of contemporary political slogans is purposefully ambiguous.[24] The apparent effect is not so much to compress information or to simplify for ease of expression and persuasion as it is to make no generalizations or simplifications at all. In effect, the uttered or typographic slogan becomes a part of a larger field of perception, and is designed not to obtrude with distracting "information". This may well explain why political sloganeering is indistinguishable from commercial advertising, with its repertoire of phrases aimed at evoking unspecifiable positive emotions with virtually no accompanying context, information or persuasive strategy: "This is Marlboro country". "Coke. It's the real thing." Thus in the 1976 U.S. presidential election, one party had no difficulty in capitalizing on an automobile advertising slogan, adopting it outright—"This is Ford country"—and gaining the added benefit of the humorous pun.[25] Just as the phrase had nothing to do with automobiles or their merits, it had nothing to do with the presidency, and this irrelevancy seemed to be its chief merit as a slogan. It offended no one, contradicted no ideas or facts, conveyed no information, contentious or otherwise; but it vaguely conferred perhaps a mildly gratifying status upon those who were already inclined to buy the product.

If we were to look for the social and political implications of post-literacy, we should be taken far beyond the scope of this study, which has endeavoured to limit our analysis to the relationship between political language and communications technology, and the way this interplay has been articulated in rhetorical theory. We have argued, in essence, that political rhetoric has virtually lost its standing as a separate technique of communication, and that oral performance in its surviving manifestations is an archaic, subsidiary method in comparison with electronic technology. At the same time, communication theory and information theory in their recent elaborations[26] have very little to do with grammatical language and nothing at all with oratory. It is in this sense that we see political society, so far as functional communication is concerned, to be both post-rhetorical and post-literate. The conclusion seems foregone that the "political language" of contemporary society is a species of human performance practically unrelated to theories and techniques of communication. What remains as identifiable political language is an obsolete grouping of literate performances, the precarious status of which is under-scored by their appropriation and transformation by post-literate, electronic technology. It is really difficult to know when "speech" and "utterance" become meaningless terms for language performances which are split into audio and video "tracks", reassembled in various contexts, or used purely as phonic or visual components of a non-linguistic electronic transmission. In any case, our conclusion certainly does not imply that political rhetoric has vanished, that people no longer use language in ordinary discourse, or that communication as a social function has ceased to exist. Rather, we have contended that the relationship between the first two and the third of these elements has been deprived of a common set of linguistic techniques.

One effect of post-literacy and a proper subject of speculation in a study of political language and public discourse is "cultural amnesia". If oral discourse and even grammatical language in printed form are receding in importance as techniques of communication (and as widely performed skills), the retention of specialized information and its availability or distribution in society become critical political issues.

The retentive capacities of language have been frequently noted, and the cultural importance of this linguistic function is obvious. If, however, post-literate society amounts to a variation of pre-literate orality, it is understandable that this transformation will be accompanied by not just a "loss" of literate culture but by a continual transiency of cultural information and identity available to the general public unless suitable oral devices for retention are adopted. Cultural amnesia—a narrowing and temporality of identity due to a reduced capacity for retaining and articulating cultural information with a technique of communication broadly available —therefore results from the failure to develop techniques (oral or otherwise) to preserve such information.

The distribution of information in society—its availability and practical accessibility—is increasingly recognized as a crucial political issue. While retention of information is obviously a significant aspect of its availability for distribution, the post-literate society depends upon techniques of communication which generate, store and use masses of information with skills and techniques which are only partly linguistic and are available to only small élites. In short, maldistribution—the removal of specialized information from public discourse—is implied by the obsolescence of linguistic techniques of communication in post-literate, technological society.

Post-literate society is, therefore, characterized by symbolic indeterminacy: not only by an amnesia concerning the past and one's identity within a tradition, but also by a low capacity to use more than a narrow range of oral formulae—slogans, clichés, slang —to articulate ideas and interpret events.[27] Public discourse, of course, supports and retains a stock of expressions and an idiom of popular speech. But as a means of communication, this level of oral discourse is increasingly remote from the symbols, ideas and information—to say nothing of the performing skills—communicated by post-literate techniques of electronic communication. In effect, post-literate society is a return to a distinction between the *lingua franca*—the vulgar tongue—and the learned official language used skilfully only by those in the corridors of power. The crucial difference between this modern period and earlier eras is that this official language is no longer an integral linguistic medium, but is comprised of a virtual Babel of semiotic techniques whose only common characteristic is their resistance to translation into the grammar and vocabulary of ordinary discourse.

Although much more might be said of a speculative nature about cultural amnesia that would be of interest to psychologists, sociologists and literary critics,[28] our remarks here will merely take note of the fact that we must be aware of modern tendencies which describe a kind of cultural forgetfulness. Movements for preservation and conservation of historical objects and interests would seem to be exceptions proving the general rule that change, progress, newness, innovation, the future and the unknown are the dominant characteristics (and identify the primary values) of modern society. On a personal level, the acquisition of a "life style" appears to be the fundamental aim, and it is noteworthy that this life style has little if anything to do with traditional goals, values or productive activities. Moreover, the personal or "self-actualizing" nature of this aim renders it largely inarticulable, a condition which appears in no way contradictory to those who pursue or market it. It seems, further, that the underlying aim is to be a "new person"—or simply "a person"—and that until one is, one remains bogged down (or "hung up") in the past. Thus "authenticity", "self-hood", and so forth, are little more than expressions for rejecting the past, of forgetting oneself and the features or conditions of life which tie one to the past.

Political rhetoric also may carefully avoid, and even assist one in forgetting, the past.[29] The vocabulary and slogans of ceremonial oratory lend the appearance of tradition to formal discourse, but this is precisely an example of the way in which oral tradition provides a limited range of symbolic content, especially when old-fashioned speech-making offers itself as a living heir of an ancient tradition while actually being *unable* to communicate newly-specialized, technical information. This is just another way of saying that ceremonial rhetoric is archaic in an essential way. Turning the past into simplistic legend is one way of forgetting details that literacy might have preserved. On the other hand, the presence of political oratory might as well be credited, as a "folk genre", with preserving the past and retaining in public discourse a stock of vocabulary, images, ideas and values. However archaic, oratory is a remnant of literacy and a form of linguistic retention. It is for this reason—the retentive capacity of formal oratory—that political rhetoric, although archaic, is such a rich resource for modern communication techniques to appropriate and transform into non-linguistic forms. The resulting "rhetorical devices", with their audio-visual slickness, are obvious examples of post-literacy, providing the viewer little if any linguistic information.

We have noted how, since Descartes, the discovery and disposition of information has had little to do with received stores of wisdom, or with methods which test new experiences by their conformity with axiomatic truths. With the reforms of modern rhetorical theory, from Ramus to the Port-Royalists to John Stuart Mill, it is not surprising that rhetoric has gradually moved away from the centre of scientific and technical communication, or to put it another way, that the discovery and disposition of information have proceeded well enough without the techniques of oral discourse preserved by rhetoric. In this sense, we find in rhetoric a bent to retention, tradition and internal consistency through the skilful use of a grammatical system. The bent of science toward discovery, new information, and truth based upon repeated experimental results marks a very early point of departure towards what we have called post-literate amnesia. This is not to say that modern science is somehow to blame for these phenomena. Quite the contrary is the case if we take Descartes's assumption at face value: that science is a gradual accumulation and purification of knowledge. Still it is the case that scientific investigation could, as it did, dispense with rhetoric as a theory of communication, and build in its place a quickly changing body of communicative techniques whose abstraction and power have eventually weakened, beyond theory, the techniques of public discourse to the point at which linguistic retention—the rudimentary socially communicative power of language—appears to be diminishing. Against this transformation in communication technology stands the genre of political oratory as a memento of classical rhetoric. If the retentive capacity of this language technique appears archaic and obsolete in the face of other techniques, this is perhaps not nearly as politically significant as the concomitant withdrawal from public discourse of the linguistic capacity to express ideas, concepts and factual material. The demise of this language function from political discourse effectively denies the public a medium for addressing the topics of change, protest or dissent, except insofar as these may be retrieved from a stock of rituals and formulae. Thus political language is circumscribed within a closed universe of discourse, and is unable to offer itself as a technique of communication for public participation. Other "languages" may be available for the communication of information and the consideration of ideas, concepts and the disposition of resources, but these languages are only partially linguistic in form and their use is limited to those few who possess the skilful techniques.

This transformation is tantamount to a weakening of the public character of language. The change is deeper than the feeling that political rhetoric is a quaint and generally embarrassing anachronism, or the fear that declining literacy and a forgotten literary heritage will lead to a cultural decay. The fundamental change has to do with the very relationship between language and communication or, more exactly, with the *separation* between individual linguistic competence and the technological requirements of specialized communication. In the realm of contemporary political discourse, both speakers and listeners are painfully, often cynically, aware that the simple rhetorical setting is inadequate for expressing and comprehending the complexities of public policy, or for winning and holding public office. Similarly, specialists in advanced technological communication are rarely able to express themselves intelligibly to the public or even to specialists in other fields of endeavour. In this circumstance, the ordinary citizen, not unlike the medieval subject, trusts and believes, supports himself with a dense fabric of opinions and sentiments, and tries to achieve a practical mastery of the immediate problems of daily life.

Although specialists and non-specialists rarely enter into mutual discourse about the more complicated facts and dilemmas which define the conditions of political life, such information nevertheless exists. If we are hardly aware of this information, and can understand little of it when we do encounter it, the information multiplies and is effectively communicated through an interwoven network of production, retention and application. But this is a silent process, audible only at the dispersed points of technical intersection as a jumble of esoteric jargon. This ineluctable function of communication occurs outside the domain of public discourse in increasingly smaller circles of technical proficiency. This constriction of public discourse and the separation of political rhetoric from specialized communication have already made traditional parliamentary institutions ceremonial anachronisms so far as the making and administration of public policy are concerned.

What passes for public discourse after the withdrawal of the function of communication from the sphere of linguistic performance is merely a residue of speech in forms increasingly reminiscent of the incantory displays of oral culture. The "image" and the "mood" of the performance, more than content and coherence, are essential. Replaced as techniques of specialized communication, political language and rhetoric remain as archaic structures of emotional declamation or, increasingly, as a curtain of insubstantial images whose task is to veil, rather than to reveal, information about the conditions of life.

Notes

1. I am indebted to Peter B. Mayer for bringing this passage to my attention.
2. This seems especially true of English-speaking countries. The journalistic accounts of alleged declines in literacy are too numerous and familiar to discuss at length. The following titles are representative of a range of viewpoints. In America, Oliver Todd, "The Triumph of Newspeak", *Newsweek* (29 September 1975) and Edwin Newman, *Strictly Speaking: Will America be the Death of English?* (New York, 1974). In Australia, Graham Williams, "Do-It-Yourself Illiteracy", the *Australian* (30 August 1975); Mark O'Connor, "The Great 'Spelling Reform One' Rumpus", *Meanjin Quarterly* 35, 2 (June 1976), pp. 158–66; Clement Semmler, "The Decline of Language", *Quadrant* (June 1978), pp. 53–54; and Alan Barcan, "The Anti-Education School", *Quadrant* (January 1978), pp. 23–25. George Orwell's "Politics and the English Language" (1946) remains the classic English complaint about language. Professor George Steiner has discussed the social and cultural contexts of declining literacy in *Why English?*, The English Association Presidential Address (Oxford, 1975); also see Robert Skidelsky, "Language and Politics", *Spectator* (18 June 1977). Steiner effectively summarized the concerns of many critics in his controversial appeal for a reform of the entire system of British education (quoting from the *Australian*, 4 October 1974):

   > There is a current crisis of articulacy, the resort in social and generational conflict to debased language and diminished, nerveless modes of speech and sub-speech. . . .
   > The monosyllabic reduction of vocabulary and syntax to a crude fraction means these are among the most violent weapons being used against the coherence of the community, against the conventions of debate and self-correction whereby a free society disagrees and then moves forward in and from disagreement.

   Educational journals have published extensively on the question of declining standards of literacy in schools and universities. D.H. Douglas, "Is Literacy Really Declining?", *Educational Record* 57, 3 (1976), pp. 140–48; J.J. Larson *et al.*, "Trends in College Freshman Reading Ability", *Journal of Reading* 19 (February 1976), pp. 367–69; J. Gray, "*The Roots of Reading:* A Critical Reanalysis", *Research in Education* 14 (November 1975), pp. 33–47, which discusses the controversy surrounding the "Report of the Commission of Inquiry into Reading and the Use of English", better known as the (Sir Alan) Bullock Report on standards of literacy in the British school system. For the political reaction upon its release, see *The Times* (19 February 1975), p. 5, and *The Sunday Times* (23 February 1975), p. 40, for the Commission's dissenting opinion.

3. There is a countervailing view which regards "literacy" as a barrier between social classes and ethnic or racial groups, with the corollary that demands for "high standards" are really veiled claims for the protection of cultural forms traditionally reserved for privileged classes. This argument accepts the idea of equality between dialects or sub-cultural speech and "standard" grammars, and holds the perhaps romantic view that the rich and creative expressiveness of slang is actually to be preferred to standard literacy. An argument on behalf of oral speech patterns at variance with grammatical literacy may well be an indication of the emergence of post-literate culture. For a discussion of this debate and bibliographical references see D.E. Eskey, "Standard/Nonstandard English: Toward a Balanced View", *English Journal* 65 (Dec. 1976), pp. 28–31.

4. *Enumerate* and *enumeracy* are becoming accepted terms in academic circles.

5. It is sufficient to note here that there is no simple cause and effect relationship between technique and content, but rather a kind of reciprocal emergence.

6. George Steiner, *Language and Silence* (London, 1967), pp. 281–82.

7. McLuhan's indignation may well be minimal, given the underlying historio-graphical assumptions of his thought regarding the inexorable emergence of successive communications technologies. McLuhan's indignation appears to be directed at remnant and obsolete manifestations of technology which are supported out of ignorance of progressive technology. This attitude is effectively conveyed in an article by Tom Wolfe, "Suppose He Is What He Sounds Like, The Most Important Thinker Since Newton, Darwin, Freud, Einstein, and Pavlov—What If He Is Right?", in *McLuhan: Hot & Cool* (New York, 1967) ed. by G.E. Stearn, pp. 15–34.

8. See Chapter II, *supra.*

9. The coincidence between social status, including power roles, and the possession of privileged language has been noted as a common feature of all stages of social organization. In oral society, privileged possession may be assigned to individuals such as a medicine man or tribal head, or to orders, such as the old men, a priesthood or proven warriors. Larger and diverse portions of the community participate in its oral tradition through songs, chants, epithets, etc., a more "common" but no less important form of cultural retention.

10. In fact, it is necessary to disavow on historiographical and epistemological grounds any attempt to establish a "cyclical" account of post-literacy as a "return" to primeval society or an "advance" to a higher stage of history. Both oral society and post-literate society are analytical constructs, and they are used here as such, rather than as terms of reference to objective historical "epochs" with distinct and identifiable characteristics. It is important to under-score the intended use of the terms "oral society" and "post-literate society" *inter alia*, precisely because of the danger of confusing analytical theories with a "theory of history". For example, to point out certain similarities between contemporary society and pre-literate society with regard to oral performance

is very different from proposing that this proposed similarity amounts to an "historical return", or that the observed similarity constitutes evidence that there are broader correspondences between these two periods (which are themselves arbitrarily the object of analytical focus). The first error results from intrinsic illogic in the very idea of an historical return, and the second error, among other difficulties, is due to the logical fallacy of composition unavoidable when any analogy is carried too far, that is, as an argument for equivalency. As Hume pointed out, we may be excused for being "habituated" to making cause and effect relationships between observed data, but the habit —e.g., of discovering cultural "advances" or concluding that similar effects can be taken as evidence of similar or identical "patterns" of causes—is no less false as logic (and history) for being easy and attractive.

11. References to support this observation are really unnecessary, so frequently has the subject been treated in popular journalism. Most speculations about the psychological and cultural effects of rock music appear to be a mixture of common sense and popular religious and political prejudices. It is interesting that books written primarily to advertise and celebrate rock music are generally enthusiastic in conceding that the music form has all the powers alleged to exist by its critics. See Nik Cohn, *Rock: From the Beginning* (New York, 1969); J. Eisen, *The Age of Rock: Sounds of the American Cultural Revolution* (New York, 1969); Albert Goldman, *Freakshow* (New York, 1971); J. Marks, *Rock and Other Four Letter Words* (New York, 1968); Editors of *Rolling Stone, The Rolling Stone Interviews* (New York, 1971); Greil Marcus, *Rock and Roll Will Stand* (Boston, 1969).

12. It is not incompatible with the analysis of political language to identify status and power, not simply as a linguistic phenomenon, but also as a function of social and economic sub-groups. Our argument as already proposed that obsolescent communications techniques become identified with an institution or group interested, in this case financially, in its "anachronistic" preservation.

13. This point was perhaps first argued by Mary Wollstonecraft in *Thoughts on the Education of Daughters* (1787) and *A Vindication of the Rights of Woman* (1792). Recent feminist writers have also noted this condition: Sheila Rowbotham, *Woman's Consciousness, Man's World* (Harmondsworth, 1973), and *Hidden From History* (Harmondsworth, 1974); Shulamith Firestone, *The Dialectic of Sex* (St. Albans, England, 1972), esp. Chs. 8 and 9; Juliet Mitchell, *Woman's Estate* (Harmondsworth, 1971), esp. pp. 131–36.

14. For example, it may easily be argued that the folk singer as entertainer is actually "liberated" so far as effective communication is concerned: liberated from being a mere instrument of received and repetitive materials so that he may become a creative singer in his own right. The form that has become, in one sense, obsolete has, in another, become revived by transformation.

15. This point is discussed *supra*, Chapter I.

16. Although this observation can be of no empirical value, among my personal acquaintances physicists have remarkably poor handwriting, with mathematicians just marginally more decipherable.

17. The replacement of letter-writing by the telephone may be added to this list. Another domestic literary activity, the personal journal or diary, has also probably become less popular due to the pace of life and intrusions of radio and television. One may speculate that such a personal memoir might be revived through the use of electronic recording devices.

18. Ancient Chinese society, with its tradition of Mandarin scholar–rulers, would appear to be an exception to this proposition. Nevertheless, China was otherwise an outstanding case in point of the coincidence of élite power and literacy.

19. This, of course, is a debatable point, and it will not be argued here. George Steiner offers in a number of his works persuasive arguments to the effect that the richness of European literature up to the eighteenth century can never be achieved again. See Ch. I of *After Babel: Aspects of Language and Translation* (Oxford, 1975); also *Extraterritorial: Papers on Literature and the Language Revolution* (London, 1971), pp. 155ff.; and *Language and Silence,* pp. 58, 62 and 205–11.

    It should also be noted here that the great achievements in systematic philosophy, epistemology and historical scholarship in recent centuries have resulted from a confrontation with and adoption of the general aims and empirical methods of science.

20. We refer here to the political campaign advertisements modelled after commercial advertising, especially on radio and television. This similarity is not coincidental, since the campaign spots are routinely made by advertising agencies which exploit the same audio-visual techniques found to be effective in commercial advertising.

21. The 1976 U.S. presidential campaign debates would seem to be a case in point. Journalistic commentary on the debates centred almost exclusively upon how dull, vague, predictable and uninformative they were—although critics generally agreed that the candidates themselves intended to convey precisely such a "low profile" and avoid controversial issues. The predictable character of the three debates did not prevent tens of millions of people from watching them.

22. See esp. *supra.,* Chs. II and VI.

23. Political campaign oratory again provides an important case in point. Especially during extemporaneous speech, "blunders" and frank statements become the transitory subject of sensational journalism until the speaker or his aides attempt to obliterate the "misstatements" with "clarifications". During the 1976 U.S. presidential debates, Gerald Ford deviated from ritual positions when he committed his "blunder" concerning Soviet-East European relations, just as Jimmy Carter violated the implicit constraints of oratory by introducing large quantities of economic statistics into his answers. Surveys following the debates indicated that the candidates suffered in the estimation of the viewers by interjecting these and other instances of unfamiliar material into the debates.

24. Several cases are discussed below. Every election campaign seems to coin a few outstanding slogans that are simple, catchy and virtually lacking in semantic content or power of reference: e.g., "Nixon's the one"; "Turn on the lights"; "It's Time"; "He cares"; "You'll know he's there".

25. Another Ford Motor Company slogan—"Ford has a better idea"—perhaps offered an even more humorous pun at the President's expense since it ironically raised the otherwise unkind subject of his less than adroit mind.

26. Colin Cherry, *On Human Communication,* 2nd ed. (Cambridge, Mass., 1966) Chs. 2 and 5, provides a brief review of the technical orientation of information and communication theory. The book also offers a useful bibliographical guide to the technical literature.

27. A particularly illustrative example of this is the phrase, "Like . . . you know what I mean?", which suggests that neither the speaker nor the listener knows what he means.

28. The concept of cultural amnesia is certainly a part of a broader inquiry carried out on many fronts. Psychologists and sociologists have developed the themes of anomie, the declining superego, and crises of identity. Writers have debated the good or ill effects of social movements aiming at "consciousness raising" and counter-cultural efforts at returning to "nature", or possibly even transcending it through drugs or meditative religions. Art and literary critics have

had to struggle with artists whose works seem purposefully to repel both audience or understanding, especially when the "objects" self-destruct, melt, are too large or small to be actually seen (as in "earth sculpture"), or exist only as an existential event. In all these cultural phenomena, there seems to be the common issue of the uncertain relationship of the present to the past (whether of personal identity or artistic tradition), associated with the idea that the creation of objects (canvases, cities , technology) in the present is somehow a malignant encumbrance on future society just as it is an exploitation of present society. Spontaneity and the ephemeral are therefore the primary values within this "amnesiac" cultural tradition, although it must be said that "amnesia" may be an unnecessarily pejorative term for a tendency described by its advocates as "liberation".

29. This argument has been most recently made by astute journalists and critics with regard to American political discourse since the Vietnam war. See Sheldon S. Wolin, "From Jamestown to San Clemente," *The New York Review of Books* (19 September 1974); various authors, "The Meaning of Vietnam", *ibid.* (12 June 1975); William Shawcross, "A Whiter Wash", *ibid.* (17 July 1965).

Index